D1263532

The Papers of the
Henry Luce III Fellows
in Theology

ats Series in Theological Scholarship and Research

The Papers of the Henry Luce III Fellows in Theology
Matthew Zyniewicz, Editor

The Papers of the Henry Luce III Fellows in Theology

VOLUME IV

Matthew Zyniewicz, Editor

ats Series in Theological Scholarship and Research

The Association of Theological Schools in the United States and Canada
Pittsburgh, Pennsylvania

The Papers of the Henry Luce III Fellows in Theology

VOLUME IV

edited by
Matthew Zyniewicz

Library of Congress Cataloging in Publication Data

The papers of the Henry Luce III Fellows in Theology / edited by Matthew Zyniewicz
p. cm. — (Series in theological scholarship and research)
ISBN 0-7885-0297-2 (alk. paper)
ISBN 0-9702-3460-0 (alk. paper) vol. IV
1. Theology. I. Henry Luce III Fellows in Theology. II. Series.
BR50.P24 1996
230—dc20 96-27815
CIP

Printed in the United States of America
on acid-free paper

Acknowledgment

The Association of Theological Schools expresses its profound appreciation to The Henry Luce Foundation, especially, Henry Luce III, John W. Cook, and Michael F. Gilligan, for their generous support of the Henry Luce III Fellows in Theology program, the annual Luce Conference, and this volume.

Contents

Introduction

Matthew Zyniewicz, Editor
THE ASSOCIATION OF THEOLOGICAL SCHOOLS
PITTSBURGH, PENNSYLVANIA

Since 1994, supported by a grant from The Henry Luce Foundation Inc., the Henry Luce III Fellows in Theology program has assisted the development of faculty research at member institutions of The Association of Theological Schools through salary replacement and research funds. The program solicits projects that offer significant and innovative contributions to theological studies, enhance the theological understanding of people of faith, and enrich the experience of church life in North America. The program also encourages faculty to develop ways for scholarship to inform contemporary culture.

The essays collected in this volume represent the work of the eight 1997-98 Henry Luce III Fellows in Theology. The topics cover a range of theological issues from the doctrine of original sin to adolescent girls' fascination with horror and the connection between this fascination and the development of their spiritual voices. Individually these essays provide a window onto some of the most innovative theological scholarship and give witness to the diversity of theological thought. Collectively these essays illustrate the deep respect and concern that theological faculty have for the rich treasury of Christian traditions and wisdom.

Necessarium Adae Peccatum (the necessary sin of Adam) argues that the story of Adam and Eve is only intelligible in light of the end of biblical history. Yet, very few modern biblical scholars consider this history of religions' concept as a necessary part of Genesis 1-3. The doctrine of original sin, then, appears suspect and ill matched to modern existence. Since many scholars claim that we can no longer accept the historical existence of Adam and Eve, is not the story of Adam and Eve's sin and redemption stripped of any significant meaning? And, if so, should not the church refine or even discard entirely what she theologically confesses about the doctrine of original sin? Gary Anderson explains in his essay that, according to tradition, Adam's sin need not lead to a grim and stark understanding of our human condition. Rather, if the beginning is correlated with its end, Adam's humiliation paradoxically leads to his exultation. In this way Adam and Eve serve the narrative purpose of "affirming that all human existence stands under the broad canopy of a merciful God," and the doctrine of original sin remains a viable, theological attempt to sketch the profound mystery and experience of God's love and mercy.

Herod's Hit Man: Horror and the Development of Girls' Spiritual Voices examines adolescent girls' fascination with horror and the connection between this fascination, the horrific elements in their lives, and the development of their spiritual voices. In her essay Patricia Davis explores issues of sexuality and violence, allowing girls in their own voices to talk about their questions on these subjects and their feelings of being ignored or betrayed by adults in the church. Davis concludes that not helping girls face difficult questions such as these may negatively affect their spiritual development and their relationships with adults, the church, and even with God.

The Word of God in the Theology of Friedrich Schleiermacher questions the underlying general description of Friedrich Schleiermacher's theology as a "theology of experience." Dawn DeVries argues on the basis of a close textual analysis of Schleiermacher's works that his theology might more correctly be seen as a distinctive type of theology of the Word of God. If DeVries's interpretation is persuasive, her work could have major implications. It may entail some changes in the way Protestant theology is told, and may affect the way that one lays out the theological options present at the end of the twentieth century and beginning of the twenty-first.

Natural and Divine Law: Retrieving the Roots of Christian Ethics sets forth the main lines of the scholastic concept of the natural law and its contemporary significance. Jean Porter is convinced that the medieval discussions of the natural law are some of the richest and yet most undervalued traditions to be found in the long history of Christian theological ethics. She examines the concept in her essay with the aim of recovering it as a resource for contemporary Christian ethics, particularly in relation to issues of sexuality and medical practice.

Rehabilitating "The Preacher": Qohelet's Theological Reflections in Context argues that Qohelet's theological message in Ecclesiastes was context conscious and suggests a possible environment wherein Qohelet's message might make sense, being shaped by the intersection of tradition and contemporary life. Choon-Leong Seow maintains that Qohelet drew on and engaged the traditions as he taught his audience knowledge and prodded them on as a preacher might, reflecting upon the contemporary world in which his audience lived. The people were preoccupied with all sorts of social and economic issues, and Qohelet often drew on those concerns and employed idioms that were familiar to them in order to subvert their preoccupations and to proclaim the absolute sovereignty of God.

Protestant Christianity and the Conundrum of Islam reflects on the deep distrust and misunderstanding that have long characterized relations between Christians and Muslims, relations that are slowly giving way to greater mutual appreciation and increased efforts at interfaith conversation. Some of this progress is reflected in, or even generated by, rethinking on the part of theologians, missionaries, and scholars about Christian understanding of Islam. Jane Smith focuses on Protestant theology in relation to Islam as it has developed over the past several hundred years in various contexts, with particular attention to writings and responses that have appeared in the last half-century.

The Gap Between Liberty and Equality: Christian Faith and the Civil Rights Movement addresses the Civil Rights Movement from 1954 to 1970. Mark Toulouse examined editorials and articles written between 1955 and 1995 in six major independent and Catholic periodicals to address a broad range of questions about Christian debate in various public arenas. He intends to lay out in his forthcoming book the Christian arguments and positions in response to selected controversial issues of the last forty years, such as Viet Nam, Civil Rights, feminism and homosexuality. Toulouse's essay in this volume offers his preliminary findings that, though sympathetic, and even active for short periods of time, white Christian church leadership eventually failed to appreciate and respond to the growing awareness among African Americans that the achievement of liberty, or legislative guarantees of individual rights, did not guarantee equality.

Imagination and Improvisation: Holy Play dares to suggest that we play with the story of God. Janet Walton urges us to play with Christian symbols steeped in traditions and memories, as if tossing balls at one another, so that the symbols live among us. Christians must continue to find ways to engage their symbols, to play with them, so that they can discover the symbols' meanings for themselves. Holy play, or improvisation, is not a disregard for tradition but is essential for effective ritualizing. In her essay Walton offers a strategy for such play based on her study of improvisation among artists. She explores an approach to worship that uses what she learned about improvisation in artistic venues to encourage active, collaborative, "holy play," and she proposes "that worshiping congregations develop an artistic mind set and a schema for improvising as a way to enjoy the freedom and the power worship can provide."

Necessarium Adae Peccatum

Gary A. Anderson
HARVARD UNIVERSITY DIVINITY SCHOOL
CAMBRIDGE, MASSACHUSETTS

The story of Adam and Eve's transgression, though surprisingly brief, did not prevent subsequent interpreters from pouring enormous attention upon it. The great English Puritan and poet, John Milton (1608-1674), expanded the several dozen verses of this story into his epic poem, *Paradise Lost*, a work comprised of twelve books, with each book containing nearly a thousand lines. Moderns are frequently wont to characterize such expansions of the Biblical original as classic examples of *eisogesis* (reading into the text what one expects to find). The label is not inaccurate, but neither is it particularly apt. To understand even a few lines of a work like *Paradise Lost*, or nearly any other Jewish or Christian elaboration one must bear in mind another theological and deeply scriptural principle. *The story of human beginnings is only intelligible in light of its end.* In other words, like any good novel, short story, or play, the first scene almost invariably hints, in some way, how the story will unfold. Upon completing a story, a good reader will return to the opening to see how the end illuminates the beginning.

Much of Milton's expansion of the story of Adam and Eve is dependent on the exegetical principle that the end will illuminate the beginning. Consider what happens when Adam transgresses the interdiction regarding the tree of knowledge:

> Earth Trembled from her entrails as again
> In pangs, and nature gave a second groan,
> Sky loured and muttering thunder, some sad drops
> Wept at completing of the mortal sin
> Original. (*Paradise Lost*, IX: 1000-1004)

These remarkable lines surprise. Where in Genesis 3 do we see signs of cosmic disturbance in the wake of Adam's sin? Has Milton used his poetic license to embellish the terse original? Hardly. These depictions of nature's groaning point forward to nature's travail at Golgotha. As Christ, the creator of the world, hangs on the cross, the earth quakes, the skies darken. So shocking is this sight that one anonymous homilist from the fifth century wrote:

> Not even the sun was able to endure this sight but completely darkened itself to block the eyes of others. Neither did it take thought of the commandment to give light (Gen 1:16) but from that moment on dared to transgress it, seeing the Lord, the giver of commandment, suffering at the hands of man.[1]

But there is no reason to be shamed by this sight, our patristic homilist argues, "for if we see the reason for which the Lord suffered, we no longer blush but stand in awe before his goodness and love for mankind."[2] Milton's depiction of the cosmic disturbances that attended Adam's sin orients the reader to the larger drama of Christian redemption.

And so it was for every Jewish and Christian reader of the Bible. The most important matter for their interpretations of Genesis was an awareness of where the story reached its climax.[3] Though this procedure may sound rather simple, in practice it was not. Christian and Jewish perceptions of the story of man's beginnings differ widely. This is because each tradition has a very different idea about what the "end" of the Biblical story is.

The Beginning in Light of the End

According to the Bible, the sin of Adam and Eve and all that it engendered (banishment from Eden, toiling upon the land, suffering in childbirth and the return to the soil at death) was a first stage in a progression of general human rebellion. After the Fall we read of Cain's slaying of Abel, the strange tale of the intercourse between the "sons of God and the daughters of men," the various evils that led to the flood, and finally the building of the tower of Babel. Humanity was progressively alienating itself from its divine creator. This escalating fall from grace took a dramatic turn toward restoration when God appeared before Abraham and promised:

> Go from your country and your kindred and your father's house to the land that I will show you. I will make you a great nation and I will bless you, and make your name great, so that you will be a blessing . . . Through you all the families of the earth shall bless themselves. (Gen 12:1-3)

Because the land promised to Abraham was thought of in near-Edenic terms ("a land flowing with milk and honey"), the possession of that land by a specially favored nation was thought to constitute a fitting redress to the fall. At first, the selection of Abraham, the progenitor of Israel, appears to be an improbable way to restore mankind. This special address, directed to one man from amid the many nations, could be seen as unmotivated, unnatural, and even unfair. Yet the mystery of this choice seems to be part of the intention of the author. As Gerhard von Rad observed: "The narrator does not explain why God's choice did not fall upon Ham or Japheth, but rather upon Shem, and [...] upon Abraham."[4] This act of unmotivated choice is most often labeled the mystery (or even, the scandal) of election; God has chosen to redeem the entirety of creation through the agency of a single nation. The nation that is imagined by this promise is not simply Israel, but the grand kingdom of Israel realized in the days of Kings David and Solomon. For during their reigns, the borders of the Biblical kingdom had an enormous reach, they encroached on the greatest nations of the ancient world.

Gerhard von Rad identified the author of this promise to Abraham as the "J" or Yahwistic-source, a writer who lived during the grand days of the Davidic kingdom. In his view, the achievements of this kingdom constituted a fulfillment of the promise made to Abraham and hence, a redress of the imbalance wrought by the fall. This hypothetical reconstruction of the narrative history of the Bible has persuaded many, but by no means all Biblical scholars. Even if we grant von Rad his hypothesis, it is nevertheless true that for most of the Biblical period, specifically the many years that followed the reigns of David and Solomon, the promise given to Abraham was always viewed as unfulfilled and open-ended. Through the course of time, Biblical authors assumed a flexible posture toward this promise. No subsequent Biblical or later Jewish author felt constrained or hemmed in by the specific intention of the text's author. For the Yahwistic writer had penned this text in a very broad and generic fashion. As a result it possessed an enormous temporal reach: It extended to the most distant of futures, the consummation of human history. In the words of von Rad this text "refused any [singular and detailed] description of its final end."[5]

If we survey the broadest outline of Biblical history we will see that the fulfillment of the promise to Abraham reached an initial apogee with the deliverance of Israel from the hand of Pharaoh and the gift of the Bible or "Torah" to Moses at Mt. Sinai. At that moment in time, Israel was formally adopted as God's firstborn or favored son. This moment of election and law-giving was meant to culminate in the taking of the promised land, the very heart of the promise made to Abraham. The gift of the land, however, was never fully realized. From the very first moment, when Moses commissioned spies to reconnoiter the boundaries of Canaan, the taking of the land was beset with problems. During the reigns of David and Solomon, Israel came the closest to realizing the grandeur of the promise, but her moment of glory was ever so brief. Eventually Israel lost the land they occupied when the Babylonian armies invaded. Ever since, Israel has awaited the final ingathering of those who were dispersed, the rebuilding of the temple, and a renewed commitment by the entire nation to return with repentant hearts to the Torah.

As the hope of realizing the promise slipped further and further into the future, the end itself, as Paul Ricoeur notes, changed in meaning. And as the tale of Israel "end" changed so did her beginning:

> The fulfillment of the Promise [to Abraham] which at first appears to be at hand, is constantly postponed. In the meantime, the revelation at Sinai, the knowledge of the Law, the setting up of a cult, and the experience in the wilderness take place. The wealth of the interval is such that the end itself changes its meaning. [...] Henceforth the "Promise" will express its tension through the mythical images of the end; those images and the figures in which they will be crystallized will supply the true answer to the images and figures of the beginning.[6]

In the time of Jesus, when Rabbinic Judaism was taking root in Palestine, Judaism was slowly transforming itself from a religion whose "end" or central purpose centered around a temple and sacrifice to a religion focused on prayer and Torah study. According to the Rabbis, Moses received two Torahs at Mount Sinai, one written on tablets, the other transmitted orally. It was the duty of all subsequent generations to pass on this legacy of a twofold Torah and to bring the Jewish nation to a position of faithful obedience of its norms. It would be difficult to find a Jewish writer from this time period who did not draw careful comparisons between the creation of man and the gift of the Torah. In the mind of the Rabbis, God himself consulted the Torah in order to create man and the world he was to inhabit. The end of man's existence, obedience to Torah, was correlated to his very origins.

Christian writers do not take a similar interest in Torah. The writings of St. Paul and the results of the first ecclesial council in Jerusalem (Acts 15) show us that at a very early date, the nascent Christian movement decided to part company with their Jewish brethren over certain aspects of Jewish law. This was because Paul, and others like him, felt that the resurrection of Christ had ushered in a new epoch in human history. This new epoch had no need for the ceremonial details of the Jewish law code, namely those that dealt with sacrifice, bodily purity, and food laws. The goal of human creation was no longer thought to be the giving of the Torah to Israel but the birth, life, and death of Jesus Christ.

It has frequently been noted that Jesus himself made no mention of the story of Adam and Eve in any of the four canonical gospels. Though he dealt with topics of human sin, the need for repentance, and the promise of salvation for the entire created order, he never once elucidated the story of Eden in the course of his teaching. This should not be overly surprising. For it is a basic feature of each Gospel that Jesus' true identity, and hence the purpose of the incarnation itself, was not known until after his death. The Gospel of Mark is perhaps the most radical on this point; only the Roman centurion standing at the foot of the cross would figure out who Jesus was when he exclaimed, "*Truly this man was God's son*!" (15:39). To be sure, the other disciples, especially Peter, would on occasion identify Jesus as the Christ. But the disciples believed that this Messianic office precluded any tinge of ignominy. Jesus, they thought, was to fill this office in a glorious manner. The moment Jesus alluded to the necessity of his suffering, the disciples rebuked him severely. Only at the resurrection, did the disciples finally come to understand the nature of Jesus' identity. In other words, the particular goal or "end" toward which Jesus moved was not made clear until after he had died. Only after his death could the purpose or "end" of Christ's life be joined to the narrative of human beginnings.

The very first Christian document to make this connection was St. Paul's letter to the Corinthians. This letter can be dated to within a couple of decades after the death of Christ (56 or 57 C.E.), not too long after Paul's own conversion to the movement. In the fifteenth chapter he takes up the problem of certain members of the community who lack a clear conviction about the bodily resurrection of Christ. Paul begins his argument by acknowledging that his own teaching is simply a handing on of what he had received. Christ, Paul declares, was buried and "rose on the third day in accordance with the scriptures. He appeared to Cephas then to the twelve. Then he appeared to more than five hundred brothers and sisters at one time.... Then he appeared to James, then to all the apostles, last of all, as to one untimely born, he appeared also to me." (I Cor 15:4-8) From this brief resume we can see that Paul has established the facticity of Christ's resurrection on evidence greater than his own personal authority. The teaching is founded on a tradition for which Paul is merely a conduit, and more importantly, Jesus' appearance is an event whose witnesses number in the hundreds.

Paul's interest is not to establish merely the truth of the resurrection. Taken on its own, the event of Jesus' bodily resurrection would seem a wondrous miracle that befell one particular person. For Paul, the event was epoch-making and had cosmic significance. In order to underscore the universal dimensions of this event, Paul introduced the figure of Adam (I Cor 15:20-23):

> But in fact Christ has been raised from the dead, the first fruits of those who have died. But since death came through a human being, the resurrection of the dead has come through a human being; for as all die in Adam, so all will be made alive in Christ. But each in his own order: Christ the first fruits, then at his coming those who belong to Christ.

Paul was aware, as would any Jewish reader of the Bible, that Adam was both the personal name of a literary figure in Genesis but also a noun designating mankind more generally. What happened to Adam in Genesis 2-3 was not limited to him alone; by virtue of his name ("mankind") it had ramifications for all persons. If the first (*protos*) Adam died, Paul reasoned, then all must die through him. Since Christ was the second or final (*eschatos*) Adam, his death and resurrection must have had universal dimensions. The resurrection was not an isolated or singular event in world history for it did not involve one man alone but all mankind. Paul brings this argument home by considering the character of the resurrection body (I Cor 15:42-49):

> So it is with the resurrection of the dead. What is sown is perishable, what is raised is imperishable. It is sown in dishonor, it is raised in glory. It is sown in weakness, it is raised in power. It is sown a physical body, it is raised a spiritual body. If there is a physical body there is also a spiritual body. Thus it is written, "the first [*protos*] man, Adam, became a living being" [Gen 2:7]; the last [*eschatos*] Adam became a life-giving spirit. But it is not the spiritual that is first, but the physical, and then the spiritual. The first man was from the earth, a man of dust; the second man is from heaven. As was the man of dust, so are those who are of the dust; and as is the man of heaven, so are those who are of heaven. Just as we have borne the image [*eikon*] of the man of dust, so we will also bear the image of the man of heaven.

What is striking about this argument is that Paul believes that two epochs characterize the growth of human history, the age of the first and the second Adam. From the first Adam, a being created from the dust, came a frail and corruptible body, from the second Adam, a life-giving spirit. Those who have faith in the second Adam "bear the image of the man of heaven." It should be carefully noted that Paul begins his argument about the significance of Adam with the fact of Christ's resurrection. It is the last Adam who sets the stage for an understanding of the first.

Lest one think that only Christians understood the beginning in terms of the end, it is worth attending to a Jewish text written in an era roughly contemporary to that of Paul. The book of *IV Ezra* is a document written shortly after the destruction of Jerusalem in 70 C.E. Although this book was written by a Jew for a Jewish audience, it was not included within the Rabbinic Bible. We owe the happy fact of the book's preservation to the early church. But this should not obscure the fact that this book is an important witness to Jewish thinking in the first century about the problem of theodicy, that is, why God inflicts such unmerited suffering on his chosen people. Many have seen in this book a striking parallel to Paul's notion of original sin. In his most despairing moment, the author of *IV Ezra* complains that human life is simply not worth enduring given the painful legacy of sin and death that Adam has bequeathed to us (7:116-117):

> This is my first and last comment: it would have been better if the earth had not produced Adam, or else, when it had produced him, had restrained him from sinning. For what good is it to all that they live in sorrow now and expect punishment after death? O Adam, what have you done? For though it was you who sinned, the fall was not yours alone, but ours also who are your descendants.

One is tempted to interpret these lines as bearing on a *general* proclivity of the human race toward sinfulness. The earth produced Adam, and Adam in turn produced sin and death. These basic features are common to all human life. But to understand the text this broadly would not fit the context of the book. The writer wants to know why *the elected nation of Israel* has suffered so grievously for her sins. Why has she, of all nations, lost her Temple and national capital?

As pessimistic as this description of Adam's legacy may sound, it must not be isolated from the larger picture of what the Jewish Bible is all about. In an earlier portion of *IV Ezra*, the author retells the story of the six days of creation. When he arrives on the sixth day, the day of man's creation, he writes (6:53-43):

> On the sixth day you commanded the earth to bring forth before you cattle, wild animals, and creeping things; and over these you placed Adam, as ruler over all the works that you had made; and from him we have all come, the people whom you have chosen.

It is striking that Adam's creation is wed to the notion of Israel's special status in God's eyes. *In Ezra's view, the creation of Adam in the image of God points forward to the election of Israel.*

The problem can be brought into bolder relief. The issue is not simply that of why do the good suffer, but why does Israel in particular—that nation which represents the very pinnacle of human creation—suffer worse than all the rest of humanity (6:55-59):

> All this I have spoken before you, O Lord, because you have said that it was for us that you created this world. As for the other nations that have descended form Adam, you have said that they are nothing, and that they are like spittle and you have compared their abundance to a drop from a bucket. And now, O Lord, these nations which are reputed

> to be as nothing, dominate over us and devour us. But we are your people, whom you have called your firstborn, only begotten, zealous for you, and most dear, have been given into their hands. If the world has indeed been created for us, why do we not possess our world as an inheritance? How long will this be so?

The imagery used to depict Israel is striking. The elected nation is understood as God's "firstborn" and "only begotten"; these are precisely the same titles used by Paul and other New Testament writers to describe Christ.[7] This similar choice of words allows us to draw a close parallel between Paul and *IV Ezra*. As Paul saw creation culminate in the figure of the second Adam and drew his picture of the first Adam as an antitype to him, so *IV Ezra* saw the figure of Adam culminate in the choosing of the people Israel. The nub of Ezra's problem is the fact that the nations have risen up and usurped the rightful position of glory that should belong to the nation Israel. Why have those who have descended from Adam overtaken those who claim their origins at Sinai? For *IV Ezra*, the story of Adam's creation and its bearing on world history cannot be understood apart from the act of God's decision to give Israel the Torah at Mt. Sinai. The Bible's beginning must be correlated with its end. Strikingly, very few modern Biblical scholars consider this history of religions' concept a necessary part of Genesis 1-3. As a result, it should occasion no surprise if the doctrine of original sin has fallen upon hard times.

The Problem of Original Sin

For many today the most pressing problem created by an emphasis on Adam's sin is that it implies a low estimation of the human person. How can human nature improve and flower if it is defined from the very start as wayward, recalcitrant, and worthy of death? In our modern secular age, an age in which the continued existence of religion itself is questioned, it is difficult to advance an argument for the inherent sinfulness of each and every human being. Why would any modern man or woman define their essential humanity in terms of a transgression committed by a primal couple whose very historical existence they do not believe? If the fossil record has made the historical existence of Adam and Eve improbable, why should we accept the conclusion that their sin continues to hound and even damn us? It is little wonder that the doctrine of original sin has fallen on such hard times. As one astute observer, Edward Oakes, has observed:

> No doctrine inside the precincts of the Christian Church is received with greater reserve and hesitation, even to the point of outright denial, than the doctrine of original sin. Of course in a secular culture like ours, any number of Christian doctrines will be disputed by outsiders, from the existence of God to the resurrection of Jesus. But even in those denominations that pride themselves on their adherence to the orthodox dogmas of the once-universal Church, the doctrine of original sin is met with either embarrassed silence, outright denial, or at a minimum a kind of halfhearted lip service that does not exactly deny the doctrine but has no idea how to place it inside the devout life.[8]

The doctrine of original sin appears woefully ill matched to modern existence. This teaching outlines our common human condition in such stark and grim terms that it no longer inspires. Indeed, the effect is far worse. Its pervasive pessimistic outlook is crowded out by competing views of the human person that are more affirming and joyful. Little room is left for contemplating our vast potential for grandeur. In the eyes of many, the task of successfully navigating the turbulent seas of the late twentieth century demands that we jettison this burdensome cargo.

The writings of the former Benedictine priest, Matthew Fox, provide a good barometer of how strong this cultural suspicion is. Angered by the recalcitrance of current religious thinkers to reconsider past truisms about the fall of man, he outlined his own proposal in the book, *Original Blessing*.[9] Fox argues that the concept of original sin is rooted in an incorrigible attitude of self-loathing. When the church demands that we ponder deeply our own wretched state, we not only make ourselves miserable, but we undermine our sense of connection and integration with the larger created order. For it is from this very sense of connection and integration, Fox argues, that our civic responsibilities grow. Absent these delicate roots that bind us to each other and to our planet, there is no telling what evils will surface in their place.

Fox's solution seems a sensible one. Replace the difficult and irreformable notion of human depravity with a different story of our origins. The Bible itself, Fox argues, presents its own competing view of the created order, a view of a more optimistic tenor. In the so-called wisdom traditions of the Old Testament, we are beckoned to become disciples of lady wisdom and give heed to her kind teaching. Lady Wisdom appears in the book of Proverbs as the very artisan of creation. "*When God marked out the foundations of the earth,*" Lady Wisdom reveals (Prov 8:29b-31), "*I was there beside him, like a master worker. I was daily his delight, rejoicing before him always, rejoicing in his inhabited world and delighting in the human race.*" Lady wisdom gives no thought to human depravity; her expectations for human life are of a different order. No preacher of fire and damnation, her pedagogy assumes a kinder, gentler air. She built her home, set her table, prepared a feast, and then sought students (Prov 9:5): "*Come, eat of my bread, and drink of the wine I have mixed. Lay aside immature thoughts and truly live, walk in the way of insight.*"

For Fox, the way of wisdom is the way of mother earth. Wisdom affirms our world as good and blessed and seeks to establish us as responsible stewards over this created order. Reflection on this order through the tutelage of lady wisdom will result in human wholeness. Human proclivities to destroy our planet will be checked; the potential for intercultural dialogue and understanding will be realized. An affirming, feminine God who reveals to us our most profound potential replaces the menacing patriarchal God who laid the notion of depravity at the doorstep of all.

Unfortunately, much of Fox's argument depends on a very narrow slice of Biblical teaching about lady wisdom. His euphoria over those points of overlap between this ancient Biblical theme and his very modern, New Age spiritual predilections, blinds him to some of the darker aspects of wisdom in the Bible. The book of Job, for example, certainly the Bible's most profound exploration of the nature and consequence of evil, is not at all optimistic about Wisdom's capacity to lay bare the fundaments of our created world. Has God ordered his creation so that those who act rightly will be rewarded?

Job's friends present the expected answer—yes!—and are subsequently rebuked. For Job the matter is far from clear. Innocence need not be rewarded; evil is frequently left unpunished. "*Where can Wisdom be found*," Job cries. (Job 28:12) The answer is not one of reassurance: "*It is hidden from the eyes of all living, and concealed from the birds of the air*." (Job 28:21) Not even the dead have a privileged point of access. "*We have heard*," Death and Hell confess, "*only a rumor of it with our ears*." (Job 28:22) Wisdom, in any full sense of the term, is in God's hands alone. Do not be too hasty in your desire to define Wisdom's scope, another Wisdom writer warns: "*God is in heaven and you are on earth; therefore let your words be few*." (Eccl 5:2)

Even if we reject Fox's overly buoyant hopes for a creation-centered spirituality, we still have not countered his stinging criticism of original sin. Even more challenging is the seconding of Fox's criticisms by other scholars whose intellectual preferences do not rest on the moral platitudes of New Age spirituality. Consider the Requiems written by Gabriel Fauré (1845-1924) and Urban Duruflé in our own time. Both of these composers left out the haunting words of God's harsh judgment on the unjust, the *Dies Irae*. Both composers had a strong distaste for the punitive words of God at the moment of death; far better in their eyes was a funeral mass that laid sole emphasis on the merciful hand of God. Or consider the noted and notable Presbyterian Biblical scholar, Sibley Towner.[10] He begins his essay with the formulation of original sin that appears in the *Scots Confession of 1560*. This was not an insignificant document; indeed it was publicly read line by line in the Scottish Parliament. This confession of faith declares that by Adam's "transgression, generally known as original sin, [. . .] he and his children became by nature hostile to God, slaves of Satan and servants to sin." However powerful such a declaration might have been in its own day, Towner claims that it has also "wrought incalculable mischief in the hearts of believers."[11] The failure of the doctrine of original sin does not simply rest in depressive ambiance about human nature that it has produced. Its very claim as historical fact is simply preposterous.

> Modern believers and unbelievers alike tend to hold as patent nonsense the notion that all human sin

> and all death are generically descended from a single act by a single pair of human beings who lived at a single moment in time, or that the cause of their original transgression was Satan in the guise of a snake.[12]

What are we to make of such a doctrine? Towner's answer is simple and forthright. We must act with the courage of our convictions and seek to move beyond it. "The concept of a Fall-less history," he argues, "requires some further maturation in me away from the religion of my Sunday School and my dogmatics textbooks."[13] This rewriting of Christian tradition will be difficult, Towner concedes, but it will also be a bracing tonic for twentieth-century man, whose self-esteem has suffered the outrageous slings and arrows of narrow dogmatism for too long. "Perhaps I can at last see us," he concludes, "not as creatures helplessly mired in sin, helpless to extricate ourselves in any way, but rather as people and peoples who can hope to make significant strides toward emancipation from the evils of hatred and greed."[14] It would take a real curmudgeon to fault Towner for these laudable desires for emancipation. And I should also add that Towner has adequately described the problems of adhering to Genesis 1-3 as a literal account of human beginnings. Modern theologians and Biblical scholars are agreed that we must move beyond *historical* literalism. But is Towner accurate regarding what the church confesses *theologically* about *peccatum originale*?

O Necessary Sin ... O Happy Fault!

A good place to test this notion is the figure of John Milton. Raised on the theological writings of Augustine and deeply committed to the rigorous Puritan tradition, Milton is deeply aware of how weak and prone to sin and error the human creature is. The Puritanism of Milton was not far removed from the strain that produced the *Scots Confession of 1560*, a document much abhorred by Sibley Towner and numerous other moderns. If the tradition of original sin is as gloomy as Towner and Fox believe, we would expect Milton's grand epic, *Paradise Lost*, to end on a somber note. Adam's loss of grace and eviction from Eden would be a matter of profound tragic loss and deepest despair. Satan's triumph, on the other hand, should have been a moment of ecstatic delight in the kingdom of darkness. After all, Adam and Eve had proved sufficiently gullible for the most simple of temptations to take fertile root.

In fact, we find nothing of the kind. True, Satan achieved his desire; Adam and Eve fell. Yet Satan's last appearance in *Paradise Lost* is not a happy one. His return to hell is greeted with lamentation, not celebration. His is a pyrrhic victory. Adam and Eve on the other hand have lost all that they held dear. Condemned to permanent exile, we would expect their mood to be morose as they leave the Garden. Such is not the case. As *Paradise Lost* draws to a close, Adam is exultant as he makes his way out of Eden.

The poem had begun with Satan in the bowels of hell, gathering his compatriots in crime and rebellion to embark on the task of alienating God from his beloved creatures, Adam and Eve. Through some nine books, each nearly a thousand verses, we follow his peregrinations from hell to earth and then back to hell. On the surface, Satan has the best of it. His power to tempt Eve proves insurmountable. Despite all God's precautions—and there were many—the creatures he loved so dearly rebel against His rule. The reader has every right to expect that as Satan rejoins his comrades in Pandemonium, Milton's name for hell, all will rejoice. Milton subverts this expectation. As Satan enters Pandemonium, he recounts the circumstances of his mighty triumph and closes with these words (*P.L.* X:501-503):

> Ye have the account
> Of my performance: what remains, ye gods,
> But up and enter now into full bliss.
> But his cohorts see no cause for celebration.
> Instead of cries of joy Satan hears,
> A dismal universal hiss, the sound
> Of public scorn.

The mood turns even more mordant as these unlikely celebrants consider their present state. In hopes of alleviating their aching pains the demonic host turns to consider the fair fruits of hell. These fruits appear enticing; perhaps they would be a balm for their ills. As the demons reach for this "fruitage fair" an unexpected result ensues (X:564-566):

> Thinking to allay
> Their appetite with gust, instead of fruit
> Chewed bitter ashes.

In a surprising parallel to the fall of Adam and Eve, the fruits of Hades prove deceptive. When the demons chew its bitter ashes they undergo the first stage of that ancient curse pronounced on the serpent, *"you shall eat the dust of the earth."*

This is our last glimpse of Satan in *Paradise Lost*. The fall, which should have been his moment of glory, has confirmed his eternal condemnation.

Our last glimpse of Milton's Adam is also quite striking. The archangel Michael stands with Adam and Eve at the edge of Eden. Just prior to driving them out he briefs Adam on what life outside will be like. Michael outlines the entire Biblical story beginning with their own children, Cain and Abel. When Michael finishes describing the life of Christ, he pauses to catch his breath. Adam cannot endure the pause, however brief. His loses his composure as he hears these mysteries. He exclaims (XII:469-471):

> O Goodness infinite, goodness immense!
> That all this good of evil shall produce,
> And evil turn to good.

But Adam does not stop here. Not only will his evil deed be turned to good, but it shall also become the necessary prelude for the appearance of a far greater good.

Milton's brilliant and surprising ending is not solely the work of his own poetic genius. His narrative is dependent upon a theological tradition that viewed Adam's sin as a true boon for mankind. This notion of the *felix culpa*, or "happy fault," has a long pedigree in Christian thought. An ancient liturgy of Easter opens with a hymn reciting God's mighty deeds in history, the *Exultet*. This hymn compares the Israelite's exodus from Egypt to the resurrection of Christ. On that first paschal night, the slaying of the Passover lamb proved instrumental in overturning the tyranny of Pharaoh; on this second paschal occasion, the sacrifice of the Lamb of God will destroy a second Pharaoh, Satan and his kingdom. In consideration of the great redemption that Christ has wrought, the cantor sings of Adam's sin. In the wake of the long period of Lenten penance that had preceded Easter, a time in which all Christians must ponder their sinful ways, the memory of Adam's transgression should stir up thoughts of condemnation. But the text of the *Exultet* knows no such thought. In words that delight as much as they shock, the cantor sings,

> O *necessary* sin of Adam,
> that Christ has blotted out by his death;
> O *happy* fault (*felix culpa*)
> which has earned for us such a great redeemer.

How unexpected are these words. But their strangeness reveals the central mystery of Easter: the human capacity for rebellion has not led to eternal condemnation but to the miracle of God's loving and steadfast mercy.

Milton understood well the theology of "the happy fault" and makes it the basis of Adam's own self-reflection after the fall. To the surprise of many readers, Adam cannot decide whether he should repent of his sin or rejoice all the more. His sin has provided the necessary condition for making God's boundless mercy manifest. Adam declares (XII:473-478):

> Full of doubt I stand,
> Whether I should repent me now of sin
> By me done and occasioned, or rejoice
> Much more good thereof shall spring
> to God more glory, more good will to men
> From God, and over wrath grace shall abound.

Our present day "cultured despisers" of original sin do not lack good reason when they criticize this doctrine in its raw and naked form. I sincerely doubt whether Milton or the composer of the *Exultet* would have warmed to the assertion that our nature is corrupt to the core and that we merit nothing less than unending punishment and damnation. Such a view advanced too stridently would veer toward the blasphemous. When these writers condemn Adam, and through Adam all humanity, they do so in the context of a larger narrative that exalts him. Adam's humiliation leads ineluctably to his exultation. This is the paradox of original sin, a paradox that has been little noticed in our day.

Original Sin and Redemption

Original sin is not a self-contained philosophical doctrine, but depends on the religious experience of redemption. The moment we isolate the sin of Adam from this broader framework we lose its larger meaning. One of the most profound thinkers of the twentieth century, Karl Barth (1886-1968), devoted considerable energy toward recovering what Christian thought meant by the doctrine of original sin. Barth was raised on the liberal theology standard in German theological education at the close of the nineteenth century and the beginning of the twentieth. The optimism regarding the human condition that had been a formative part of that tradition was brutally undercut, Barth thought, by the tragedy of the first World War. His turn to the Bible as a source of inspiration for theological work was born, in part, from a deep distrust of what he felt was an overly optimistic assessment of what philosophical knowledge could and would yield. One might have expected Barth to begin his work by returning to the classic Protestant teachings on original sin.

But this was not what he did. Instead, when Barth sat down to write his greatest theological work, *Church Dogmatics*, he did not take up the topic of original sin until the end of the work. And this was not accidental. As he wrote:

> But the question immediately poses itself: Why is it only now that we have come to speak of this matter? Why have we not followed the example of the dogmatics of all ages, Churches and movements and begun with a doctrine of sin, first stating the problem, then giving the decisive answer to it in the doctrine of the incarnation and atoning death of Jesus Christ?[15]

Traditional Protestant teaching had attempted to erect the edifice of Christian belief on an objective portrayal of human depravity. Deep reflection on one's depravity was thought to be one short step from perceiving one's need for a redeemer. For Barth, this argument was foolish on two grounds. First, if all human beings were so depraved, one could just as easily rationalize one's own evil in a self serving way: "My actions may be despicable, but they are no worse than anyone else's." My sinful state is simply a part of the general human condition. Far from impelling the individual into the arms of a merciful redeemer, such a doctrine could just as easily serve to comfort sinful persons in their wrong doing.

Barth had another, more Biblical manner of getting at this question. He argued that no one could understand his status as "a lowly sinner" apart from the miracle of redemption. "We can never have the negative knowledge [of sin]," Barth declared, "except in [light of] this positive faith."[16] Barth fervently denied the capacity of any person to understand his fallen condition by contemplating his wayward ways. We may become aware of our limited and deficient nature by doing so. We may even incline toward despair and hopelessness. But this is not what the Bible means by sin. The fathomless depth of sin can only be glimpsed under the tutelage of the Redeemer. The experience of redemption, in Barth's eyes, was always that of an unmerited *bonum*, or gift, to the believer. Not asked for and not deserved, redemption always comes as an unexpected act of grace. *The notion of human sin and fallenness is nothing other than a considered reflection on the unmerited and unfathomable moment of salvation.*

Barth's claim about the love of God can be paralleled in our own deepest attachments. Nearly any romantic tale worth its salt will accent the profound power of love by showing its ability to transform both the lover and the beloved. Yet the power and the strength of that love nearly always is established on the fragile and frail foundation of human nature. The attitude of the beloved is never one of merit or entitledness: "I had this coming," but precisely the opposite: "I don't deserve this." As the poets are well aware, the beloved never feels worthy of the advances of the lover. When Jewish or Christian mystics appeal to their divine lover to "*draw me after you, let us make haste [to your bed-chamber]*" (Song of Songs 1:4), they utter these words in awe. True love is unmerited love.

In a profound way, the same process informs the teaching of original sin. In the religious life, human sinfulness can only be grasped as a reflection on the unmerited advances of the divine lover toward his beloved. When the church prays, "*Let him kiss me with the kisses of his mouth*," (Song of Songs 1:2) she is directing her erotic desire toward the advances of her divine lover. Yet the erotic appeal of the church to her divine lover is born from the consciousness of her own unworthiness of that love.

In a similar fashion, consider the gospel reading that introduces the period of Lenten penance in both the Eastern and Western liturgies. It is, quite ironically, the story of the prodigal son (Luke 15:11-32). The prodigal son is a young man who received an inheritance which he subsequently squandered through a life of luxury and abandon in a foreign land. Coming to his senses, he sets out for home in order to redress his ways. Arriving at home, he begs for mercy and his father is overcome with joy. His expectations, born of his penitential demeanor, are minimal. "I will get up and go to my father," the son exclaims, "and I will say to him, 'Father, I have sinned against heaven and before you; I am no longer worthy to be called your son; treat me like one of your hired hands'" (Luke 15:18-19). The other son, who never exhibited such rebellious behavior, is angered by the festivities that attend his brother's homecoming. "Listen!" he says to his father, "For all these years I have been working like a slave for you, and I have never disobeyed your command; yet you have never given me even a young goat so that I might celebrate with my friends." (Luke 15:29) No doubt, this upright brother had every right to be jealous. But the gospel reading requires this motif of unfairness to make a point: Nowhere is there more joy and thanksgiving than when a wayward person rights his course. The gospel narrative brings home, in a powerful way, that the depth of human sin is seen most clearly from the vantage point of one shown mercy. The prodigal son felt himself unworthy of being treated as a son, but his merciful and loving father saw the matter differently. His father did not see a rebellious, wayward son; he saw a son who had once been dead come to life, a son who had been lost but now was found. The unfair reception of the prodigal son serves a profound theological point: The lower one falls, the greater the joy at one's return. Or to reverse the matter, the more powerful one's sense of redemption the more profound is one's sense of sinfulness. As the church enters the Lenten period, the context against which Adam's sin is considered is that of the prodigal son. We are all, in some sense, wayward sons making our way back to a merciful father. The promise of Easter is that the power of sin and redemption are inversely related.

Elsewhere in the Bible we find a similar tendency to correlate human unworthiness with divine grace and mercy. In the Old Testament, the crowning achievement of God's created order is the election of the people of Israel at Mt. Sinai and the pronouncement of the Ten Commandments. These Ten Commandments, the first of the six hundred and thirteen to be revealed at Sinai according to Jewish tradition, are heard directly by the people Israel. So awed are they by this encounter that the people become afraid and tremble. Standing at a distance, they beg Moses to intercede on their behalf. For mere mortals to witness the stark purity and overpowering holiness of the Deity was a reckless venture. Who could behold the living God and not die? Aware of their waywardness, they appealed to Moses to approach God on their behalf.

> So now why should we (Israel) die? For this great fire will consume us; if we hear the voice of the Lord our God any longer, we shall die. For who is there of all flesh that has heard the voice of the living God speaking out of fire, as we have, and remained alive? Go near, you yourself (Moses), and hear all that the Lord our God will say. Then tell us everything that the Lord our God tells you, and we will listen and do it. (Deut 5:25-27)

Everywhere in the Bible when God appears before his people in order to save them, He strikes fear in the hearts of those so blessed. The experience of the divine calls one to reflect on one's frailty. Isaiah begged leave when he entered the presence of God, "Woe is me! I am lost, for I am a man of unclean lips." (Isa 6:5) Other prophets begged similar exemptions when God called them by name. *Those graced by the very presence of God are the very persons who reflect most poignantly on their sinful human condition*.

One of Barth's favorite illustrations of this dilemma is the story of Peter's denial of Christ as told in Luke's Gospel (22:31-34; 54-62). Luke, like the rest of the Gospel writers, presents the messianic office of Jesus of Nazareth as a mystery. This vocation was publicly announced at his baptism. Yet throughout his entire earthly life Jesus was rejected for claiming this identity. Those he was sent to redeem sought to destroy him. Even the eleven faithful disciples deserted him during his last hours, and he was left to suffer alone. Christ had predicted the denial of one of his most beloved disciples, Simon also known as Peter. "Simon, Simon" Christ said, "Satan has sought to test you as one winnows grain. I have prayed on your behalf that your faith not fail. But you, when you have turned back, strengthen your brothers." (Luke 22:31-32) Then Peter, acting with a sincerity that is as touching as it is human, counters this prediction with a foolhardy vow, "Lord I am ready to go with you to prison and to death!" Jesus replies, "I tell you Peter, the cock will not crow this day until you have denied me three times." (Luke 22:33-34) Later that evening Jesus is betrayed, arrested, and taken by force to the High Priest's home for interrogation. Peter, following at a distance, enters and takes a seat near an open fire, warming himself outside as Christ is interrogated within. Once, twice, finally a third time, Peter denies ever having known this man from Galilee. As in the other Gospel accounts, the cock crows. Luke's story has not ended. As the cock crows, Jesus looks away from the High Priest and his court which sits ready to condemn him and catches his precious disciple's eye. "Peter remembered the word of the Lord," Luke records, "and he went out and wept bitterly." (Luke 22:61b-62)

Peter's earlier words, although they border on bragging, are hardly contemptible. We err badly if we begrudge him his feeling of confidence. Peter's confidence, whatever its source, runs aground on the shoals of his own fears and self-interest. But his awareness of his failure is contextualized by Luke in the face to face encounter with his Lord. As Raymond Brown has remarked: "Jesus had [earlier] prayed for Peter that his faith might not fail, now Jesus is leading his disciple to repentance so that having turned around, he may strengthen others."[17] Peter learns of his sinful predisposition, not as a sterile dogma, nor solely as a moment of hatred and loathing turned inward. His sinful inclination becomes clear only through the loving glance of his Lord, a glance that forgives even as it renders judgment.

Peter's failure is revealed in a face-to-face glance by his redeemer who hastened to forgive even as he issued judgment. And so our paradox: Peter's profound knowledge of this forgiving love, like the knowledge of the prodigal son, springs from a moment of abject failure. The greatness of Peter, which will come to light in the wake of Easter, originated in the weakness he reveals during Jesus' trial.

In the experience of unmerited redemption, the advances of the divine lover seem too grand for words. In the attempt to characterize their awe at this act of God's condescension to humanity, Biblical writers give voice to their own sense of inadequacy for such an encounter. It is from precisely this nexus—the merciful approach of God to an unexpectant person—that the notion of original sin takes life. And so Barth's profound insight: original sin is not a reasoned, philosophical consideration of human waywardness and evil, however true these concepts might be on their own terms. The doctrine of original sin is a theological attempt to sketch how profound this mystery and *experience* of redemption truly is.

Adam as Microcosm

To Karl Barth we owe the modern articulation that the depth of human sin can only be known by the redeemed. As the story of Peter's denial of Christ and the parable of the prodigal son illustrate, the locus of human sin is precisely the spot where God's capacity for mercy shines most brilliantly.

Yet one may wonder whether the mercy shown to Peter or the prodigal son are isolated examples or representative of a larger pattern. Would it be more honest to say that the occurrences of love and mercy are distributed randomly across the face of human history? Would the world be better defined as an arbitrary and unjust place?

Christians answer this question with a resounding "*No*!" For Christians, the affirmation that God's mercy defines the very ground of human existence is founded on the basis of Adam's sin and redemption. As we could not understand the prodigal son's confession of sin apart from the loving father anxious to forgive and restore him to his place in the family, so we cannot understand Adam's sin without setting it against the backdrop of his redemption. Not by accident, both readings are lenten texts.

In individual stories of repentance we see the effects of divine mercy in *microcosm*; in the history of Adam this work of redemption is writ large across the *macrocosm*. Any particular moment of tearful confession and redemption is not a random act; it is a participation in the most fundamental structure of the created order. All have died in the first Adam; all will rise through the second. And this is precisely the reason why the Christian tradition has ascribed the fall of man to the sin of just one man. The defeat of that first man is swallowed up by the victory of the last man—Jesus Christ. This is no exercise in literary artistry, as though the writers of the Bible had merely aesthetic interests at stake when they closed this story as it had opened. The purpose was theological. The story ends as it began in order to bring home the point that God's forgiveness of Adam through Christ defines *all* human creation. Individual acts of mercy are not random and episodic; they participate in that grand act of mercy that defines the poles of creation.

Many have claimed that since we can no longer accept the historical existence of Adam and Eve, the story of their sin and redemption can no longer have any meaning. But such a narrow view of how the Bible discloses its meaning misses the entire point. Adam and Eve are significant as individuals not because they represent the very first persons on planet earth, but because they serve the narrative purpose of affirming that all human existence stands under the broad canopy of a merciful God. Forgiveness and grace are not arbitrary moments in the lives of random specimens of the species *homo sapiens*. They are the very center point around which all creation turns—and flourishes. This is the teaching of original sin.

Endnotes

1. "Homily on the Passion of Our Lord," falsely attributed to St. Athanasius, Patrologia Graeca 28.204.

2. Ibid.

3. On the importance of knowing the full narrative horizon of the scriptural story see the essay of Robert Jensen, "How the World Lost its Story," *First Things* 36 (1993): 19-24. His remarks on the poetics of Aristotle are particularly relevant, "[T]he sequential events [of any realistic narrative like the Bible] are understood jointly to make a certain kind of sense, a dramatic kind of sense. Aristotle provided the classic specification of dramatically coherent narrative. In a dramatically good story, he said, each decisive event is unpredictable until it happens, but immediately upon taking place is seen to be exactly what 'had' to happen. So, to take the example of Aristotle's own favorite good story, we could not know in advance the Oedipus would blind himself, but once he has done it instantly see that the whole story must lead to and flow from just this act."

4. Gerhard von Rad, *Genesis, a Commentary*, trans. John H. Marks (Philadelphia: Westminster, 1961), 159.

5. Gerhard von Rad, *Genesis*, 160.

6. Paul Ricoeur, *The Symbolism of Evil* [*Symbolique du Mal*] trans. Emerson Buchanan (New York: Harper and Row, 1967), 263.

7. On the terms "first-born" and "only begotten" and their relationship to the theme of election, see the comments of Michael E. Stone, *Fourth Ezra: A Commentary on the Book of Fourth Ezra* (Hermeneia; Minneapolis: Fortress Press, 1990), 188-189.

8. Edward Oakes, "Original Sin: A Disputation," *First Things* 87 (1998): 16. Much of this section of my essay has been inspired by this excellent article.

9. Matthew Fox, *Original Blessing: A Primer in Creation Spirituality in Four Paths, Twenty-six Themes, and Two Questions* (Santa Fe: Bear Press, 1983).

10. W. Sibley Towner, "Interpretations and Reinterpretations of the Fall," in *Modern Biblical Scholarship: Its Impact on Theology and Proclamation*, ed. Francis A. Eigo (Villanova, PA: Villanova University 1984), 53-85.

11. Cited in W. Sibley Towner, "Interpretations," 56-57.

12. W. Sibley Towner, "Interpretations," 57-58.

13. Ibid.

14. W. Sibley Towner, "Interpretations," 82.

15. Karl Barth, *Church Dogmatics,* vol. 4 (Edinburgh: T &T Clark, 1956), 359.

16. *Church Dogmatics*, vol. 4: 413.

17. Raymond E. Brown, *Death of the Messiah: From Gethsemane to the Grave: A Commentary on the Passion Narratives in the Four Gospels*, vol. 1 (New York: Doubleday, 1994), 622.

Herod's Hit Man: Horror and the Development of Girls' Spiritual Voices[1]

Patricia H. Davis
PERKINS SCHOOL OF THEOLOGY
SOUTHERN METHODIST UNIVERSITY
DALLAS, TEXAS

> ... girls between the ages of ten and nineteen present special problems of interpretation. On the one hand, the evidence of their involvement in witchcraft proceedings is remarkably full and vivid; on the other, there is hardly any evidence about their experience apart from such involvement.[2]

Nilla was twelve years old, the sister of three older sisters, and the daughter of the most eccentric parents in her rural township. Their gray old house was set back from a dirt road, surrounded by untidy fields. Their barn was teeming with dogs, cats, kittens, baby pigs, a ragged old horse, and assorted wild children. Their back woods were rumored to be the site of cult rituals, and Nilla herself said she'd found possible sacrificial remains by the overgrown pond there.

Halloween was the family specialty. On Halloween nights Nilla's father became a vampire, and her mother became a particularly horrible-looking witch. The combination of the two monsters and their enthusiasm for their roles scared local trick-or-treaters out of their wits on a yearly basis. It was a rare child who had the courage to accept the candy offered. For several years fundamentalist churches in the area picketed the house in hopes of shutting down the family's extravagant Halloween enterprise. Even without the vampire and witch on the porch, however, the house had a spooky aura. Even the family's minister tried not to visit at night.

Despite her family's eccentricities Nilla had many friends; usually she looked and behaved like most of the rest of them, except that she got better grades in school. She was, in most ways, a "normal kid" with strange tales to tell. She loved to tell her stories of ghosts in her bedroom, and of tapping noises in her basement, and of candles that would burn without having been lit by human hands.

Although neither she nor her sisters or parents attended worship regularly, she had a keen interest in traditional Christianity and was a regular attender at the local Methodist church Sunday School. She was the student who could be depended upon to notice the odd subtexts in the Bible stories and the one who demanded explanations of difficult passages.

The year she was in sixth grade she and her parents decided that it would be a good thing for her to be in the church Christmas Eve pageant being organized by the new pastor's wife.

Being sensitive to avoid leaving anyone out, or casting people in roles they didn't want, the pastor's wife was determined to allow the children to choose their own parts. She assigned Mary and Joseph to two older children, then gathered all the others and began slowly to read the familiar story of Jesus' birth. As she read, the children called out the characters they wanted to play: angels, shepherds, kings, lambs, donkeys, camels—all claimed their roles. At the end of the story Nilla hadn't found a role to suit her.

Mrs. Alexander, the costume manager, tried to coax Nilla into being a king or shepherd, to no avail. Nilla finally asked if she could have the Bible. She took it to read by herself. For fifteen or twenty minutes she was hardly noticed, reading intently, amid all the confusion of trying to find wings and crowns and tails for all the angels, kings, and beasts.

After ten minutes she returned. "Mrs. Alexander, I've found my role."

"Yes, Nilla—who are you going to be?"

"A hit man."

Mrs. Alexander swallowed hard, noticing the upward glance of the minister's wife. "There are no hit men in this story, honey."

"Right here: 'Rise, take the child and his mother, and flee to Egypt, and remain there till I tell you; for Herod is about to search for the child, to destroy him.' I want to be Herod's hit man."[3]

"What would a hit man wear?"

"All black—to hide—and he'd carry a sword."

"You're sure that's what you want?"

"Yes, Ma'am."

"Okay, Nilla. That's you."

On that Christmas Eve night—thanks to Mrs. Alexander and Nilla—their Methodist church saw and heard a fuller version of the story of Christ's birth, with both the wonder and the horror intact. In this church the wise men traveled to King Herod before they arrived in Bethlehem; they were accompanied by a shadowy figure on their way to the stable. Outside the stable, a hit man lurked as Mary cherished the baby and the angels sang. On that Christmas Eve, Nilla's church may have been the only church in Christendom to remember Christ's birth in this more complete narrative including not only the beauty and glory, but also the fear, the evil, the grief, and the "hit man."

Girls' Lives and Voices

Horror.

Nilla was an expert. Even girls less attuned to it than Nilla seem to understand it. Most church people don't. Girls seem to live in different worlds than adult church members. Girls, even those not as attuned to horror as Nilla, live in a strange and dangerous reality, and they know it.

Research on criminal victimization rates of girls has shown that one in three girls will be sexually abused before she is eighteen.[4] Of these girls eighty-nine percent will be abused by a family member.[5] The Department of Justice *National Crime Victimization Survey* from 1993 reports that girls ages twelve to twenty-four are almost ten times more likely to be raped than females of other ages.[6] Murder rates are also much higher for adolescents (both boys and girls) than for other age groups.[7]

In addition to violence, girls are also subject to such cultural factors as racism, classism, and ageism. Undoubtedly some of girls' appreciation for horror stems from their relatively dangerous social locations in the culture, the reality of which they are just beginning to be able to comprehend.

Television programmers understand the attraction of horror for girls and have capitalized on it. Shows such as *Buffy the Vampire Slayer* and *Xena: Princess Warrior* weekly attract huge audiences of adolescent girls. Publishing houses have also realized the power of girls' fascination with the horrific sides of life. The best selling young adult author of all time, R.L. Stine, churns out little novels authenticating girls' horrific vision on an almost monthly basis.[8] V.C. Andrews writes more substantial novels about girls whose lives are touched by evil and marked by their resistance to it.[9] Books about girls who are addicted to drugs,[10] are in love with serial killers,[11] are sexually abused,[12] and are living with physically abusive relatives[13] are currently girls' favorites. Both *The New York Times*[14] and *Publishers Weekly*[15] have run articles in the last several months wondering about girls' predilections for such "grim" topics.

The answer to that question has to do with girls' realities and their newly forming abilities to comprehend them. Adolescence is a time when girls begin to develop the mental capacities to think in new and more complex ways. Robert Kegan, a developmental psychologist, describes the changes that take place in adolescent meaning-making as they move from "categorical" to "cross-categorical" ways of thinking and feeling. Young children think "categorically," living inside their social realities in such a way that they are unaware that the realities could be different. They can't imagine things outside of the categories they believe are "normal." They cannot understand, for example, that their parents could be different, that their teachers could be more or less fair, that their churches could be more or less open to hearing their feelings and thoughts about God and their faith.

As girls become adolescents, however, they move out of merely categorical thinking and are able to begin to comprehend their worlds at deeper levels, moving toward "cross-categorical" mental capacities. They begin to develop abilities to reason abstractly, to think about their own thinking, and to understand others' points of view empathically.[16] They also become aware that their realities could be different than they are, that violence could be stopped, that abuse and oppression are not normal, that religious people have responsibilities to take action against injustice.

Girls have trouble, however, being understood and taken seriously by the adult world that has so much power over them. Because of their age, gender, inexperience, and relative powerlessness, their awareness of social realities does not often translate into an ability to make changes. Often it does not translate into the ability, or opportunity, or safety even to *speak* of the things they see.

They often feel, in fact, that telling what they think, expressing preferences, lobbying for what they want, or asking for what they need are all hopeless and/or dangerous enterprises. Educators note that this struggle for "voice" arises, in part, because of another cultural factor—a "hidden curriculum"—that teaches girls in subtle ways that they don't matter.[17]

Carol Gilligan writes that because girls' voices are cut off, and because their visions of life are undervalued or disregarded by adults, many girls retreat to places unseen by others. They seem to begin to live significant portions of their lives "underground."[18] Gilligan's research aims at meeting girls in their underground caverns of knowledge, where they keep their most precious thoughts and insights. Many girls stop talking altogether in the "above-ground" world; they remain silent in classes, in church, and in their families. They stop talking, but they don't stop watching. They see and understand the reality of the danger and horror around them.

Horror in Our Culture

In 1997 Mark Edmundson, an English literature professor at the University of Virginia, published an excellent volume of provocative popular theology entitled *Nightmare on Main Street.* In this book he attempts to explain the resurgence of what he calls gothic horror in our culture at large.[19] He writes that he found himself strangely drawn to a whole set of current and cult horror movies, with titles like *Scream, Dawn of the Dead, Last House on the Left, Nightmare on Elm Street,* and *Texas Chainsaw Massacre.* He not only watched these films, he became somewhat obsessed with them. Then, he analyzed his obsession.

In brief, he decided that he had tapped into a cultural undercurrent (almost undertow) of horror—gothic horror—"possession narratives"—running from the O.J. Simpson trial, to Oprah, to horror movies, to rumors of ritual cult abuse, to the evening news.

Gothic, Edmundson writes, "is the art of haunting. . . . It shows us time and again that life, even at its most ostensibly innocent is possessed, that the present is in thrall to the past. All are guilty. All must, in time, pay up."[20]

Why this undercurrent of horror? Edmund's almost throwaway answer is that people have stopped believing in God.

> Though most of us Americans claim to believe in God, few of us seem able to believe in God's presence. That is, we do not perceive some powerful force for good shaping the events of day-to-day life in accord with a perceptibly benevolent master plan. Most of us don't have a story that we can believe about the way God's designs are unfolding among us. Whatever God is up to, he is not busying himself unduly with worldly events.[21]

How can we escape the horror of a God-less world? Edmundson notes there is another strong undercurrent in our culture—one he identifies with angels and Forrest Gump—which he calls "facile transcendence." Forrest is faced with many challenges and heartbreaking circumstances, but none touch his essential goodness. And, he is richly rewarded for remaining simple.
Edmudson writes:

> Through [all his trials] Alabaman Forrest is magnolia sweet. . . At the core of Forrest Gump is the sugary fiction that dull virtue in tandem with humble, unrelenting poverty is well rewarded.[22]

Forrest Gump is the culture's vacation from horror. He is the respite—to whom we turn when we need a breath of cleaner air. It's not satisfying, because it's honeysuckle sweet. But, it's some sort of relief.

My Research

How does spirituality shape the ways girls understand themselves and their worlds, their experiences of safety and their experiences of horror? Between 1993 and 1997 I undertook research designed to try to hear from girls—from their underground worlds (as much as they would allow it)—from various geographic, economic, racial/ethnic, and religious backgrounds. I used a questionnaire and an interview format and talked with girls in churches, community agencies, and schools. The methodological premise was that to understand girls' spirituality it was necessary to engage and to encourage their voices. During the four-year period I talked to more than 100 girls from Boston, New York, Philadelphia, Dallas, Denver, Indianapolis, and Atlanta.

Interviews took place in church youth groups, in dance troupes, in prep school lounges, and in a church "attic" with girls after an annual youth service. The girls represented diverse religious communities; they were Presbyterian, Methodist, Episcopalian, Roman Catholic, charismatic, Southern Baptist, agnostic, and those who categorized themselves as "nothing" or "atheist." They also represented diverse ethnicities: Arab American, African American, Anglo, Eurasian, and Latina.

Some of the girls had very strong positive spiritualities. They had begun to learn to relate to God in mature ways, tolerating ambiguities and paradoxes, even making sense of silence. For these girls, their spiritualities were beginning to give them a positive sense of identity and life's meaning.

Most girls who participated in this study, however, also revealed ways in which their spiritualities were troubled. Many of these girls described having deep spiritual questions that arise out of their new comprehension of their worlds. They wanted answers to questions. They wondered if God listens; they often wondered if God cares about them. They also wondered what God expects from them, and why it isn't communicated clearly. They were very troubled about God's seeming tolerance of evil and violence.

Many of the girls I talked to bear witness to a gothic vision of the world arising from their own experience, their view from the underground, and their cultural heritage. They are also, however, struggling to find a way to believe in God in this world. They often turn to the church for help in this struggle. But they are startled, unhappy, and disillusioned to find that, for the most part, the God they are presented in church is a God derived from the facile transcendent world Edmundson describes. It is the God of Forrest Gump, present in the world, but only capable of the most innocuous goodness. A God who is essentially unaware of evil. A God who seems not to give answers to hard questions.

Two topics that seem to hold special interest, and to pose very difficult problems for the girls I talked with are sexuality and violence. For the girls, both of these issues have strong connections to their visions of God and their feelings of insecurity in the world.

Sexuality

Today's adolescents have much more exposure to sex than teenagers of previous generations. From television, to movies, to books, to the Internet, sex acts are performed before their eyes and ears, and sexuality is discussed in both healthy and unhealthy forums. Sexuality is tied to horror for girls through first- or second-hand knowledge of sexual abuse and rape, through their observations about the culture's general attitude about young women's supposed "uncanny" sexual powers, and through their observations that, for instance, girls who are sexually active are often the first/prime victims in the sorts of horror movies Edmundson watched.

It is natural that adolescents would turn to the church and to God for guidance on this matter so important to them. It is natural that they connect sexuality with spirituality and with horror, as they recognize the new power and vulnerability that is theirs in sexuality.

Sadly, for many of the girls I interviewed there is a large gap between what they are being presented by their churches and what they wish would be addressed. Girls want to discuss sex and sexuality with adults who are not embarrassed; they want to learn about the emotional as well as physical aspects of sex; they want help in making decisions; they wonder why their sexuality is not encouraged and celebrated. They wonder what God thinks of them as sexual beings. Even those churches that provide sexuality education for adolescents often "miss the point" as far as the girls are concerned, and avoid the questions the girls are really asking about God and their sexualities.

The following conversation took place with a group of six girls at a large Midwestern church, the week after they had all participated in a sexuality education seminar called CPR (*Creating Positive Relationships*). The conversation began with an acknowledgment that the class was an embarrassment for most students:

> Liz (15): Our [church] had a thing on CPR and we talked about sex and things like that, but most people were embarrassed about it and they really didn't want to talk about it. But we had this whole lesson. Most of the people really just laughed at it and were very immature about it.

According to Liz, the problem stemmed from the fact that the teacher was uneasy about teaching sexuality, and conveyed this to the students. She wonders if she was the only one who thought this ("Am I crazy?"):

> I could tell the teacher sort of felt uncomfortable in a way. Or maybe it was just me that felt that way. It just—

Clair (14) interrupts, and expresses her gratitude for any information:

> I'm in the eighth grade, and with this CPR thing, I've never heard of this before in my entire life. . . I never knew any of this, 'til this Sunday and last Sunday, and I knew about saving sex for when you're married. But like nobody ever explained it to me or anything, and I think a lot of the eighth graders who are in my class, feel the same way . . . I think it's a really really good thing to talk about, because it just helps you plan your life, basically.

But, she acknowledges that the answer to her real question—How do I know what the limits of sexual activity should be at my age, before I'm married?—was not provided:

> We've asked questions like "How far is too far?" and stuff like that, but our teacher didn't really answer. He just said, you know, "Sex before marriage is wrong," which we all knew that.
>
> . . . Well, you know, what do you think about what comes before—like until you can't stop from going on and having sex and stuff? . . . So we really didn't get an answer on that, and I was wondering about that.

Why, she wonders, won't the teacher answer her question? Why did he try to substitute an easy, and well-known, answer for a harder one—the real one?

Missy (15) agrees that the subject needs to be discussed because girls her age are not aware that other sexual activities besides intercourse are also wrong:

> I believe that we don't talk about the other things that go on, because there's sex and then there's other contacts. . . that are sinful also. And we don't talk about that. [Girls] are like, "Well, as long as I'm not having sex I'm O.K." But I don't agree with that—because in a guy's eyes sex and all those other things are equal. I don't know if you guys believe that or not, but I think if you're doing something that you're

> not supposed to, it's still a sin. And so I think this is overlooked. And I don't think it's talked about enough in school, and that it's not O.K. to do that.

When I asked her to be specific about what is sinful and what isn't:

> Well, kissing's obviously not [a sin]. I guess, yeah, don't go on beyond a kiss. Removing clothes or going up someone's shirt or something like that. . . I don't think you should be going beyond a kiss, or whatever.

She begins to hesitate and stumble over words when she hears the rest of the girls disagreeing with her. She thinks maybe she has set the boundary too high. Then, she returns to her original argument, stressing the need for people to be told about all kinds of sexual expression, because knowing that it is wrong might make girls think more (although it might not change their behavior much):

> I wish people would know. Because when you think back more, if people actually knew, it would make them stop and think that what they're doing is wrong. And they wouldn't do it. As much.

Where is God in sexuality? For these girls it must appear that God either doesn't provide answers for hard questions. Or that their real questions are too embarrassing to be talked about. Or that they are too young to hear. Girls make all sorts of excuses for God and for adults who aren't helpful. Even so, it makes them wonder about their God and their church:

> So we really didn't get an answer on that. And I was wondering about that.

Violence

The second set of examples has to do with the violence girls experience in their lives and the church's lack of attention to it.

Girls who have experienced violence often have a difficult time relating to God and the church. Beliefs about God change, or God begins to fade from their immediate concern. Sometimes they try not to think about religion, because they can't reconcile the violence they've seen with their images of a God who loves them and the world. Their churches don't seem able or willing to help them in this struggle.

Maria (18) is the secretary of her church, an ethnically diverse congregation in an urban area in the Southwest. Three years earlier she had been a member of the youth advisory team and president of her youth group. Then one of her good friends was shot and killed. She talks about the shooting:

> One of my friends, one of the members of the youth group was murdered about three years ago. . . Eric. He was shot. He was the vice-president of the youth group, and in charge with me. He was in a house and they broke in, and they shot him point blank, so—there was no struggle or anything.

Eric's death was her first real experience of loss due to violence, and it shattered her belief that the world is a safe place. The morals and values her mother instilled in her didn't protect her from losing a friend:

> I've always been and I still am kind of sheltered from everything. My mother is so strict with me, and she's brought me up with morals, and values, and things, and I've always been sheltered from violence and things that are going on. So it was a shock and kind of hard to handle, because that has been the only time I've had to deal with losing a close friend.

In the aftermath of the shooting she felt close to God and alienated from God at the same time:

> In this situation I felt closest to God and distant from Him. I think this situation kind of pulled me away from Him, but at the same time it made me feel close. I felt closest to God, because I feel that He got me through it. Without Him I don't think I would have, and it was also with friends and family that supported me. But at the same time I felt distant from Him, because that's the time that I started questioning Him and doubting Him, and you know, wondering, "Why me?" or "Why my friend?" So it goes both ways, me feeling close to Him and me feeling distant.

Maria continues to attend church and to participate in national youth events in her denomination, but God is not currently an important part of her life. Between the time of the shooting and my interview with her, God had become more and more distant.

> I'm in this stage, kind of, right now where I feel kind of distant from God. Religion hasn't been that important, hasn't been up there in a long time.

Her problem with God stems from Eric's death, and from her realization that violence and cruelty are pervasive in her world. She has begun to reckon with the problem of theodacy in her own way: I think I kind of don't understand why, if He is such a powerful God, I don't understand why we have so much crime and so much death and things like that. There's so much cruelty in the world and it seems like things are just getting worse. They're not getting any better and, I think, I don't understand. If He's supposed to be so loving and powerful, then why are so many things going on? So I think that's the only thing I have with God.

She has repeatedly asked adults in the church, including her ministers, to answer her questions. She is not satisfied with any of the explanations given, and is not willing to forget the questions in order to restore a closer relationship with God:

> It's been explained to me so many times why things like this happen. But I still kind of have doubts. I don't think it's going to get any better unless someone changes it.

It's up to "someone" else to change the world. She has doubts that God or the church will be much help.

Kim, De Andree, and Vanesia from South Dallas are frustrated that the church has done little to change the dangerous situations in their neighborhoods and at school. They describe having grown up with kids who are now in gangs, and having to learn to negotiate relationships with those kids and the gangs. They talk about drugs and weapons in their schools, and police dogs sniffing their lockers. They talk about worrying about drive-by shootings, and hearing little voices in their heads always telling them to be careful because, "The next time it could be you."

Kim is frustrated that the church seems to be more concerned with its own peace than her safety: "The church could do something about it, but they're scared."

De Andree believes that God is furious with the perpetrators of violence, and with the church. God is also, in her view, shamed by the pervasiveness of violence. She wants to encourage "everybody" to take part in working to change their neighborhoods.

> God does not like this—is probably very angry—angry at everybody. I'm SERIOUS!! He feels disgraced by it.
>
> And everybody would have to suffer just because of some people. Everybody needs to work together.

When asked if the church helps them to stay out of trouble, they respond with giggles. Their community leaders have obviously let them know that gangs, drugs, and other kinds of violence are not acceptable: "They just put the fear in us so we will know not to do something like that. It would be all over."

According to these girls, the church can help them to stay beyond the reach of perpetrators of violence by encouraging them and standing by them as they resist the temptation to join in. It also provides activities for them to "keep them off the streets." They believe, however, that the church will not fight to reduce the influence of gangs and violent people in the community, because it is afraid to be involved. They are grateful for any help they can get in their struggles with violence—grateful that the church is a safe place for them—but, they are frustrated and confused about the church's unwillingness to take on the real battle.

For Maria, Kim, Vanesia, and De Andree, who see the reality and pervasiveness of violence in their communities very clearly, adults and the church are disappointments. From their perspective adult Christians fail them in two ways: (1) by hypocritically denying the extent of the violence and (2) by failing to "work together" to solve the problem. They are hesitant to talk about God, but when they do, it is clear that they are disappointed with God also: "If He's supposed to be so loving and powerful, then why are so many things going on?" "I wonder . . . how anyone can allow children to die like that."

The explanations given to them by adults don't make sense, and this leaves them more prone to doubts about God's power and love. They believe that most adults are not able to appreciate the seriousness of their situation.

Conclusion

I don't agree with Mark Edmundson's theory that our cultural undercurrent of gothic horror would be less pervasive if people really believed in God. I think that girls have it more right: The real struggle is to try to find God in the midst of horrors. Girls, if we listen to and encourage their newly developing voices, will help us to see enough of their lives—and our own—to appreciate the reality of horror, violence, and hard questions about sexuality. Girls—if they are given safe spaces in which to speak the truth, and if their voices are attended to—can give churches an antidote to Forrest Gump theologies. They can give us the gift of clearing the air of honeysuckle sweetness.

But, girls need something in return. They need models of adults who have wrestled with God, who have experienced and not turned from the horrible questions of faith, adults who can talk with clear voices about sexuality in realistic and wholesome terms—and help them to find God's grace as well as "sin" and horror in sexual expression. They need adults who will face up to the reality and horror of violence in their lives—and not try to cover it over. More than easy answers, they need adults who will listen carefully, who will not assume they can easily understand, and who will act to protect them from any identified ongoing violence.[23]

Girls from families and faith communities who address the hard questions will be better able to resist cultural messages that their voices aren't important. They will also be better able to live in relationship to God notwithstanding their important questions. Life can be hard, unfair, and unjust; "hit men" lurk to ruin even the most innocent pleasures. For girls who are just developing their voices, and just beginning to understand the realities of their world, a God who smells like honeysuckle may be more of a horror than an absent one.

Endnotes

1. I am grateful for many helpful insights from those who have heard or read an earlier version of this paper and especially for the wisdom of M. Shawn Copeland, Paula Buford, Carolyn Bohler, and Kathleen Greider.

2. John Putnam Demos, *Entertaining Satan: Witchcraft and the Culture of Early New England* (New York: Oxford University Press, 1982), 157.

3. When she identifies herself in the story, Nilla chooses a male figure. She might perhaps be unusual in that regard. She is not unusual, however, in describing powerful figures in male language. Nearly all of the girls interviewed in my study named God as "he." See Patricia H. Davis, *Counseling Adolescent Girls* (Minneapolis: Fortress Press, 1996), 39-49 for more discussion of this phenomenon. Also see Carol Saussy, *God Images and Self Esteem: Empowering Women in a Patriarchal Society* (Louisville: Westminster/John Knox, 1991), for a discussion of the negative effects of an exclusively male God-image for women and girls.

4. David Finkelhor, *Childhood Sexual Abuse: New Theory and Research* (New York: The Free Press, 1984); Gail Wyatt, "The Sexual Abuse of Afro-American and White Women in Childhood," *Child Abuse and Neglect* 9 (1985): 507-519.

5. Diana Russell, *The Secret Trauma: Incest in the Lives of Girls and Women* (New York: Basic Books, 1986).

6. U.S. Department of Justice, *National Crime Victimization Survey, 1992-1993*, "Female Rape Rates, by Race and Age of Victim, 1993."

7. Federal Bureau of Investigation, *Supplementary Homicide Report*, 1992.

8. A few recent titles include: *Chamber of Fear* (New York: Golden Books, 1998); *Cheerleaders: The New Evil* (New York: Pocket Books, 1994); *The Hitchhiker* (New York: Scholastic Books, 1993); *Scream* (New York: Golden Books, 1998); and *Forbidden Secrets* (New York: Pocket Books, 1996).

9. Recent titles include: *Darkest Hour* (New York: Pocket Books, 1993); *Hidden Jewel* (New York: Pocket Books, 1995).

10. Melvin Burgess, *Smack* (New York: Holt, 1998).

11. Robert Cormier, *Tenderness* (New York: Delacorte Press, 1997).

12. Brock Cole, *The Facts Speak for Themselves* (Arden, N.C.: Front Street Press, 1997).

13. Norma Fox Mazer, *When She Was Good* (New York: Arthur A. Levine Books, 1997).

14. Sara Mosle, "The Outlook's Bleak," *The New York Times Magazine*, August 2, 1998, 34, 36; Alison Lurie, "Reading at Escape Velocity," *The New York Times Book Review*, May 17, 1998.

15. Jennifer M. Brown and Cindi Di Marzo, "Why So Grim?" *Publishers Weekly*, February 16, 1998, 120-123.

16. Robert Kegan, *In Over Our Heads: The Mental Demands of Modern Life* (Cambridge: Harvard University Press, 1994), 15-36.

17. Myra and David Sadker show the particular ways girls are silenced in their school environments in their volume, *Failing at Fairness: How America's Schools Cheat Girls* (New York: Charles Scribner's Sons, 1994).

18. Carol Gilligan, "Teaching Shakespeare's Sister: Notes from the Underground of Female Adolescence," in *Making Connections: The Relational Worlds of Adolescent Girls at Emma Willard School*, Carol Gilligan, Nona P. Lyons, and Trudy J. Hanmer, eds. (Cambridge: Harvard University Press, 1990), 6-27.

19. Mark Edmundson, *Nightmare on Main Street: Angels, Sadomasochism, and the Culture of Gothic* (Cambridge: Harvard University Press, 1997).

20. Ibid., 5.

21. Ibid., 67.

22. Ibid., 75.

23. Excellent resources are available on issues of abuse and healing for girls and women. See Christie Neuger's article in Mark Edmundson's *Nightmare on Main Street: Angels, Sadomasochism, and the Culture of Gothic*, and other resources such as Carol Adams and Marie Fortune's, *Violence Against Women and Children: A Christian Theological Sourcebook* (New York: Continuum, 1995); Linda H. Hollies, *Inner Healing for Broken Vessels* (Nashville: Upper Room Books, 1992); Barrie Levy, ed., *Dating Violence: Young Women in Danger* (Seattle: Seal Press, 1991); Patricia H. Davis, *Counseling Adolescent Girls* (Minneapolis: Fortress Press, 1996), 66-81; and S. Amelia Stinson-Wesley, "Daughters of Tamar: Pastoral Care for Survivors of Rape," in *Through the Eyes of Women: Insights for Pastoral Care*, ed. Jeanne Stevenson Moessner (Minneapolis: Fortress Press, 1996), 222-239.

The Word of God in the Theology of Friedrich Schleiermacher

Dawn DeVries
UNION THEOLOGICAL SEMINARY AND
PRESBYTERIAN SCHOOL OF CHRISTIAN EDUCATION
RICHMOND, VIRGINIA

> Christianity properly so called [is] faith in a revelation of God in the person of Jesus.
> —Schleiermacher, *On the Glaubenslehre*

> The infinite significance of Holy Scripture is not in contradiction to its hermeneutical limitations.
> —Schleiermacher, *Aphorisms on Hermeneutics*

Introduction

There is a common tradition of interpretation that attributes to Friedrich Schleiermacher (1768-1834) the dubious honor of ushering in the distinctively modern phase of Protestant theology. According to this account, the honor truly *is* dubious, for the fate of the type of theology he initiated has not been a happy one; in one way or another it has led to a dead end. The story has several alternative endings, each highlighting the putatively insurmountable difficulties associated with Schleiermacher's "theology of experience." But perhaps no single version of the story has been as powerful in asserting itself in the theological landscape of the twentieth century as that of Emil Brunner and Karl Barth. Brunner offered a sustained critique of Schleiermacher's theology in his 1924 book *Mysticism and the Word*.[1] He argued that the father of modern theology betrayed the Reformers' commitment to the Word in his turn to experience as a source for dogmatics, and thus surrendered to the hopeless confusion of mysticism. Barth, in his voluminous *Church Dogmatics*, set out to provide the antidote to the theology of experience: a straightforward and unabashed theology of the Word of God.[2] For better or for worse, not in small part as a result of Barth's own work as a historian, Schleiermacher and Barth are almost always catalogued in the history of doctrine as polar opposites. But does this characterization really correspond to the facts? This, in part, is the question I sought to answer in the research begun during the year of my Luce Fellowship.

It needs to be admitted at the outset that Barth's version of the story of modern Protestant theology has been under attack for some time, and were my project simply a blow-by-blow refutation of Barth's interpretation of Schleiermacher, it would have a limited value. To serious Schleiermacher scholars, it will come as no surprise that Barth was not an accurate reader and interpreter of Schleiermacher.[3] My goal in this study is another one: that is, to question the underlying general description of Schleiermacher's theology as a "theology of experience." Although it is certainly correct to say that Schleiermacher understood doctrines as articulations of Christian faith and not as supernaturally revealed propositions about God,[4] it does not follow that therefore he had no concept of revelation or of the Word of God, or that these concepts had no role in his dogmatic system. Schleiermacher, it seems to me, is justified in his dismay at others' failure to understand him, especially on this point.[5] How can a theologian who claims that "Christianity properly so called is belief in a revelation of God in the person of Jesus"[6] be accused of substituting anthropology for theology, the word of man for the Word of God?

I am arguing, then, on the basis of a close textual analysis of his works, that Schleiermacher's theology might more correctly be seen as a distinctive type of theology of the Word of God. If my interpretation of his work is persuasive, it will entail some changes in the way the history of Protestant theology is told. On the one hand, if I am right about Schleiermacher, it will be impossible any longer to present Barth's and Brunner's theology of the Word as a radical break with liberalism's theology of experience. Although there are undoubtedly many individual points of continuity and discontinuity, it will not do to characterize their theology as a recovery of the Reformation emphasis on the Word, which had been lost in Schleiermacher's anthropological starting point. Moreover, a fresh estimation of Schleiermacher's theology would also affect the way in which one lays out the theological options present at the end of our century. The historical account of modern theology that undergirds at least some postmodernist or "postliberal" theological proposals relies on a similarly inaccurate interpretation of Schleiermacher and his legacy.[7]

As a work in the field of historical theology I intend my study to contribute to *theology* as well as to the history of theology, and perhaps it would be useful here to suggest why I think it may still be important to think about what might be meant by the phrase "Word of God." In common parlance, "Word of God" is used as a synonym for revelation or for the Bible. In the technical vocabulary of theology, the "Word of God" may also refer to Jesus or to the second person of the Trinity. Rarely, the Word of God is also used to describe a contemporary divine communication—particularly in the act of preaching. Each of these uses of the term points to ongoing matters of theological debate, but, for the moment, let us consider only the first two.

Questions about revelation lie behind much of the contemporary debate about theological method. Does ultimate reality disclose itself to us in some way that we are capable of receiving it, or is the very concept of a "reality" that somehow transcends the natural order and communicates with us untenable? Depending upon one's answer to that question, the work of theology will be described differently. The alternatives in the present discussion are fairly sharply cast, between those who see theological language as realistic and referential, corresponding in some way to an ultimate reality, and those who argue that all theological and religious statements are imaginative human constructs, which represent nothing more than the wishes, fears, or values of their authors.[8]

But if such debates about theological method seem to occupy the rarified stratosphere of the ivory tower, those debates surrounding the claim that the Bible is in some way the "Word of God" are fought in the streets. Whether one thinks of the bitter debates about the ordination of homosexuals that have plagued the mainline denominations in recent years, or of the recent statement of the Southern Baptist church on the doctrine of women's submission, it seems that appeals to the divine authority of Scripture are ubiquitous in America's culture wars. People occupying diametrically opposed moral or theological positions claim to be doing so on the basis of the Word of God they discovered in the Bible. The dilemma this poses for Christian believers is not, of course, a new one. One thinks, for example, of the use and abuse of Scripture in the debates about slavery during the last century. But the present debates are held in the brave new world of critical biblical scholarship, where it is not only the interpretation of the text, but the text itself that cannot be reliably determined. In this climate of uncertainty, theologians have been increasingly called upon to say something reassuring about the Bible. But once again, the alternatives seem to be sharply drawn in the present context: between those who have given up on the Bible either in triumph or despair, and those who have, through a variety of means, reasserted its unique and unsurpassable authority.[9]

As a historical theologian writing a monograph on Schleiermacher's doctrine of the Word of God, I cannot directly engage in these debates. But I believe the historical theologian does contribute to the present state of theological knowledge, if only indirectly, precisely in the work of retrieving ideas from the past that are not informing the current conversation. Schleiermacher's doctrine of the Word of God has not been well understood, and for a variety of reasons it has also not been very influential. I am attempting to offer a fresh interpretation because I suspect that his way of thinking about these matters may still have relevance.

Schleiermacher himself uses the phrase "Word of God" in several senses, including all four mentioned above. The main body of my research involves a close reading of his work in its historical context aimed at unpacking the precise meaning given to the concept in each instance. For example, Schleiermacher states that the Word of God is "the divine activity expressed in the form of consciousness."[10] Grammatically, that is a relatively simple phrase. But to understand what he means entails explicating his understanding of divine causality and of consciousness. Each of these ideas, in turn, in order to be understood, needs to be placed in the context of the discussions of them in eighteenth and nineteenth century theology, metaphysics, epistemology, and psychology. For the purposes of this article I want to focus on Schleiermacher's understanding of Scripture, explicating in particular a section of *The Christian Faith* that is rarely discussed in the secondary literature.[11] I am sharing the details because I think they give a better indication of the nature of the project than would oversimplified generalizations.

The Word of God and the Treasure of Scripture

Curiously, although Schleiermacher himself works out a sophisticated doctrine of Scripture in several of his writings, and although he himself lectured more frequently on New Testament than on dogmatics, he is often presented as a theologian who radically subordinated the authority of Scripture to that of experience and accordingly limited severely the role of the Bible in theology and church. In laying out his thoughts on Scripture in some detail, I hope to demonstrate just how unfair these charges are.

The Dogmatic Function of the Doctrine of Scripture

The discussion of the doctrine of Scripture in the *Glaubenslehre* falls under the rubric of ecclesiology in the second part. Scripture is identified, along with ministry of the Word, the sacraments of Baptism and Lord's Supper, the power of the Keys of the Kingdom, and prayer in the name of Jesus, as one of the essential and unchanging marks (*Grundzüge*) of the Christian church as it exists in history (*im Zusammenbestehen mit der Welt*). These are contrasted with other characteristics of the empirical church that are changeable, and which, under the sway of the Kingdom of God, are destined to disappear: namely, the plurality and fallibility of Christian churches.[12]

Schleiermacher begins his discussion from an assumption that is fundamental to his entire dogmatic project: that the Christian faith is always and everywhere brought about in the same way, namely, through the proclamation of Christ.[13] For the Apostles, this proclamation was received immediately from the mouth of Jesus. Whatever may be the actions of Christ in us that produce our faith, the only way we can be certain that they come from him is to demonstrate their identity with the original faith-evoking activity of Christ. Thus, all subsequent generations of Christians are continually led back to the Apostles' representations of the personality of Christ. Furthermore, Schleiermacher contends, even the disciples themselves could not have become active agents of the Kingdom of God through the communication of the Holy Spirit without the faith-evoking influence of the Word. The efficacy of the presentation of

Christ in the Word, then, is always an indispensable condition of the communication of the Holy Spirit.

Schleiermacher is quick to point out that, if in the first instance what we seek in turning to the apostolic witness is to discover the same efficacious proclamation that produced the first disciples' faith, this proclamation in no way extends to the entire text of the New Testament, nor could everything that is taught on the basis of the New Testament text be developed from it. Indeed, an appeal to authorizing witness—an evangelical core of Scripture—does not even require a fixed written text. We must admit the possibility of a preached or oral propagation of the gospel, and insofar as this is possible, the most we could guarantee about it would be an unimpaired identity of transmission (*Überlieferung*). Thus, we can conclude that the particular, written form in which the person of Christ is represented to us (i.e., the canonical New Testament) does not belong unavoidably to the essence of the church (*Sein*), but to its wellbeing (*Wohlsein*).[14] While the church truly is for Schleiermacher, as it was for Luther, the *creatura evangelii*, it is not constituted by the canonical Scriptures in their final form, for this would be to place the apostles and the first several generations of Christians outside the church.

The part of the New Testament that is not, properly speaking, evangelical, performs two functions. First, it shows that Christ's promised church-building activity really did proceed from his own efficacious actions and from the testimony he commanded from his disciples, so that they are the source of the church as we have it. Second, it provides a supplement to the immediate teachings of Christ. We can look at the ordinances and actions of the disciples and try to infer from them what must have been their sources: the instructions and expressions of the will of Christ.

Scripture as we now have it, both the individual books and the collection of the canon as a whole, is a treasure preserved for all later generations of the church, and must be seen as a work of the Holy Spirit.[15] It is, however, only a particular case of the more general category "testimony about Christ," to which also the ministry of the Word belongs. To speak of the general category as "testimony" captures the truth that originally the oral and written teaching and narratives about Christ were the same, and only came to be distinguished from each other fortuitously through the vicissitudes of historical development. Now, however, Scripture constitutes a special case (*ein Besonderes*), for its preservation without changes establishes the identity of our testimony with the original witness to Christ in a peculiar way. Yet without the living witness to Christ (ministry of the Word) that is the common duty and calling of all Christians—a witness that refers back to Scripture to be sure—the canonical Scriptures would be a dead possession. These two taken together, then, Scripture and the ministry of the Word of God (*Dienst am göttlichen Wort*), are constitutive of the essence of the church.[16]

The Authority of Scripture

Having established the appropriate function of a doctrine of Scripture in dogmatics, that is, to identify the distinctive essence of the church, Schleiermacher moves on to a discussion of the doctrine itself. Following a pattern he uses throughout the *Glaubenslehre*, he distinguishes his own constructive treatment of the questions from a critical engagement with the confessional tradition of the Protestant church.[17] Positively, he argues that Scripture is not the foundation of faith in Christ, but rather faith in Christ is the foundation of the authority of Scripture. Thus Scripture is regarded as an expression of faith in Christ—the first in a series of such expressions, but normative in a way that later presentations of faith are not (§§ 128-129). Critically, he gives an interpretation of what the confessions mean when they speak of the inspiration of Scripture and canon, and of Scripture's authenticity and sufficiency (§§ 130-131). The discussion closes with addendum on the role of the Old Testament in the Christian Scriptures (§ 132).

Schleiermacher argues that confusion about the relationship between biblical authority and faith is a wide-spread problem. Insofar as textbooks or confessions actually begin with the doctrine of Scripture, they invite the thought that Scripture is the source of faith. But if faith in Christ were in fact based on the authority of Scripture, on what would the authority of Scripture be based? One approach might be to prove the authority of Scripture by reason. But there are at least two problems with this approach. First, it would involve a kind of intellectual exercise that not all people are capable of, and hence the ground of faith would not be immediately available to all in the same way. Some would believe because they could demonstrate the authority of Scripture, others would have their faith second-hand. Second, if it really were possible to prove the authority of Scripture through reason alone, it would seem that any right-thinking person could be reasoned into belief. And yet, on the one hand, it is conceivable that such a person might "believe" without ever having felt the need of redemption, without ever having experienced repentance or conversion. But such a conviction would not really be faith at all, since it would not of itself lead to living communion with Christ. On the other hand, where the need for redemption makes itself known, faith could rest upon a knowledge of Christ that is in no way connected to convictions about how the writings of Scripture were produced.[18]

If we come to faith in the same way as the Apostles, however, perhaps it will be admitted that they came to faith as a result of their belief in the Old Testament Scripture. Schleiermacher avers that this reasoning is just as flawed. The disciples did not believe in Christ because, after careful study, they came to recognize that he was the promised Messiah foretold by the Prophets. Rather, precisely because they believed in Jesus, they applied the prophetic writings to him.

The faith of the apostles arose from Christ's own proclamation of himself, and in the same way all Christian faith has taken rise from the preaching of Christ. The New Testament itself is a collection of such preaching come down to us, and insofar as it is a collection of preaching, it too produces faith. But this is not the result of special doctrines concerning Scripture, attributing its beginning to a special divine revelation or inspiration. And it must be admitted that Scripture could produce faith in this way even if it contained many errors alongside the essential witness to Christ. Thus, just as the Apostles had faith before they were able to produce Scripture, so we must have faith before we are led, through our reading of it, to accept the truth of propositions concerning its unique character. Doctrines such as the inspiration of Scripture are only credible to those who already believe. Scripture, then, must be seen primarily as the expression of the Apostles' faith in the form of testimony about Christ.[19]

The Normative Character of Scripture

The next step in Schleiermacher's constructive argument is to identify more precisely the kind of normativity exercised by the New Testament. Although Scripture as an expression of faith in Christ is simply the first in a series of similar (*gleichartig*) presentations of Christian faith, it is not superseded by what comes later. This is because, within the apostolic age, at least some of the teaching about Christ was actually Judaism or heathenism with a thin veneer of Christian expressions. Alongside this material, the preaching of the immediate disciples of Christ stood as a corrective, for their proximity to him and to his own teaching, purified their testimony of alien elements. Thus within the apostolic age itself the distinction between the *canonical* and the *apocryphal*, as respectively the most perfect and the most imperfect elements of the original witness, began to be drawn. This distinction cannot arise in precisely the same way in any other age. This is so, Schleiermacher argues, partly because the liability to corruption through foreign elements decreases in proportion to the number of Christians who are born and raised in the church. Further, it is impossible for later Christians to generate truly canonical materials since their representations cannot be purified through an immediate encounter with Jesus.

The normative authority of Scripture, then, extends primarily to what might be called its canonical elements. Schleiermacher maintains that the peculiar normative honor (*normale Würde*) granted to the canonical does not extend to every word of the New Testament. It is reserved for materials produced to restrain error or corruption, so that many occasional remarks (*gelegentliche Äusserungen*) and merely subsidiary thoughts (*bloße Nebengedanken*) do not share the same degree of normativity as the chief subject matter in each case. Further, the normative authority of Scripture does not imply that every later presentation of Christ must be derived from the canon in the same way, or that every later idea be contained in it, at least in germ. Since the Spirit has been poured out on all flesh, no age can be without its own peculiar originality in Christian thought. Scripture makes normative these later presentations in two ways. First, all later proclamation must be able to be harmonized with the original (canonical) teaching. And second, the original Scripture can guarantee the Christian character of a representation or expose what is non-Christian with a degree of certainty granted to no later presentation.[20]

The Meaning of Inspiration

As he turns to a critical conversation with the confessional heritage of the Evangelical churches on the question of Scripture, Schleiermacher takes up in turn a number of concepts connected with the traditional presentation. The first of these is the concept of inspiration. The term strictly speaking, he notes, is not a scriptural one, though two passages in the New Testament are commonly mentioned in connection with it. The first, I Timothy 3:16, refers only to the Old Testament writings, and speaks of them as *theopneustos*, "God-breathed." This could lead to the idea that in the act of writing, the Holy Spirit had a special relationship with the writer that was otherwise non-existent. Such an interpretation does not follow as easily from II Peter 1:21, which speaks of "men moved by the Holy Spirit" who "spoke from God"—a passage that seems to suggest a more stable state of being so moved.

Because the term "inspiration" is not one regulated by Scripture itself but rather a figurative term, it needs to be illuminated by other, related terms that describe the ways in which persons arrive at ideas. Schleiermacher contrasts the inspired (*das Eingegebene*), the learned (*das Erlernte*), and the excogitated (*das Ersonnene*). Often the first two types are contrasted with the last, as the products of outside influences over against the self's own activity. At other times, however, usage distinguishes the inspired from the learned. In this usage what is inspired is understood to depend on a purely inward communication, as opposed to something learned from external communication, in which case the inspiration of Scripture might include the whole freedom of an individual's productivity.[21]

At this point in the argument Schleiermacher makes a distinction that is crucial for his entire doctrine of Scripture. He states: "The general custom of calling Holy Scripture as such 'revelation' not infrequently causes the two concepts to be treated as interchangeable; but this cannot occur without confusion."[22] If it is taken to mean that God made known to the authors of Scripture in detail what they were to write, this is a totally unfounded assumption, because they themselves trace everything in their teaching back to Christ. Thus, God's original act of disclosure (*Kundmachung*) of everything contained in Scripture must already be in Christ himself—not as a series of discrete bits of inspired information, but rather as a single and indivisible revelation that develops organically (that is to say, under the conditions of space and time). The conclusion is that "the speaking and writing of the apostles moved by the Holy Spirit was thus at the same time simply a communication from the revelation of God in Christ."[23]

The church applies the notion of inspiration not only to the composition of the individual books of Scripture, but also to the collection of them into the canon. This, however, is the result of the complex interaction of cooperative and competitive forces in the church, and not everything that has been achieved in this way can be attributed in the same measure to the Holy Spirit. For this reason, Schleiermacher himself refers to the collection of the canonical Scriptures not as a case of inspiration, but as a product of the guidance (*Leitung*) of the Holy Spirit.

Because the Holy Spirit is the source of all spiritual gifts and good works, all thinking about the Kingdom of God must be traced back to and inspired by the Holy Spirit. Schleiermacher argues that this holds true both of the apocryphal and of the canonical elements of the thinking of the Apostolic age. Yet it is also true that the efficacious work of the Spirit is most perfect and penetrating in the circle of those singled out by Peter (Acts 1:21ff) as men who had accompanied Christ from the beginning of his public ministry. Inspiration, in the case of these individuals, extends beyond the writing of Scripture to the whole exercise of their office as apostles. In this sense, the peculiar inspiration of the Apostles is not something that belongs only to the New Testament writings—on the contrary, these books only share in it. Dogmatics can ignore a whole set of questions about the extent of inspiration in the production of the text. Only dead scholasticism would try to draw lines of distinction within the process or would focus on the final form in its sheer externality (*Äusserlichkeit*) as a special product of inspiration.[24]

The most suitable analogy for understanding the mechanics of inspiration, Schleiermacher argues, is provided by Christology. The divine essence unites with the human nature of Jesus in a person-forming way, but it does not thereby destroy the true humanity of Jesus.[25] So, too, *mutatis mutandis*, the divine Spirit indwells the Christian church, inspiring the thoughts and actions of the Apostles, but in a way that does not wipe out their full humanity. This is why Schleiermacher rejects a special hermeneutics for the New Testament.[26] Although the texts are truly disclosures of God's self-communication, they may be understood at the very same time as completely human compositions, susceptible of being understood in the same way any other human writings are understood. And the difference between God's incarnation in Christ and in the church should not be overlooked: only in Christ was the God-consciousness absolutely powerful; in the church, in its struggle with sin in the historical process, the permeation of the Holy Spirit is never complete. Thus, even the church's witness to the revelation of God in Jesus Christ can be tinged with error.[27]

The Formation of the Canon

Schleiermacher does not assail the credibility of Scripture in the manner of the deist or rationalist skeptics. Such a stance was not possible for a man who confessed in public that his highest goal was to be a "servant of the divine Word."[28] Yet woven throughout his treatment of Scripture, even in the *Glaubenslehre*, is an account of how errors and unworthy elements can creep into the text. Scripture itself, as we have seen, must not be understood as a direct and immediate product of divine revelation. The apostolic authors were reporting out of the revelation of God in Christ. And although Christ's own life and teachings might be presupposed to be a perfectly transparent case of divine revelation, the human witnesses could, and *did*, interpret it in various ways. The movement toward distinguishing canonical from apocryphal accounts witnesses to just such a variety of interpretations. Even under the best of circumstances, it must be conceded that the scriptural authors were reproducing their memories, and such an act is a form of historical composition. The conclusion is this: "The effort to make the Redeemer appear [in the biblical narratives] as he really was is likewise the work of the Spirit of Truth, and it is only insofar as they are this that such narratives have a place in Holy Scripture."[29]

Schleiermacher was an early pioneer in historical-critical New Testament scholarship, and he was one of the first to suggest that independent fragments of tradition were later woven together into the larger narrative of a Gospel.[30] Inspiration, he argues, must also be thought of as extending to the collection of stories and sayings and their incorporation into larger accounts. But once again, it is important to remember that this does not, in itself, remove the possibility of the introduction of errors.

The potential fallibility of the text is gradually regulated and minimized through the canonization process, which takes place under the leading of the Holy Spirit, but the process must be understood at the same time as a thoroughly human and historical one. Schleiermacher introduces as an analogy for understanding the Spirit's work in the church the model of an individual's regulation of his or her own thinking. Just as individuals know how to distinguish their ideas—identifying excellent ones, reserving others for further thought, rejecting some—so the Holy Spirit works through the whole Christian body in distinguishing the canonical from the apocryphal. The debate that occurred in the early church about the inclusion or exclusion of individual books shows that the process was one of gradual approximation to an ideal. The same kind of process persists in the church to this day as it carefully weighs the different degrees of normative dignity to be attributed to individual portions of Scripture and decides how to interpret all kinds of gaps and interpolations. Thus, "the judgement of the Church is only approximating ever more closely to the complete elimination of the apocryphal and the pure reverencing (*Heilighalten*) of the canonical."[31] Whatever contributes to the achievement of this ideal is from the leading of the Holy Spirit; whatever prevents its realization comes from the persisting influence of the world on the church.

Schleiermacher rejects any attempt to see the canon as irrevocably fixed. For one thing, since the determination of the canon as we have it was made after the age of the Apostles, there is no genuinely apostolic indication for how to distinguish what is normatively canonical. But even more, through the natural, gradual process of sifting the early church writings, many things could have crept into the sacred books that could be recognized and definitely proved as uncanonical in a later age. "The sense for the truly apostolic is, as history teaches, one of the gifts of the Spirit that is gradually increasing in the Church."[32] Thus, it would be a mistake to try to prevent further unrestricted research into the matter, even though several of the confessional standards represent the canon as closed. It can only contribute to the well-being of the church if what does not truly belong to Holy Scripture is distinguished clearly from it.

The Sufficiency of Scripture

Holding an open canon, and positively encouraging critical investigation of the New Testament texts, it is not surprising that Schleiermacher, whose skills as a classicist had been honed in his translations of Plato's dialogues, turned his own pen to biblical criticism. In 1807, he published an essay "On the So-Called First Letter of Paul to Timothy," which argued, on internal grounds, that the text could not have been written by Paul himself.[33] He was a good enough New Testament scholar to know that more, not fewer, questions would soon be raised about other books of the New Testament. So his reading of the confessional tradition on the authenticity of Scripture starts from the presupposition that this cannot depend upon each book having been written by the author to whom it is attributed. Not only could manuscripts be wrongly attributed quite unintentionally, but also a biblical author's modesty or prudence may have led him to take a pseudonym. There is nothing "inauthentic" about these texts. What the confessions are denying with the concept of "authenticity" is the thought that the texts were written with the intention to mislead. As Schleiermacher puts it:

> [The Confessions assert] that we trust universal Christian experience as the testimony of the Holy Spirit, that the canon we received through the tradition of the Church has not accepted into itself through deceit or ignorance components belonging to a realm of Christianity suspected of being apocryphal or heretical. . . . Nevertheless, we admit that not all these books are equally suited in content and form to effectively assert their canonical dignity.[34]

We can make good our confidence in the authenticity of Scripture, he argues, by approaching the canon with the utmost freedom as well as with the most rigorous conscientiousness. No prejudice should hamper free inquiry into the authorship of the texts. Interpretation should not be diverted from the purest hermeneutic out of fear that the resultant reading of the text would uncover an unworthy view of the Christian faith.

The normative sufficiency of Scripture is of two kinds: constitutive and critical. As a *constitutive* norm, the New Testament actually creates Christian thought and language. Through the use of Scripture, the Holy Spirit is able to lead into all truth. This is Scripture's productive sufficiency. Thus, if some day the most perfect image of Christ's living knowledge of God were at hand in the church, we could with perfect right understand this to be the fruit of Scripture. The proper utterances of Christian piety take their rise from Scripture and its interaction with the peculiar linguistic and intellectual environment in which individual readers of Scripture live, and the common Christian orthodoxy of every age is formed this way by the reigning interpretation of Christian faith called forth by Scripture.[35] Thus for Schleiermacher the language of piety is not created anew by each individual believer, or chosen freely to express inner experiences; it is not, in short, "experiential-expressivist."[36] Rather, it is formed in every age through the encounter with Scripture, and each age's articulation of the faith must be appropriate to *(gemäss)* the distinctive expressions of the Bible.

The *critical* sufficiency of Scripture—which is often the only kind of normativity one has in mind when discussing the concept of sufficiency—relates to the constitutive as a strictly subordinate function, almost as a shadow. As a critical norm, Scripture tests the adequacy of religious thinking that means to be Christian, though not itself produced under the influence of the Holy Spirit in Scripture. As the constitutive use of Scripture grows, and as more perfect understanding of the text renders its misinterpretation less likely, this critical use should decrease.

If Scripture truly is sufficient, there can be nothing superfluous in it. That material is repeated in the New Testament is completely understandable given the way in which the text took shape. But the repetition has only the appearance of superfluousness. The doctrine of sufficiency articulates the conviction that cases of repetition ought to be taken as significant: They provide further assurance of the authenticity of particular traditions or teachings, and they provide potentially complementary material.[37]

The Status of the Old Testament in the Christian Canon

In an addendum to the doctrine of Scripture, Schleiermacher sets out a view that has been regarded, alternatively, either as prescient or as heretical (making him a Marcion *redivivus*): that the Old Testament cannot be seen as possessing the same normative authority for Christian faith as the New.[38] He was well aware that this view was not yet generally recognized by church theologians, but he felt sure that it was destined in some future time to be widely shared. The argument against the authority of the Old Testament rests on three grounds. First, the inspiration of the Old Testament texts, with the possible exception of Messianic prophecies, was not the activity of the same Spirit of Christ at work in the church. Schleiermacher develops his case through a reading of Paul's treatment of the Law in Galatians and Romans, but he also notes that Christ himself does not represent the sending of the Spirit as the return of One who had been present already. Second, the Old Testament cannot, strictly speaking, serve as a productive or language-forming norm for Christian piety. Even in the noblest Psalms, ideas are present that Christians cannot appropriate as pure expressions of their piety, and only by deceiving oneself through unconscious editing or supplementation could one construct a Christian doctrine of God from the Psalms and the Prophets. Finally, the Old Testament is also ill-suited to function as a critical norm. Even though one could find throughout the history of the Church attempts to prove virtually every doctrine from the Old Testament, why should we choose the less clear premonitions of the prophets over the clear self-proclamation of Christ? The history of Christian use of the Old Testament makes clear just how such use actually hindered honest exegesis, and how it raised a myriad of complex problems that Christian theology had no need to address. The best course of action, then, would be to give up Old Testament proofs for specifically Christian doctrines and to lay aside those doctrines that rest primarily on such proofs.[39]

One might ask why the Old Testament is in the canon at all. Schleiermacher argues that there are primarily two reasons for its inclusion. First, the preaching of Christ himself and of the apostles was based on portions of the Old Testament read aloud, and this practice continued in the early Christian community before the formation of the New Testament canon. Second, Christ himself and the apostles refer to the Old Testament books as divine authorities favorable to Christianity. In both cases the mere fact that they were so used by Christ is not in itself sufficient to establish that they should continue to be used in this manner. Because the connection between the apostolic proclamation and the Hebrew Scriptures is a historical one, it could be expected that gradually the need for references to the Old Testament would diminish, and accordingly it would retreat behind the New Testament in the church's usage. Although he did not recommend the removal of the Old Testament from the Christian Bible, Schleiermacher thought it would perhaps be better to include it as an appendix after the New: then it would be clear that is was in no way necessary first to work through all of the Old Testament in order rightly to understand the New.[40]

Conclusion

Much more, of course, could be said about Schleiermacher's views on Scripture. The exposition of the doctrine of Scripture in *The Christian Faith* needs to be filled out by what he says in the *Brief Outline on the Study of Theology* (1811 and 1830) about the task of exegetical theology, and the material there is further illuminated by his posthumously published *Lectures on Introduction to New Testament* and *Hermeneutics*. Moreover, it is important to remember that Scripture is, for him, only one of two forms of testimony to Jesus Christ that are essential marks of the church. His views on the other form, the ministry of the Word, would require at least as much exposition as I have given to the doctrine of Scripture here.[41] In his *Practical Theology* he discusses the uses of Scripture in preaching, catechesis, and church hymnody. And we can test how the theory is put into action in several technical exegetical works and ten fat volumes of published sermons. For now it must suffice to go back to some of the theological debates mentioned at the beginning, and to show how a careful reading of Schleiermacher might contribute to the conversation.

One of the most widely discussed books in North American theology in the last fifteen years—a book that has given rise to a new movement in theology called "postliberalism"—has been George

Lindbeck's *The Nature of Doctrine*. In it he suggests that there are primarily three models for understanding the nature and function of doctrines in the Christian community, only the third of which is adequate. The first conceives of doctrines as propositional claims about reality with defensible cognitive viability. This model, he argues, presents virtually insurmountable difficulties in the face of modern (and postmodern) epistemology. The second model, which he attributes to Schleiermacher, suggests that doctrines are the expression of inner, pre-linguistic religious experiences. The problem with this model, according to Lindbeck, is that it does not describe what really goes on in the formation of doctrine. The language of Christian doctrines actually shapes experience, not the other way around. There is no universal, basal religious experience that is expressed through the various religions. Each faith or church is thoroughly grounded in the historical, social, and linguistic environment in which it lives. Thus, a more adequate third alternative is to see doctrines as cultural-linguistic rules. To be a faithful religious person, one does not subscribe to certain beliefs, or have particular experiences, but rather one lives through a specific tradition, following the rules (i.e. doctrines) that organize its life.[42]

While many theologians have found Lindbeck's thesis suggestive and helpful, he has also been the recipient of pointed criticism.[43] Perhaps the most serious difficulty the critics have noted surrounds the question of the truth of doctrinal statements or of the beliefs that they are supposed to regulate. For Lindbeck and other postliberals, the "truth" of doctrines is judged primarily by how faithfully they represent the core claims of a tradition, and how effectively they build character and identity within the community. But what to do when one is confronted with conflicting traditions, playing different games, according to different rules? How might one know what most nearly approaches truth?

Contrary to Lindbeck's account, Schleiermacher does not hold an experiential-expressivist view of doctrine. Recall, for a moment, what he says about Scripture as a constitutive norm. He says that Christian piety receives its proper or rightful utterances, in every age, through the constitutive normativity of Scripture. That is to say, Scripture, as understood in a particular historical, linguistic, and social context, actually creates the language of piety in one religious community. Doctrines are second-order reflection on the language of Christian piety (§ 15) and not, as Lindbeck would have it, the expressions of individuals' interior and pre-linguistic experiences. Even the feeling of absolute dependence is awakened in us by the "communicative and stimulative power of expression or utterance."[44] No more than anything else that is human can piety "be conceived entirely separated from all communication."[45] Up to this point, Schleiermacher's view of doctrine is rather close to Lindbeck's, but they depart from each other in a way that has relevance to the truth question.

Doctrines for Schleiermacher can and must be continually criticized and reworked, because they are human reflection on human testimony to a truth: God's revelation in Jesus Christ. The Christian community is constituted, not by its commitment to live according to certain doctrinal rules, but by its confidence that Jesus Christ is the Word of God made flesh. Still, human testimony to that event—even the testimony of Scripture—is liable to err. For this reason Schleiermacher was not at all inclined simply to defer to the doctrinal authority of the ancient and undivided church, or to a supposedly inerrant book, or to any other human words. At the same time, we can surely infer from his famous Proposition 11 that he would be unwilling to give up the centrality of Christianity's great truth claim: that God was in Christ reconciling the world to himself.[46] And that truth claim, even though it is not, strictly speaking, rationally demonstrable (Schleiermacher is also not a foundationalist!),[47] *can* be probed as to its intersubjective intelligibility. The best insurance against the possibility that my experience is corrupting my hearing of God's Word, then, would be provided by comparing my views to those of others who claim to be hearing the same Word. That is why Schleiermacher speaks of *universal* (*allgemein*) Christian experience as the testimony of the Holy Spirit. The "universal" here is not the foundationalist's projected fiction of an unassailable belief from which all other beliefs are derived. It is the historicist's appeal to collective empirical data. Whether or not Schleiermacher's understanding of doctrine still works (or ever did), it clearly represents a view not accounted for in Lindbeck's typology.

A second issue on which a fresh reading of Schleiermacher may prove pertinent is on the relative roles of experience and the Word of God as sources and norms for theology. Here the classic criticism of Schleiermacher comes from Karl Barth. Over and over again, Barth hammers home the point that Schleiermacher starts in the wrong place. Theology ought to be about the Word of God. One cannot speak about God by speaking about humanity in exalted tones. What has experience to do with the Word?[48] The later Barth is somewhat more cautious in his criticisms, less confident that he has correctly understood Schleiermacher. He even admits to a point that is lost on many of his disciples: that the experience Schleiermacher is interested in is not universal human experience, but the experience of the human being "under the gospel." Nevertheless, even the experience of *homo evangelicus*, Barth argues, is something other than the Word of God.[49] The alternatives are sharply opposed: either theology is about experience, or it is about the Word.

On this question, too, a close reading of Schleiermacher may suggest another alternative: that theology *ought* to be about the Word of God, but precisely for that reason it dare not ignore the role of experience as the recipient of the Word. The temptation will always be, in a world still subject to sin, to confuse the human and the divine.[50] Schleiermacher states, in defense of his theological method, that "the verse John 1:14 is the foundational text for all of dogmatics and for the entire practice of ministry."[51] The Word became flesh, and *we beheld its glory*. Human testimony to the revelation of God in Jesus Christ, starting with that of the disciples themselves, is being led by the Spirit toward all truth—but it hasn't gotten there yet. Analysis of experience as the receiver of revelation, then, so far from being a case of anthropocentric self-absorption, actually functions as a form of self-criticism, testing the adequacy of human descriptions of the Word made flesh. After Freud and Foucault, such attention to the role of experience in theological constructions is, it seems to me, even more pertinent than it was in the early nineteenth century. I do not mean to imply that Barth ignores the "prism" of the human act by which the light is appropriated.[52] The point, rather, is that the gap between him and Schleiermacher is narrowed if one acknowledges that for Schleiermacher, too, it is the revelation in Jesus Christ that is seen refracted in the human faith and experience of the Christian.[53]

A final issue I would like to mention is the question of biblical authority. At the present time, there seems to be a general sense of confusion and frustration surrounding the Bible among church people. There are many reasons for this, and we cannot explore all of them within the limits of this essay. Certainly one set of difficulties is raised by the ongoing quest for the historical Jesus. The way in which historical critics chip away at the Gospel narratives is alarming, not just to lay people who have not had the benefit of a theological education, but also to highly trained ministers and scholars. Where does it all end? Of course, this problem, too, is a complex one, and a fresh reading of Schleiermacher's theology certainly will not solve every aspect of it. But Schleiermacher's discussion of biblical authority is worth bringing into the discussion. The historical critics seem to pose a threat to the authority of the Bible. Why? Because they discover errors of fact, or because they reduce the core of genuine sayings of the historical Jesus to very little. The assumption is that the Bible possesses authority because of something special about it that a historian could conceivably take away: its veracity, its reliable reportage, or some such thing. Schleiermacher, you will remember, would understand this to be a case of grounding the authority of Scripture in the wrong way. We do not believe Scripture because it is special—it is special because we believe it. It is our faith in Christ that gives Scripture authority, and presumably our faith was not the gift of historical criticism. But what about those historical critics, ever chipping away at the texts? What do we do with them? The answer for Schleiermacher would certainly be: "Let them get on with their business! We have nothing to fear from them."[54] Scripture as living Word, in the preaching and teaching of the church, has reliably been evoking faith for nearly 2000 years, and it is unlikely that the latest word from the Jesus Seminar will alter that fact. The authority of Scripture rests on our complete confidence that through it the Holy Spirit can lead us into all truth. If we really believe that, we will want to be assiduous students of Holy Scripture.

Endnotes

1. Emil Brunner, *Die Mystik und das Wort: Der Gegensatz zwischen moderner Religionsauffassung und christlichem Glauben dargestellt an der Theologie Schleiermachers* (Tübingen: J. C. B. Mohr [Paul Siebeck], 1924). For a careful critique of Brunner's arguments in comparison to Schleiermacher's *Glaubenslehre*, see

Brian Albert Gerrish, *Tradition and the Modern World: Reformed Theology in the Nineteenth Century* (Chicago: University of Chicago Press, 1978), 13-48, 190-98.

2. Barth's doctrine of the Word of God is treated in the prolegomena to his system. See Karl Barth, *Church Dogmatics*, vol. I/1: *The Doctrine of the Word of God: Prolegomena to the Church Dogmatics* (Edinburgh: T. & T. Clark, 1936); vol. I/2: *The Doctrine of the Word of God: The Revelation of God, Holy Scripture and the Proclamation of the Church* (Edinburgh: T. & T. Clark, 1956.)

3. Erwin H. U. Quapp has shown in detail how Barth misread Schleiermacher's *Weihnachtsfeier (Barth Contra Schleiermacher: "Die Weihnachtsfeier" als Nagelprobe: mit einem Nachwort zur Interpretationsgeschichte der Weihnachtsfeier* [Marburg: Karl Wenzel, 1978]). Also helpful is Dietmar Lütz, *Homo Viator: Karl Barths Ringen mit Schleiermacher* (Zurich: Theologischer Verlag, 1988).

4. Friedrich Schleiermacher, *Der christliche Glaube nach: den Grundsätzen der evangelischen Kirche im Zusammenhange dargestellt*, 7th ed., based on the 2nd German edition, ed. Martin Redeker, 2 vols. (Berlin: Walter de Gruyter, 1960), §§ 15-16. Hereafter cited by proposition number and paragraph as *Gl*. English translation: *The Christian Faith*, trans. from the 2nd German edition, ed. H. R. Mackintosh and J. S. Stewart (Philadelphia: Fortress Press, 1976).

5. Schleiermacher complained, after the reviews of the first edition of the *Glaubenslehre*, that his critics, especially those from the Tübingen school, were "engaged in a controversy with a Schleiermacher whom I in no way recognize as myself" (*Schleiermachers Sendschreiben über seine Glaubenslehre an Lücke*, ed. Hermann Mulert (Giessen: Verlag Alfred Töpelmann, 1908), 12. Hereafter cited as *Sendschreiben*. English translation: Friedrich D. E. Schleiermacher, *On the Glaubenslehre: Two Letters to Dr. Lucke*, trans. James Duke and Francis Fiorenza (Chico: Scholars Press, 1981), 37.

6. *Sendschreiben*, 37; ET, 62. My first epigraph is taken from this passage.

7. A recent example is Nancey C. Murphy, *Beyond Liberalism and Fundamentalism: How Modern and Postmodern Philosophy Set the Theological Agenda* (Valley Forge: Trinity Press International, 1996), especially 11-61.

8. One could cite many different contemporary theologians to illustrate this division between "critical realists" and "constructivists." On the realist end of the spectrum, see Schubert M. Ogden, *The Reality of God* (San Francisco: Harper and Row, 1963), and Ian Barbour, *Myths, Models, and Paradigms: A Comparative Study in Science and Religion* (San Francisco: Harper and Row, 1974). On the constructivist side, compare Gordon D. Kaufman, *An Essay on Theological Method*, 3rd ed. (Atlanta: Scholars Press, 1995), and Sallie McFague, *Models of God: Theology for an Ecological, Nuclear Age* (Philadelphia: Fortress Press, 1987).

9. Once again, one could cite many theologians to illustrate this general feature of the theological landscape of the late 20th century. Among those who have given up on the Bible somewhat triumphantly, one could mention many post-Christian feminists, such as Margaret Daphne Hampson. See her *Theology and Feminism* (Oxford: Basil Blackwell, 1990). Kenneth Cauthen, on the contrary, sounds somewhat more regretfully resigned to the Bible's failures to solve ethical issues in his *Toward a New Modernism* (Lanham: University Press of America, 1997), especially 31-60. There are many interesting proposals for retrieving the concept of biblical authority and uniqueness, but among the best I have recently read is Nicholas Wolterstorff's *Divine Discourse: Philosophical Reflections on the Claim that God Speaks* (Cambridge: Cambridge University Press, 1995). See also *Reclaiming the Bible for the Church*, ed. Carl E. Braaten and Robert W. Jenson (Grand Rapids: Wm. B. Eerdmans Publishing Co., 1995).

10. *Gl.*, § 96.3; cf. § 55.1.

11. It is worth noting that there *is not* much secondary literature on Schleiermacher's understanding of Scripture. Terrence Tice states that there have really only been two substantial studies of Schleiermacher's biblical work (Friedrich Schleiermacher, *Luke: A Critical Study*, trans. Connop Thirlwall, ed. Terrence N. Tice [Lewiston: Edwin Mellen Press, 1993], 13). See Karl Heinrich von Weizsäcker, "*Schleiermachers Arbeiten zum Neuen Testament*," Bonn Diss., 1972 (Bonn, 1972), and Ian Staunton Wishart, "Schleiermacher's Interpretation of the Bible: The Doctrine and Use of Scriptures in the Light of Schleiermacher's Hermeneutical Principles," Knox College, Toronto, Th.M. Thesis, 1968. The 1984 Schleiermacher Congress in Berlin devoted one of its sections to the general topic, "Schleiermacher as Exegete and Preacher," but as it turned out, the papers submitted all had more to do with preaching than with exegesis. See *Internationaler Schleiermacher-Kongreß Berlin 1984*, 2 vols. ed. Kurt-Victor Selge, (Berlin: Walter de Gruyter, 1985), 643-770. I find it strange that the authors of a book on the Bible in modern culture would develop their view of Schleiermacher almost completely without reference to the doctrine of Scripture in the *Glaubenslehre* or to the understanding of exegetical theology in *Brief Outline on the Study of Theology*. See Roy A. Harrisville and Walter Sundberg, *The Bible in Modern Culture: Theology and Historical Critical Method from Spinoza to Käsemann* (Grand Rapids: Eerdmans, 1995), 66-88.

12. *Gl.*, §§ 127, 148, 149.

13. *Gl.*, § 127.2; cf. § 14.1.

14. *Gl.*, § 127.2.

15. Schleiermacher's reference to Scripture as a "treasure" may be derived from his reading of Matthew 13:52. See his sermon, "The Effects of Scripture and the Immediate Effects of the Redeemer," where he comments: " . . . at no time does he [Christ] fail to produce in his church those students of Scripture, well-educated in the Kingdom of Heaven, to whom God's Spirit gives from his *treasure*, along with the old and proven things, new insights . . . that enlighten us and make our hearts burn within us" (*Servant of the Word: Selected Sermons of Friedrich Schleiermacher*, trans. and ed. Dawn DeVries [Philadelphia: Fortress Press, 1987], 103), emphasis added.

16. *Gl.*, § 127.2.

17. Schleiermacher develops his own constructive position under propositions he calls *Glaubenssätze*, literally, "faith statements," whereas the confessional tradition is located under propositions he identifies as *Lehrsätze*, or "doctrinal statements." See the discussion in *Gl.*,§ 27.

18. *Gl.*, § 128.1; cf. § 14.2-3.

19. *Gl.*, § 128.2.

20. *Gl.*, § 129.1-2.

21. *Gl.*, § 130.1.

22. *Gl.*, § 130.1.

23. *Gl.*, § 130.1.

24. *Gl.*, § 130.2.

25. See the discussion of Christology in *Gl.*, § 94, § 96.

26. *Gl.*, § 130.2. Cf. Fr. D. E. Schleiermacher, *Hermeneutik: Nach den Handschriften neu herausgegeben und eingeleitet*, 2nd ed. ed. Heinz Kimmerle (Heidelberg: Carl Winter Universitätsverlag, 1974), 81. Hereafter cited as *Hermeneutik*. English translation: *Hermeneutics: The Handwritten Manuscripts*, ed. Heinz Kimmerle, trans. James Duke and Jack Forstman (Missoula: Scholars Press, 1977), 107.

27. Cf. *Gl.*, § 153.

28. See his "Sermon at Nathanael's Grave," *Servant of the Word*, 211.

29. *Gl.*, § 130.3.

30. See the discussion in *Luke: A Critical Commentary*, 9-18. Cf. Friedrich Schleiermacher, *Einleitung ins neue Testament*, ed. G. Wolde, in *Friedrich Schleiermachers sämmtliche Werke* (Berlin: Georg Reimer, 1834-1864), I/8:217-254. Hereafter cited as *Einl. NT*.

31. *Gl.*, § 130.4. Cf. Schleiermacher's discussion of the formation of the canon in *Einl. NT*, 32-75.

32. *Gl.*, § 130.4. For this reason Schleiermacher argues that the peculiar task of the part of historical theology that deals with the Bible, exegetical theology, is to establish the canon. See the discussion in Friedrich Schleiermacher, *Brief Outline on the Study of Theology*, trans. Terrence N. Tice (Richmond: John Knox Press, 1966), 50-60, esp. § 110.

33. *"Über den sogenannten ersten Brief des Paulos an den Timotheos,"* in *Friedrich Schleiermachers sämmtlich Werke*, I/2:221-320.

34. *Gl.*, § 131.1.

35. In his discussion of the use of Scripture in catechesis, Schleiermacher maintains that a genuine "living in" the language of Scripture is the foundation of all religious education (*Bildung*). Friedrich Scheiermacher, *Die praktische Theologie nach den Grundsätzen der evangelischen Kirche im Zusammenhange dargestellt*, in *Friedrich Schleiermachers sämmtliche Werke*, I/13:399.

36. George A. Lindbeck calls Schleiermacher's view of Christian doctrine "experiential expressivist" in his influential study, *The Nature of Doctrine: Religion and Theology in a Post-Liberal Age* (Philadelphia: Westminster Press, 1984), 16, 20-21, 30-45.

37. *Gl.*, § 131.2-3.

38. *Gl.*, § 132; cf. *Brief Outline on the Study of Theology*, 55-56; *Sendschreiben*, 41-42 (ET, 65-66). For a discussion of Schleiermacher's view of the Old Testament, see Horst Dietrich Preuss, *"Vom Verlust des Alten Testaments und seinen Folgen: dargestellt anhand der Theologie und Predigt F. D. Schleiermachers,"* in *Lebendiger Umgang mit Schrift und Bekenntnis: Theologische Beiträge zur Beziehung von Schrift und Bekenntnius und zu ihrer Bedeutung für das Leben der Kirche*, ed. Joachim Track (Stuttgart: Calwer Verlag, 1980), 127-60; Martin Stiewe, *"Das Alte Testament im theologischen Denken Schleiermachers,"* in *Altes Testament Forschung und Wirkung: Festschrift für Henning Graf Reventlow*, ed. Peter Mommer and Winfried Thiel (Frankfurt: Peter Lang, 1994), 329-336.

39. *Gl.*, § 132.2.

40. *Gl.*, § 132.3.

41. I have discussed his views on preaching as a part of the ministry of the Word elsewhere. See *Servant of the Word*, 1-23. See also Dawn DeVries, *Jesus Christ in the Preaching of Calvin and Schleiermacher* (Louisville: Westminster/John Knox Press, 1996), 48-70.

42. *The Nature of Doctrine*, 15-45.

43. See, for example, the review essay by Timothy P. Jackson, "Against Grammar," *Religious Studies Review* 11 (July 1985): 240-45; cf. David Tracy, "Lindbeck's New Program for Theology: A Reflection," *The Thomist* 49 (July 1985): 460-472; B. A. Gerrish, "The Nature of Doctrine," *Journal of Religion* 68 (1988):87-92.

44. *Gl.*, § 6.2.

45. *Gl.*, § 15.2.

46. Schleiermacher calls the appearance of Christ in history the "miracle of all miracles" (*Sendschreiben*, 40) and argues that it is a supernatural occurrence in the sense that it cannot be accounted for by what preceded it in human history (*Gl.*, §§ 13-14).

47. See his clarifications regarding the relation of knowledge to piety in *Sendschreiben*, 13-18 (ET, 38-45). Piety is, he says, the "*Unbegründete*"—literally, that which has no foundation in an epistemological sense (*Sendschreiben*, 17).

48. For Barth's early views on Schleiermacher, see especially Karl Barth, *Das Wort Gottes und die Theologie* (Munich: Chr. Kaiser Verlag, 1924), and *Die Theologie Schleiermachers: Vorlesung Göttingen, Winteresemester 1923/24*, ed. Dietrich Ritschl (Zurich: Theologischer Verlag, 1978. English translations: *The Word of God and the Word of Man*, trans. Douglas Horton (London: Hodder & Stoughton, 1928), and *The Theology of Schleiermacher: Lectures at Göttingen, Winter Semester of 1923/24*, ed. Dietrich Ritschl, trans. Geoffrey W. Bromiley (Grand Rapids: Wm. B. Eerdmans Publishing Co., 1982).

49. Karl Barth, *Evangelische Theologie im 19. Jahrhundert, Theologische Studien*, no. 49 (Zollikon/Zurich: Evangelischer Verlag, 1957), 15-18; English translation, "Evangelical Theology in the Nineteenth Century," in Barth, *God, Grace and Gospel*, trans. James Strathearn McNab, Scottish Journal of Theology Occasional Papers, no. 8 (Edinburgh and London: Oliver and Boyd, 1959), 66-69. Cf. Barth, "Nachwort," in *Schleiermacher-Auswahl mit einem Nachwort von Karl Barth*, ed. Heinz Bolli (Munich and Hamburg: Siebenstern Taschenbuch Verlag, 1968); trans. George Hunsinger, "Concluding Unscientific Postscript on Schleiermacher," in *The Theology of Schleiermacher*, 261-79.

50. Interestingly, Schleiermacher makes just this point in his sermon "The Effects of Scripture and the Immediate Effects of the Redeemer." He writes: "God's Word must ever remain the standard for measuring and judging everything else if we are to avoid deceiving ourselves into unintentionally confusing the human and the divine" (*Servant of the Word*, 112).

51. *Sendschreiben*, 34 (ET, 59).

52. In fact, Barth sounds very close to Schleiermacher when he says dogmatics "knows the light . . . . [y]et it knows it only in the prism . . . which . . . is still a human act, which in itself is no kind of surety for the correctness of the appropriation in question, which is by nature fallible and therefore stands in need of criticism, of correction, of critical amendment" (*Church Dogmatics*, I/1:14).

53. Equally, however, I do not mean to imply that there is after all *no difference* between Barth and Schleiermacher. Cf. *Church Dogmatics* I/1:215-17.

54. *Sendschreiben*, 41-44 (ET, 65-68).

Natural and Divine Law: Retrieving the Roots of Christian Ethics

Jean Porter
UNIVERSITY OF NOTRE DAME DEPARTMENT OF THEOLOGY
NOTRE DAME, INDIANA

The idea that we can remake ourselves indefinitely, without reference to natural boundaries, is widely considered to be one of the hallmarks of modernity. Yet even in today's secular society, we cannot dispense with some minimal concept of what is natural or appropriate to human life, particularly in relation to issues of sexuality and medical practice. As these issues become more pressing and complex, we are seeing a revival of interest in the moral significance of human nature among scientists and philosophers as well as theologians.

So far, this renewed interest has not led to much interest in examining earlier accounts of the natural law as potential resources for Christian ethics, with the exception of the account offered by Thomas Aquinas. However, while the value and significance of Aquinas's thought is beyond dispute, no one author can fairly represent the richness of an extended tradition of discussion. And the discussion of the natural law, which provides the immediate context for Aquinas's work, is one of the richest, and yet most undervalued traditions to be found in the long history of Christian theological ethics.

This conviction led me to examine the concept of the natural law as it emerged in this medieval discussion with the aim of recovering it as a resource for contemporary Christian ethics. More specifically, in the book that resulted from my research, I developed an interpretation of the concept of the natural law as it was developed through the work of scholastic canon lawyers and theologians in the twelfth and thirteenth centuries. In doing so, I attempted to present the ideas and arguments of these texts accurately but, at the same time, I evaluated them precisely as ideas and arguments, considering them in the light of our own best understanding of the issues at stake. Hence, my aim in this project was constructive as well as historical. By reflecting on certain issues with the scholastics, so to speak, I attempted to offer a contribution to contemporary theological ethics, as well as to advance our understanding of their views.

In this paper, I set forth the main lines of the scholastic concept of the natural law and its contemporary significance, as I understand it. What follows is a summary of a longer project, and I have not attempted to provide detailed documentation, which is provided in my book.[1]

The Scholastic Concept of the Natural Law

The scholastic concept of the natural law brings together three traditional loci for moral reflection: nature, reason, and Scripture. Although each of these was a familiar idea (or text, in the case of Scripture) with a long tradition of reflection behind it, or perhaps because of that fact, the meaning of these loci was far from clear, and their proper interrelationships were even less clear. Reflection on these issues set the agenda for scholastic reflection on the natural law.

In sorting through the variety of traditional definitions of the natural law, the scholastics make use of the well-established distinction between the natural and the conventional to bring order to this variety. They do not interpret this distinction in such a way as to equate the natural with the morally good *tout court*, or the conventional with what is morally bad or suspect. Rather, they use the distinction between the natural and the conventional as a warrant for interpreting human action in the light of the diverse forces that ground and limit it. These pre-conventional givens include the exigencies of our biological nature as well as both reason, which is seen as setting both normative and practical constraints on human freedom, and Scripture, seen as a revelation of divine wisdom and will.

There are a number of points of contact between the scholastic conception of the natural law and contemporary thought. For example, when we examine scholastic writings on the relationship between the pre-rational aspects of our nature and rationality, we find striking resemblances to recent scientific and philosophical attempts to come to terms with the continuities between animal behavior and human morality. The scholastics do not attempt to derive moral norms directly from observations of animal behavior, as they are often accused of doing, but they do interpret human morality as the distinctively rational expression of needs and ways of behaving that are found more generally throughout the animal kingdom.

There is a second point of contact between the scholastics and those of us who work in the field of theological ethics. That is, the scholastic concept of the natural law is a theological concept, not a purely philosophical construct such as we associate with later versions of the natural law. It is theological, first of all, because it is formulated with a view to affirming the goodness of creation and drawing out the social implications of that affirmation, in response to those such as the Cathars who denied the goodness of the material world. Moreover, and more significantly, the canonists and theologians draw on and extend the scriptural aspects of earlier natural law thought.

Most contemporary theologians are familiar with the claim that the natural law and Scripture should be seen as two mutually complementary sources of moral knowledge, each of which can serve to supplement and correct the other. But the connection between the scholastic concept of the natural law and Scripture is more substantive than this claim would suggest. For the scholastics, the scriptural grounding of the natural law provides a way of identifying those aspects of human nature that are normative. Seen in this light, the scholastic concept of the natural law offers one formulation of a natural morality, but it also leaves open the possibility of other natural moralities, grounded in different assessments of what is morally valuable or significant in human nature. Hence, the scholastic concept of the natural law offers us a way of addressing the problem set for theological ethics by the moral indeterminancy of human nature, even though the scholastics themselves do not seem to have formulated this problem explicitly.

Precisely because of its theological character, the scholastic concept of the natural law does not offer a universal moral code that can be discerned by all rational men and women. Yet it offers us other advantages, which are arguably more important for contemporary theological ethics. It offers a theology of morality that preserves central theological commitments and can be developed into a moral theology with specific content. It suggests a theological framework within which to interpret the phenomenon of human morality and to account for the variability of different moral codes. Even more importantly, it offers us a way to understand Christian morality as one distinctive expression of human nature, which is therefore not wholly discontinuous with other moral systems, and yet retains its distinctiveness as one possible development, out of many, of natural human inclinations.

In the next two sections of this paper, I examine these aspects of the contemporary significance of the natural law in more detail.

The Theological Significance of the Natural Law

The scholastic concept of the natural law is first of all a way of approaching moral issues, which consists of both a fundamental orientation toward moral reflection and, inseparably from that, a set of specific normative commitments. As such, it is something less determinate than a particular theory, yet more coherent than a set of *ad hoc* appeals or fragments from earlier traditions. In this respect, it is comparable to other more familiar approaches to morality, for example Kantianism or utilitarianism, both of which are rooted in specific theories but have now expanded into general orientations toward moral reflection that accommodate a number of specific theories.

The scholastic concept of the natural law is similar to modern approaches to moral reflection in another way. That is, like these more familiar alternatives, it emerged out of a specific tradition of reflection and was shaped by the particular concerns that generated it. Of course, in contrast to the scholastic concept of the natural law, most modern approaches to moral reflection can be traced to specific, well-articulated theories developed by a single author. Nonetheless, these latter approaches reflect the traditions of reflection that motivated and shaped their authors' work, just as the scholastic concept for its part represents a synthesis of traditional elements.

This point is worth emphasizing, because we tend to think of the natural law as emerging directly from natural or rational exigencies. In contrast, scholastic reflections on the moral significance of nature were grounded in a tradition of reflection, and the scholastics themselves were aware of this fact.

The tradition of natural law reflection received by the scholastics incorporated both classical and distinctively Christian voices.

For the scholastics, this was first of all a scriptural tradition that offered, for that very reason, a framework within which Scripture could be interpreted afresh in the light of new concerns. At the same time, however, it offered resources for incorporating the best of twelfth-century natural philosophy into Christian theological reflection. The resultant concept of the natural law thus reflected the best understandings of nature that were available at the time, and even more importantly, it reflected an attitude of openness to natural philosophy that kept it from becoming rigid and unrealistic. At the same time, it was a theological concept in the distinctively Christian sense of reflecting a particular set of theological commitments, grounded in a particular, doctrinally informed reading of Scripture.

What were these commitments? They included, first of all, the goodness and integrity of the created world, as seen through the prism of the rich and complex medieval idea of nature. This was no mere theoretical affirmation, but a response to the resurgence of dualistic movements, which considered the material world to be in the most literal sense God-forsaken. The scholastics recognized that these movements offered a profound challenge to Christian belief, and their concept of the natural law should be seen as one aspect, as it were the praxis-oriented aspect, of their response to that challenge. Secondly, and correlatively, the scholastics were committed to defending the integrity and the revealed status of Scripture, and more particularly the Old Testament, which witnesses to God's work as Creator and provident Sustainer of the visible world. Finally, these commitments included a limited yet real commitment to natural equality, seen as grounded in the commonalities of our shared human nature, especially our capacities for moral discernment and free action.

In my view, these commitments are still theologically valid, and just as important for us as they were for the scholastics. Of course, the scholastic understanding of nature, and even more, the specifics of their moral conclusions, would call for considerable revision in order to be acceptable today. Nonetheless, the scholastic concept of the natural law offers us an affirmation of the goodness of nature, together with a framework for thinking through the practical implications of that affirmation, which is still sound in its main lines.

This framework is particularly valuable for us today, because it offers a way to deal with recent scientific advances in our understanding of the biological and psychological roots of human nature. In particular, it provides us with a way to appropriate the insights of evolutionary psychology into theological ethics without allowing those insights to determine the ethic in a reductive way. Admittedly, this will only appear as an advantage to those who find the work of evolutionary psychologists to be illuminating; yet it is hard to deny that their approach is fundamentally valid, however much some of them may have exaggerated its explanatory power.

It is reasonable to expect that any moral system will reflect the pre-rational and rational patterns of behavior characteristic of us as a species. This does not mean that a particular moral system will ever be wholly determined by the givens of human nature, or much less that any given morality will be subject to a reductive explanation in terms of our evolutionary history. There is no such thing as a pure human nature existing prior to culture (as we are frequently reminded), and so we would expect any particular moral system to reflect the history and culture of the society that generates it. Nonetheless, we would also expect to see common patterns of social organization in nearly all communities, not only because all societies share certain basic needs and vulnerabilities, but also because the human being exhibits characteristic behavioral patterns, as do all other species of animals. Hence, we would expect to find what we do in fact find when we compare different moral systems, namely, some resemblance at the most general level of ideals and basic norms, combined with considerable diversity at the level of specific normative beliefs and practices. Although the scholastics drew on different understandings of nature, their concept of the natural law provides us with a framework for reflecting theologically on the beliefs and practices of human societies in accordance with our best insights into the natural givens out of which they emerge.

The affirmation of the goodness of nature implicit in the scholastic concept of the natural law is all the more important today, because it is in tension with the prevailing direction of much contemporary theology, at least in the English-speaking world. In this respect, the scholastics offer an alternative to the approach of those contemporary theologians who emphasize the distinctiveness of Christian morality. This approach offers a valuable reminder of the radical demands of the gospel and the pervasive effects of human sinfulness, and it provides, in addition, a necessary corrective to the proud assumption that we can autonomously determine the meaning of human moral goodness. Yet taken to its extreme, the current emphasis on the distinctiveness of Christian ethics leads to the attempt to create a self-referential, self-enclosed Christian discourse, within which the Christian neither needs to, nor (according to some) can engage in any alternative discourse.[2]

The difficulty with this approach is that it risks falling into another kind of pride, the pride of assuming that we can create our own world of meaning, within which we can take refuge from the ambiguities of society and the stark inhumanity of the physical universe. Over against this, the scholastics remind us that we live in a world that we did not make, under the sovereignty of a Creator whose goodness we can trust, but whose designs will always be to some extent opaque to us. Correlatively, they draw our attention to the fact that human social practice and moral reflection stem from natural givens that we did not put in place, and that condition and constrain us even within the Christian community. This does not mean that there is no element of human construction in the generation of social practices and the morality that sustains them; on the contrary, we have seen that the scholastics do allow for an element of such construction, and we would undoubtedly give it a greater role than they did. By the same token, we need not assume that we can distinguish with certainty between the natural and the conventional in any given instance, in order to acknowledge that pre-conventional constraints are operative in most social practices. What the scholastic concept of the natural law provides is not an absolutely reliable guide to determining what is natural, but a framework within which to reflect on the moral significance of the pre-conventional roots of human social practices, in accordance with our best efforts to discern what these are at any given point.

Seen from this perspective, what the scholastic concept of the natural law offers us is first of all a theology of morality, that is to say, a theological context within which to interpret and evaluate the genuine phenomenon of human morality. So interpreted, morality is neither transcendent, nor a perspicuous expression of the divine will. It is essentially a mundane reality, and as such it is both flawed and limited. Yet it is also an expression of human nature, and as such, it reflects God's creative wisdom and expresses the fundamental goodness of the human person considered as a creature of God.

Ultimately, this affirmation of the limited yet real validity of human morality implies the further affirmation of the doctrine of creation, and of the correlative view that the visible world, including the structures of human life, reflects the goodness of its Creator.

Although the goodness of human nature, comprehensively understood, is the ground for the value of human morality, it is also the case that human nature under-determines morality, and correlatively, there can be more than one authentic natural morality. Indeed, there are many such, because every indigenous moral tradition should be considered as a distinctive form of a natural morality. This brings us to the second respect in which the scholastic concept of the natural law can contribute to contemporary Christian moral reflection. That is, this concept implies a particular set of normative commitments that should guide the ongoing development of Christian morality, as well as offering a starting point for assessing other moral traditions.

These commitments take the form of judgments about those aspects of human nature that should be privileged, and correlatively, those aspects that should be given secondary importance, or even discouraged. More specifically, the scholastic concept of the natural law implies a privileging of our capacities for rational self-direction, and correlatively, it gives a secondary place to, without discounting, those temperamental and emotional capacities that are more clearly unevenly distributed. Moreover, because it incorporates commitments to non-maleficence and an ideal of natural equality, it implies that we should promote those capacities for empathy and cooperation that foster those commitments, while de-emphasizing tendencies toward aggression and hierarchical organization that tend to undermine them.

Hence, the scholastic concept of the natural law suggests a set of criteria for interpreting specific social practices. In this way, the theology of morality offered by this concept of the natural law is transformed into a moral theology with definite normative implications. The specific moral content of this concept of the natural law will not be as comprehensive or unambiguous as the moral conclusions promised by many later versions of the natural law. The theological character of the scholastic concept prevents it from serving as a universally valid moral code, and the limitations and ambiguities inherent in the concept prevent it from serving even as a comprehensive and complete Christian ethics. Nonetheless, this concept does have specific normative implications; it is not merely formal or motivational.

How are these implications to be drawn out? It is worth underscoring that the scholastics did not attempt to draw out moral conclusions by way of deducing them from a fixed and determinate human nature. In fact, the scholastics did believe that we have a species-specific nature (at least, they did in the period I considered), but that does not mean that they believed it to be sufficiently knowable to serve as a basis for a deductive system of moral rules. More importantly, they did not argue as if they believed that moral conclusions could be unambiguously established on the basis of our knowledge of human nature. Rather, their moral arguments moved dialectically between accepted moral precepts and practices, and their views on the natural and scriptural bases of those beliefs and customs, interpreting and reformulating each in the light of their best understanding of the other.

The development of scholastic thinking on sexuality and marriage offers one of the clearest examples of this. Many of the early scholastics held the view that sexual desire is intrinsically sinful, and by implication not a part of human nature. However, this view stood in tension, to say the least, with the affirmation of the goodness of marriage and procreation, an affirmation that not only reflected a widely accepted practice, but that was seen as required by fundamental theological commitments. This tension led the scholastics to modify and then finally to reject the claim that sexual desire is intrinsically sinful; in the process, they drew on their concept of the natural law to develop a new interpretation of sexual desire, according to which it is rendered intelligible through the purpose it serves in human life, and thus acknowledged as a part of human nature.

What we have here is an example of a rethinking of the meaning of human nature, prompted by fundamental moral and theological commitments, and made possible through the framework of the scholastic concept of the natural law. When we, in our turn, rethink norms for sexual activity in the light of our commitment to the value of interpersonal love, and our sense of the value of sexual activity as an expression of that love, we are not breaking with the scholastics, but continuing a process of dialectal interpretation of sexuality begun by the scholastics themselves.

A contemporary appropriation of the scholastic concept of the natural law would go beyond the scholastics in its recognition that human nature allows multiple developments, and correlatively in its acknowledgment of the self-reflexive and constructive dimensions of moral reflection. Even here, what is at stake is not so much a break with the scholastics, as an extension and development of certain lines of their thought, because the scholastics did not believe that the natural law gives rise to moral claims directly and immediately. Rather, in their view the general imperatives of the natural law must be translated into social practices through the conventions of a particular society in order to be practically effective.

These conventions are not themselves part of the natural law properly so called, and they stand in a complex relationship to it. At the same time, they can be described as natural law in a derivative sense, because they are expressions of the natural law in a more proper sense, and are in some cases very nearly as universal as the natural law itself. (For example, this would be generally said to be true for the law of nations as secular jurists of the time understood it.) Moreover, even those precepts of the natural law that are revealed by God cannot be translated directly into social practices without a considerable degree of interpretation. In this sense, there is some room for human construction even with respect to the fundamental moral precepts that are confirmed by revelation.

The scholastics do not explicitly raise the question whether the precepts of morality are discovered or constructed by human reason. If we ask what answer to this question is implied by their concept of the natural law, we must conclude that seen from this perspective, their concept is ambiguous. They emphasize the permanence, supremacy, and binding force of the natural law, considered as the pre-conventional origin of all laws and social practices. At the same time, they recognize that there is considerable room for human construction in the level of formulating specific norms. Yet this process of construction itself operates within constraints, partly set by the exigencies of reason and pre-rational nature, and partly normative in character.

Yet this ambiguity need not be regretted; seen from our standpoint, it is potentially fruitful. To the extent that the scholastics recognize that morality is a human construct, they provide a point of entry for us, who are very conscious of the extent to which morality is a social construction. Yet their concept of the natural law also implies that there are practical and normative constraints on the social construction of morality, and correlatively, it implies that the status of morality as a human construct need not imply sheer moral relativism.

It is worth noting that on this view, there is an element of construction in Christian morality itself. Through an ongoing process of reflection, teaching, and practice, the churches attempt to discern the practical implications of the Christian gospel and to shape their communal life and witness accordingly. This process typically involves some reflection on the givens of human nature, yet the moral significance of these givens can never just be read off from observation and experience. Christian reflection on human nature, or human experience or needs or aspirations, always involves an element of selective interpretation in the light of theological commitments. Furthermore, the humanity, which is the object of this interpretation, has already been given a determinate shape by the preceding history of reflective interpretation, which for us in Western societies means that it has been shaped, at least to a considerable extent, in the light of the Christian beliefs and practices of our forbears.

The claim that Christian morality is in any sense a social construct may seem to invite a charge of relativism. However, "relativism" can mean a great many things. If this term is taken to imply that the specific moral beliefs and practices that comprise Christian morality are varied, that they change over time and also differ from community to community, then it is true that I am arguing for a kind of theological relativism. Yet I do not see how any account of Christian morality (or indeed, of any other kind of morality) can avoid being relativistic in this sense. Even the most stringent divine command theory of Christian morality will necessarily leave some room for variability at the level of interpretation and implementation of what are taken to be divine commands. But if the charge of relativism is taken to imply that Christian morality develops without any constraints whatsoever, then I would deny that this account is relativistic. On the contrary, Scripture and the exigencies of human nature both place normative constraints on the development of Christian moral systems. Correlatively, it is always both necessary and meaningful to ask whether we as a Christian community are acting in fidelity to scriptural imperatives and the moral demands of our nature.

The primary task of Christian ethics, considered as a self-reflective formal discipline, is continually to raise and pursue this question. So understood, the task of Christian ethics includes both reflective and constructive elements, corresponding to the dialectic of discernment and practice within the life of the Christian community. Christian ethics as a discipline attempts to understand and articulate the ongoing processes of interpretation and formation through the historical and analytic tools of academic discourse. At the same time, the Christian ethicist is himself or herself a participant in this process, bringing academic insights to bear on the life of the community, thus contributing to its ongoing self-construction.

From Theology to Morality: Some Specific Implications of the Natural Law

What can the scholastic concept of the natural law bring to the work of contemporary Christian ethics at the level of specific moral insights?

Modern and contemporary accounts of the natural law have accustomed us to associate natural law reasoning with definite, stringent prohibitions. The scholastics certainly gave a particular set of prohibitions a central place in their concept of the natural law, and yet this concept was not in the first instance negative and limiting. On the contrary, the concept of the natural law served most fundamentally as a positive and legitimating concept. Whatever can be construed as an expression of nature, in most of its generally accepted senses, was considered to be *prima facie* legitimate and good, even though this *prima facie* assumption could be overridden by other considerations. In order to prevent misunderstanding, it should be noted that nature in this context was always understood in terms that admit of construal of some general intelligible purpose. For this reason, not everything that emerges spontaneously in human beings as a class, or in a given individual, can serve as a basis for moral legitimation, because the human constitution includes some elements that are either accidental, or harmful, and the constitution of an individual is not sufficiently general to serve as a basis for moral conclusions. Nonetheless, this way of applying the natural law offered considerable flexibility, because it allowed for an appeal to nature in any sense that admits of construal in the light of general intelligible purposes.

Applied to contemporary moral refection, this aspect of the scholastic concept of the natural law offers a way of interpreting the moral beliefs and practices of other cultures, and even of different sub-cultures within our own society, in the light of the natural human purposes that they reflect and serve. Natural purposes, in this context, can be construed broadly to include the exigencies of human social life, as well as biological needs and the basic inclinations that we share with other animals, or with the other higher primates. If the seemingly arbitrary or even repugnant practices of other societies can be seen as expressions of natural purposes, they can at least be rendered intelligible and accorded the value of expressions of a fundamentally good human nature, even if they still seem problematic on other grounds.

We have already noted that the scholastic concept of the natural law, precisely because of its specifically theological character, does not yield the universally valid moral code that modern and contemporary natural law theorists have attempted to provide. However, it can offer us another way of dealing with the moral pluralism of what is increasingly a world society. That is, it offers a framework within which to affirm the value and integrity of a plurality of expressions of human nature, even while we acknowledge that all these expressions may not be compatible with one another, or with a Christian vision of human life. As such, the scholastic concept of the natural law offers us something that is perhaps of even greater value than the supposedly universal moral code associated with later natural law theorists. It offers a space for what I believe is a more realistic recognition of the irreducible diversity of human moral beliefs and practices, together with resources for a more nuanced assessment of these diverse mores. This line of approach does not force us to judge ways of life different from our own as intrinsically iniquitous or sinful. Nor does it lead to the conclusion that any moral code that is incompatible with Christian ideals is *ipso facto* to be condemned. Rather, it allows for a positive theological assessment of diverse human mores, seen as expressions of human nature bearing their own integrity and value, even when they are not compatible with a Christian way of life.

Does it follow that we must give up any possibility of cross-cultural moral dialogue and critique? In my view, it does not. The moral and legal agreements and conventions, which today serve as a framework for international relations, are our contemporary equivalent of the ancient and medieval law of nations, and like the law of nations, they can themselves be considered as a kind of natural law. However, we must keep in mind that these agreements and conventions are not given perspicuously by nature, or by reason; like the mores of particular societies, they are a determinate expression of human nature, arrived at through a complex process of negotiation, mutual accommodation, coercion, and unreflective practice among the nations and peoples of the world. We Christians are participants in this process, and have as much claim as anyone to attempt to shape it in accordance with our best ideals, but we should not expect that ours will be the only, or even the dominant, voice in this process.

Within the Christian community, the scholastic concept of the natural law likewise offers a framework for acknowledging the value of diverse practices, but in this context, the assessment of these practices must also take account of a distinctively Christian vision of what is of primary value in human life. That is, within the Christian community we need to ask not only whether a given practice is intelligible in the light of the natural purposes it serves, but also whether it is compatible with a distinctively Christian construal of those purposes.

Here is an example. On December 14, 1998, Gustav Niebuhr, writing in *The New York Times,* reported that the Celestial Church of Christ, founded in Nigeria in 1947 by a Methodist layman, S.B.J. Oshoffa, had recently been denied admission to the World Council of Churches (WCC) because of that church's policy of allowing clergy to have more than one wife.[3] Since 1986, according to the Reverend Alexander Bada, its current head, the Celestial Church of Christ has refused to ordain men who have more than one wife, but in order to avoid splitting the community and seeming to endorse divorce, it has not required men ordained before that time to give up their additional wives. According to one senior clergyman, Olantunji Akande, the 1986 policy had "put the church back on to the path of rectitude." However, this was not enough for the WCC, which on December 10, 1998, voted to reject the church's application for membership by a 3-2 margin.

This judgment is understandable, given the consensus of the churches that make up the WCC, and yet it does not appear to take account of the distinctive practices of African societies. At the same time, almost no one would want to say that every traditional practice of every society should be accepted; otherwise, what basis would there be for a Christian critique of culture?

Consider this dilemma in the light of the scholastic concept of the natural law. In the first place, it is easy to construe polygamy as an expression of natural human purposes, if only because it reflects an efficient reproductive strategy. However, secondly, polygamy does seem vulnerable to the criticism that Aquinas lodged against it in the thirteenth century; that is, it undermines the equity that should exist between husband and wife, and reduces the wife to a near-servile status (*Summa contra gentiles* III 124). As such polygamy appears as an intelligible expression of genuine human purposes, but one that is insufficiently responsive to a Christian construal of human nature according to which the ideal of natural equality is given a central place. Hence, the WCC would appear to be justified in challenging those churches that allow polygamy among their members to repudiate the practice.

At the same time, seen from this perspective, the WCC judgment in this case appears to be excessively harsh. At the very least, the practice of polygamy is a legitimate expression of the natural law, albeit one that does not appear to be optimal from the perspective of Christian moral ideals. Given this, it is difficult to say that this practice is so fundamentally at odds with Christian ideals as to require other churches to break off communion with those churches that endorse or tolerate it. Furthermore, a natural law perspective invites us to consider how far the reaction of the WCC reflects distinctively Western sensibilities, rather than Christian commitments. I do not mean to say that equality is a Western sensibility, but is it so clear that polygamy is necessarily incompatible with equality and equity among the partners in a marriage, in the specific cultural setting that is in question here? It is also worth noting that the Celestial Church of Christ is moving away from tolerating polygamy, but it has hesitated to require monogamy of all its clergy because to do so would imply an endorsement of divorce, and this, as they rightly point out, would also be problematic from a Christian standpoint. It appears to me that a more flexible stance with respect to divorce and remarriage is consistent with Christian morality (although I cannot argue the point here); nonetheless, it is difficult indeed to claim that a church that gives great importance to the permanence of marriage, even at the expense of monogamy, is taking a stance that is radically inconsistent with the ideals of the gospel.

If the scholastic concept of the natural law were only a legitimating concept, it would offer a valuable contribution to contemporary Christian ethics, but it would not offer much in the way of concrete norms. However, this concept also incorporates prohibitions that bring greater specificity to its moral content.

In order to appreciate the true force of these prohibitions, we must be on guard against a widespread assumption about what a natural law theory must involve. That is, we commonly associate natural law reasoning with injunctions against seemingly unnatural practices. Yet as we have seen, the idea of the unnatural plays a surprisingly small role in scholastic natural law reasoning. The scholastics do stigmatize certain sexual practices as unnatural, but they have clearly been influenced in this judgment by Paul's claim that homosexual acts are contrary to nature. According to some scholastics, usury is also unnatural in a pejorative sense.[4] However, for Aquinas at least, it is unnatural in the sense of being irrational, not in the sense of violating some supposedly pre-conventional aspect of economic exchange (*Summa theologiae* II-II 78.1, especially 78.1 *ad* 3; he also observes that this view has scriptural justification, even though the practice is permitted in the Hebrew law, at 78.1 *ad* 2). Yet these kinds of judgments do not appear to be typical of scholastic natural law reasoning. In fact, the scholastics are well aware that most of the central institutions of society are not natural, and may even be said in some sense to be contrary to nature.

This reticence may seem surprising and even disappointing. Yet the scholastics' reticence to characterize specific practices as unnatural reflects, once again, the distinctively theological and scriptural character of their concept of the natural law. This concept incorporates the complexity of traditional and scriptural judgments concerning the naturalness of social practices and institutions, and for this very reason, it does not readily lend itself to condemnations of specific practices as unnatural. What is contrary to nature in one sense may well express natural purposes in another sense.

The scholastics' reluctance to judge particular practices to be unnatural in a pejorative sense should be kept in mind when we attempt to apply their concept of the natural law to specific questions of biomedical ethics. So far as I can determine, there is nothing in the scholastic concept of the natural law to suggest that interventions in the genetic code, or the enhancement of bodily functioning by technological or pharmacological means, is in itself unnatural in a pejorative sense. The scholastic concept of the natural law does not imply that there is anything morally normative about the biochemical and physical processes that comprise our bodily existence, considered in themselves. However, the proper functioning and flourishing of the organism does have a positive moral value within the framework of this concept, and this implies that interventions that enhance human health and well-being are at least *prima facie* good. For this reason, the scholastic concept would function primarily as a legitimating, rather than a boundary-setting concept in medical contexts.

In contrast to prohibitions of unnatural behavior (at least outside of sexual contexts), the norms of non-maleficence implied by the Golden Rule and summarized in the Decalogue are seen by the scholastics as centrally important implications of the natural law. This is critically important, because it had the effect of placing the notion of harm, rather than unnaturalness, at the center of the scholastic concept of the natural law. That is to say, in most instances the natural law was seen by the scholastics as prohibiting particular kinds of actions because they are harmful, to others or to the agent of the act, and not directly because they are unnatural, although of course they did appeal to their understanding of human nature in order to determine what counts as harming another and what sorts of harms might be permissible.

The scholastic emphasis on the Golden Rule and the Decalogue might seem to imply that the normative content of the natural law as they understood it is not grounded in natural law reasoning at all, but in Scripture. It is true that scriptural norms provide starting points and parameters for scholastic moral reflection. Yet it would be a mistake to conclude that for the scholastics, the basic prohibitions associated with the natural law are simply recited from Scripture, and then given a *post factum* justification as tenets of the natural law. The concept of the natural law itself provided them with criteria for the interpretation of Scripture, which enabled them to distinguish between those scriptural norms that are moral and therefore generally binding, and those other norms that are not intelligible as general norms, and are therefore to be understood as cultic or legal norms. Moreover, this concept provided them with a way of interpreting those norms that did appear to them clearly to be moral rules. For example, Bonaventure drew on this concept of the natural law to argue that the prohibition against murder should be extended to include prohibitions against injury and detraction, and similarly, Aquinas drew on this concept to argue that this prohibition does not include killing in self-defense (*Collationes de decem preceptis* IV 4; *Summa theologiae* II-II 64.7).

The scholastics drew on their concept of the natural law in such a way as to emphasize the rational and intelligible character of scriptural moral norms, without rejecting their status as expressions of God's authoritative will. Moreover, for them the specific moral norms of Scripture are intelligible precisely as expressions of the basic injunction to love one's neighbor as oneself, and that means that they must be interpreted and applied with reference to fundamental human needs, vulnerabilities and desires. In this way, they reinforce the connection between morality and non-maleficence.

This brings us to a further point. The negative prohibitions associated with the natural law convey a positive meaning that goes beyond the specifics of the prohibitions themselves. That is, they come to function as expressions of a fundamental commitment to human dignity, which is safeguarded by prohibitions against harming others in fundamental ways. Aquinas remarks that anyone who harms another, contrary to the prohibitions against murder, wrongful injury, theft, or robbery, "dishonors him by depriving him of some excellence on account of which he has honor"—a general remark, it should be noted, that is not tied to any specific status apart from shared participation in a common humanity (*Summa theologiae* II-

II 72.1). This aspect of the scholastic concept of the natural law is well captured by the encyclical *Veritatis splendor*, where, after observing that the norms of morality apply equally to all, it states:

> In this way moral norms, and primarily the negative ones, those prohibiting evil, manifest their meaning and force, both personal and social. By protecting the inviolable personal dignity of every human being they help to preserve the human social fabric and its proper and fruitful development. The commandments of the second table of the Decalogue in particular—those which Jesus quoted to the young man of the Gospel (cf. Mt. 19:19)—constitute the indispensable rules of all social life.[5]

At the same time, there is another aspect of the commitment to human dignity embodied in the scholastic concept of the natural law, which this encyclical does not fully express, and which likewise merits recovery for contemporary ethical reflection. That is, the scholastics grounded human dignity positively in the capacity for moral discernment and self-direction enjoyed by each rational adult. They are very far from claiming, as this encyclical at least suggests, that men and women must depend on their "bishops and pastors" for knowledge of the moral law.[6] By the same token, they value human freedom, seen as the capacity for self-direction on the basis of the individual's own moral discernment, and some of them at least express this through a defense of individual subjective rights. Certainly they hold that human persons ought to make right use of their freedom through obedience to God's law, but they do not equate that freedom with right moral behavior, nor do they deny that even an abused freedom has value as a reflection of the divine image in the human person.[7]

This suggests that if the Christian community is to incorporate a respect for human dignity into its social life and communal witness, it must not only respect and promote human well-being, it must also find ways to honor and foster human autonomy and self-direction. The specific forms through which this is done will vary from church to church, but it seems to me that in any case, they will include some recognition, formal or implied, of the rights of individual Christians over against the institutional church, as well as a more general acknowledgment of the independent value of human freedom, apart from any consideration of the ways in which that freedom is used.

These are arguments for another day. However, they illustrate a more general point that is worth underscoring. That is, precisely because it lies at the root of so much Christian moral reflection and practice, the scholastic concept of the natural law offers both a fresh perspective on familiar commitments, and a valuable reminder of the forgotten or unfashionable implications of those values. In addition, as I have tried to show throughout this study, this concept is fundamentally sound and can still serve as a fruitful starting point for theological reflection. For both these reasons, the scholastic concept of the natural law merits retrieval as a resource for Christian theological ethics.

Endnotes

1. This paper is adapted from my book, *Natural and Divine Law: Reclaiming the Tradition of Christian Ethics* (Ottawa: Novalis, 1999), and it is published here with the kind permission of the press. An earlier version of this paper was read at a conference of the Henry Luce III Fellows in Atlanta, Georgia, on November 7, 1998, and I am grateful to my respondent, Margaret Farley, and the other participants in that conference for many helpful comments and suggestions.

2. Among English-speaking theologians today, John Milbank probably goes the farthest in this direction; see his *Theology and Social Theory: Beyond Secular Reason* (Oxford: Blackwell, 1990), passim.

3. Gustav Niebuhr, "Polygamy Keeps a New African Church from World Council," *New York Times*, December 14, 1998.

4. On the development of a natural law argument against usury, see John Noonan, *The Scholastic Analysis of Usury* (Cambridge: Harvard University Press, 1957), 38-81.

5. "The Splendor of Truth," (*Veritatis splendor*), promulgated on October 5, 1993, para. 97.

6. This phrase is taken from *Veritatis splendor* paragraph 117; compare paragraph 53, which states that the concrete meaning of the natural law in specific historical circumstances must be determined by the magisterium, although the latter is expected to draw on the reflections of laypersons and theologians in doing so. It is also worth noting that according to the encyclical, de-Christianization will necessarily lead to a decline or obscuring of the moral sense (paragraph 106), a claim which from the scholastic perspective would be overly simple, at best.

7. Again, compare *Veritatis splendor*, which comes very close to saying that authentic freedom consists in following the moral law in accordance with Christ's example (para. 85), and dwells at length on the "weakness" and the "tragic aspects" of human freedom (para. 86), while saying very little about its theological significance.

Rehabilitating "The Preacher": Qohelet's Theological Reflections in Context

Choon-Leong Seow
PRINCETON THEOLOGICAL SEMINARY
PRINCETON, NEW JERSEY

Introduction

There is probably no book in the Bible that has been more controversial than Ecclesiastes. The rabbis of antiquity sought to remove it from circulation partly because it seemed internally inconsistent (*b. Šabb.* 30b) and partly because they feared it might lead to heresy (*Qoh. Rabb.* on 1:3). Even though it won approval at the famous gathering of rabbis at Jamnia at the end of the first century C.E., questions about its suitability for the general public continued to be raised for centuries thereafter. Indeed, long after Jamnia, Jerome reported that there were some who tried to suppress it.[1] Even in modern times, the book is often viewed as one that stands at the periphery of the canon, at best a voice of protest from "the farthest frontier of Yahwism," as Gerhard von Rad famously put it.[2]

Scholarly debates have continued to revolve around the tensions within the book and its apparent heterodoxy, and assessments of it have remained wildly contrastive. One interpreter has characterized the book as the supreme example of skepticism in the Bible, while another replies that it reflects the quintessence of piety.[3] One scholar argues that the author—known by his Hebrew pen-name, Qohelet—was "a depressed workaholic,"[4] while another calls him "a preacher of joy."[5] A majority of commentators regard the author as an unrelenting pessimist, constantly proclaiming that "all is vanity" (1:2, KJV), while others portray him as an unflappable optimist, who submits that "there is nothing better for people under the sun than to eat and drink and be merry" (8:15).

To explain the teachings of the book that seem idiosyncratic in light of the rest of the Bible, critics have argued that the author was influenced by skeptical traditions from Mesopotamia or Egypt, or that his thoughts were shaped by various Greek philosophical schools. His perspectives are usually accounted for in terms of his intellectual background—most notably the foreign influences—or his personal disposition and predilection.[6] Qohelet, it is believed, was either a pessimist or an optimist because of his training and/or simply because "that was the way he was." Then, to explain the perspectives that do not fit their portrayals of the consummate pessimist or optimist, commentators have typically sought recourse to various theories about the editorial process (e.g., multiple reductions) or rhetorical strategies (e.g., dialogues with opponents real or imagined). A few would simply explain the dissonant passages as aberrations, essentially lapses from the author's dominant posture. Thus, a recent interpreter, who argues for a thoroughly pessimistic outlook, summarily dismisses the enjoyment passages as evidence of Qohelet's "wishful thinking" that provided "psychological relief."[7]

The approach of Michael Fox is a welcome exception to such tendencies, for he views the contradictions as part and parcel of the book's message, arguing that "Qohelet is not so much contradicting himself as *observing* contradictions in the world" (italics his).[8] Yet, despite such an emphasis on observations, Fox investigates only Qohelet's "intellectual background" and reaction to traditions, maintaining that "Qohelet's complaints do not reflect specific historical-social conditions."[9] In this reluctance to consider the sociohistorical context, Fox is not alone. Indeed, only a few have reckoned that Qohelet's message might have been occasioned and informed by his particular sociohistorical context.[10]

This emphasis on intellectual background has led to the common judgment that Ecclesiastes is finally a philosophical treatise, rather than a theological work with a particular message for a particular audience. So, Sibley Towner has suggested that "Ecclesiastes is not a book about God; it is a book about ideas."[11] Similarly, R. B. Y. Scott reckons the book to be "primarily a philosophical work rather than a book of religion."[12] Yet, the motif of "the fear of God," the ancient Near Eastern idiom for religion appears prominently in the book (3:14; 5:6; 7:18; 8:12-13; 9:2; 12:13). To be sure, Ecclesiastes reads nothing like a modern systematic theology; it certainly does not offer a sustained thesis about God.[13] Nevertheless, whether explicitly or implicitly, God is considered throughout the book. One may surmise from the mere fact that *ʾādām* ("humanity") and *ʾĕlōhîm* ("God") are among the most common words that the book is largely concerned with humanity and God. Indeed, the recurrence of these and other of Qohelet's favorite terms suggests the author has searched thoroughly to find what is good for humanity in a world where mortals have no control and God is utterly inscrutable.[14]

The Context-Consciousness of Qohelet

It is noteworthy that the three most common verbs in Ecclesiastes are *rʾh* ("to see, experience"), *hyh* ("to be, happen"), and *ʿśh* ("to do, make"). The importance of the first of these lies in the fact that in some twenty-six instances, the author is the explicit or implicit subject.[15] More precisely, Qohelet *observes* the happenings in the world (1:14; 7:13; 8:9), human preoccupations and strivings (3:10; 4:4, 7; 5:12-13; 8:16), divine arbitrariness as reflected in the unequal lots of individuals (2:24; 6:1), society turned upside down (3:16; 10:7), the prevalence of injustice and oppression (3:16; 4:1; 8:9), and how the traditional rules are contradicted in reality (7:15; 8:10; 9:11, 13). Admittedly, these are situations that one may find in almost any period in history and virtually anywhere. Still, these are things that Qohelet himself tells us that he has seen; they are not presented as realities learned from traditions alone. Some of these observed situations, moreover, sound rather specific, such as the tragic case of the parsimonious man who hoarded wealth only to lose it all in a "bad venture" (5:12-13), the solitary individual who was unable to stop striving even though there was none with whom to share the fruit of his toil (4:7), the powerful person who committed an inadvertent error and paid for it (10:5), and the instance where the poor and the rich seemed to have traded places (10:7).

The recurrence of the other two of the most common verbs (*hyh* "to be, happen" and *ʿśh* "to do, act") is also suggestive, for they indicate that Qohelet draws lessons from his observation of his world—what was *happening* and what was *being done*.[16] Moreover, in terms of Qohelet's "lexicon," Dahood has identified a list of commercial terms that, to him, indicate that the book reflects "a distinctly commercial environment."[17] Dahood's overall thesis that the mercantile environment implied by this vocabulary demands a Phoenician provenance in the late fourth century B.C.E. cannot be sustained, for we now know that international trade had penetrated deeply into Palestine in the Persian period. Still, he is certainly right that the vocabulary indicates a deep concern with economics. That concern suggests that Qohelet was addressing a particular environment, whatever the precise period might have been. That is not to say that Qohelet's "epistemology" is entirely "empirical." He does draw on traditional sources as well, specifically, wisdom teachings, materials found in the Torah (most explicitly, Deuteronomy) and, of course, traditions about Solomon. There are suggestive parallels, too, with various ancient Near Eastern literary works, most remarkably, the Gilgamesh Epic, a text about the ephemerality of humanity that counsels enjoyment of life while one is able, and the Aramaic Wisdom of Ahiqar, the earliest witness to which is found on a papyrus dated to the late fifth century B.C.E.[18] There is, indeed, much that one learns through an understanding of Qohelet's intellectual background. Nevertheless, one can hardly ignore the author's own insistence that his conclusions are derived largely from what he has observed in his particular time and place.[19]

To some extent, the reticence of scholars to consider the sociohistorical context of the book is understandable, for its date is not easy to pin down. There is no reliable external evidence save the fragments of two Qumran manuscripts, the earlier of which date to about 175 B.C.E. Those who posit Greek philosophical influences will, of course, argue for a Hellenistic date of composition. Yet, there is no indisputable evidence of Greek influence and the idioms that have been linked to putative Greek antecedents may readily be shown to have Semitic parallels.[20] When all is said and done, the most compelling evidence for dating the book may be its language, and in this regard recent opinions have converged upon the postexilic period as the most likely time of composition.[21] I have elsewhere argued that typologically the language of Ecclesiastes fits best in the last 120 years of Achaemenid rule in Palestine.[22] While a Hellenistic date cannot be precluded on linguistic grounds alone, I find no compelling reason to follow scholars who privilege such a dating. Indeed, the number of terminological and thematic links with Aramaic documents of the Persian period are without parallel. There is no similar coincidence of a cluster of idioms in the Hebrew and Aramaic dialects of other periods; even though some of these terms are also attested in other periods, we do not find them all together in both languages in a single period other than the late Achaemenid.

By the same token, the idiom *hšlyṭ lśʾt mtt* ("to authorize to take up a grant") in 5:18-19 reflects an equivalent technical idiom in Persian-period Aramaic, *šlyṭ lmnśʾ dšnʾ* ("authorization to take up the grant").[23]

At all events, the purpose of my brief sociohistorical foray is not ultimately a historicist one. Rather, I want merely to argue that Qohelet's theological message was context conscious and to suggest, in light of the linguistic evidence, a possible environment wherein Qohelet's message might make sense. His hermeneutic and rhetoric, I contend, were shaped by the intersection of tradition and contemporary life. He drew on and critically engaged the traditions as he taught "the people" knowledge and prodded them on as a pastor might (12:9-11).[24]

Late Achaemenid Context

Historians have long touted the administrative reforms of the Achaemenid government, notably the infrastructural innovations and renovations that greatly accelerated economic development. Arguably the most significant of the imperial measures was the standardization of currency at the end of the sixth century to facilitate the collection of taxes, simplify the disbursement of payments by the government, and enhance international trade. The standardization of coinage democratized the use of money and, in consequence, radically transformed the economy of the Eastern Mediterranean region.

The evolution from a non-monetary economy to a monetary one is evident in government documents uncovered at the imperial city of Persepolis. Records from the late sixth century indicate that disbursements then were made entirely in goods.[25] By the first decade of the fifth century, however, payment was still in kind but the cash values of the goods were invariably stipulated, thus indicating that cash had become the principle method of accounting. Soon after that, disbursement was made partly in kind and partly in cash: initially two-thirds in kind and one-third in cash, then half and half, and then one-third in kind and two-thirds in cash. Finally, by 469 B.C.E., we have the first record of payment made entirely in cash.[26] The economy had become fully monetarized at Persepolis, it seems, partly because of government policy and, no doubt, largely because of demand for cash. Archaeological evidence indicates that the revolution took a little longer to reach Palestine. Whereas coins from the end of the sixth century have been found sporadically in Palestine, they did not become common until late in the fifth and early in the fourth, in which period archaeologists have uncovered numerous hoards at various sites.[27] The Phoenicians, always more attuned to commercial opportunities, were quick to adopt the monetary system, but the revolution was spreading gradually but surely even into newly repatriated Yehud. There is evidence of a marked increase of commercialism in the province and clear indications that money was coming into circulation before the Hellenistic era.[28]

In view of such a monetary economy, it is perhaps not surprising to hear Qohelet say that "those who love money will not be satisfied with money, nor those who love abundance with yield" (5:11). Clearly, money had become a desired commodity. Elsewhere, too, Qohelet alludes to how "money preoccupies everyone" (10:19). The indictment is all the more poignant when one realizes that the same Hebrew words may be taken to mean that "money is the answer for everything" (NIV), suggesting that Qohelet may have turned a cliché about the efficacy of money into a criticism of those who subscribed to such a notion. A similar sort of subversion is evident in 7:12, where the author equates the security afforded by money with the security of wisdom. Here the term used for the protective power of money and wisdom is *ṣēl*, a term that elsewhere connotes ephemerality (6:12; 8:13). Qohelet's point is that money, like wisdom, affords not a permanent shelter but only temporary relief like a shadow. He suffers no illusions about the reliability of money or wisdom, even though he acknowledges, perhaps tongue-in-cheek, that "wisdom is as good as inheritance" (7:11), pointing ironically to the fact that both are, in fact, ephemeral.

Ecclesiastes reflects a lively economic environment brought about in no small part by the monetary revolution. The view long held by historians that imperial taxation in this period had drained Palestine to the point of economic stagnation must be reevaluated in light of archaeological evidence. It can be shown, in fact, that the economy of the region witnessed unprecedented overall growth. All along the coast, as well as in the agricultural hinterland, archaeologists have found evidence of economic vitality.[29] This vitality is attested, too, in the portrayal of fifth-century Jerusalem under the administration of Nehemiah (Neh. 13:15-16). At the same time, however, the book of Nehemiah also attests to the volatility of the economy and the vulnerability of ordinary citizens caught in a world of taxes, mortgages, loans, and foreclosures (Neh. 5:3-5). Persian taxation undeniably placed an enormous burden on the lives of the common folk, who often had to borrow to meet their obligations. Extrabiblical inscriptions attest to the heavy price of credit, with demand for it driving up the interest rates to unprecedented levels. Default in payment often resulted in foreclosures, seizures, detention, and enslavement. Yet, people continued to borrow because of the lure of success, while others did so simply because they had no other way out of their financial predicaments. In such a world of openings and pitfalls, it is easy to understand how Qohelet's audience could never feel secure with what they had. They strove for success out of envy (4:4), hoarded out of a sense of insecurity (5:12), and toiled out of anxiety for their financial well-being and the security of their descendants (2:18-23) or simply out of obsessive habit (4:7).

There were economic opportunities as never before in the Levant. Documents from the period showed that even slaves were able to borrow substantial sums of money, earn income for their work, and invest in all kinds of business ventures. Some became exceedingly wealthy, like Ribat, a slave of one of the bosses of the business firm of Murashu and Sons in the city of Nippur. Ribat had his own slaves, issued sizeable loans, made real estate deals, charged access to a canal, served as guarantor for debtors, detained his own debtors, went into joint ventures with other enterprising slaves, and even paid taxes for an office that he held.[30] Such rags-to-riches stories no doubt induced people to yearn and strive for success. The economic revolution created an impression of equal opportunity for wealth. Indeed, as the inscriptions amply attest, there was a variety of possibilities for employment, tenant farming, small-capital investments, joint-ventures, silent partnerships, and the like. That was a world in which there was, apparently, hope of success for anyone who would strive hard enough or have sufficient skills to "work the system." So people toiled and longed for wisdom.

The free market that Qohelet observed, however, was a frustratingly unpredictable world of boom or bust. Along with the opportunities for wealth were risks of financial disaster. So one reads in Ecclesiastes of the person who was so fearful of losing his wealth that he hoarded it, only to suddenly lose it all in a "bad venture" (5:12-14). Commentators generally recognize that Qohelet must have been referring to a situation he encountered. Thus, Norbert Lohfink suggests that the man had deposited his money in a bank, but was bankrupt when the bank became insolvent.[31] Whatever the truth, the passage points to the volatility of the economy that Qohelet and his audience knew. What they had one day could be gone the next. So people toiled to acquire more and more in order to hedge against the possibility of a financial disaster. Abundance does not, however, relieve one of worry. On the contrary, the more one has the more one worries and "the surfeit of the rich does not allow them to sleep" (5:11). Even those who have already achieved success could not count on staying on top (10:5-7). Qohelet's characterization of a topsy-turvy world is not a mere figment of his imagination. If it is a "wisdom *topos*," as it is sometimes suggested,[32] he is using it to corroborate his observation of the volatile economy of his time; the situation that he *observes* (10:5) proves the *topos* true yet again. Certainly, such volatility is evident in the late-Achaemenid period, when society seemed at times, and at least in some quarters, to have turned upside down.[33] The rich and the poor alike were susceptible to the winds of political change, as well as the variable forces of the market. Even kings were vulnerable to the vagaries of the market and vicissitudes of "realpolitik." Accordingly, one reads in Ecclesiastes of an old king who, though born into royalty, ended up impoverished, while an indigent youngster rose to become king despite having been in prison, a repository for debtors (4:12-13). If this scenario reflects realities of the Persian period, one should think of the deposed "king" here not as the ruler of the Achaemenid dynasty, but of a local ruler who had fallen out of favor because of some offense against the imperial government. Like other subjects of the Great King, local rulers could also be recipients of royal grants, as we know King Eshmunazor of Sidon was in the fifth century B.C.E.[34] Still, there are no guarantees in life, as Qohelet might well point out (cf. 9:11-12). It turned out that Eshmunazor could not hold on to his possessions, for he died "before [his] time" (cf. 7:17), leaving to posterity nothing but a tomb inscription cursing would-be grave robbers with infamy among the living "under the sun" (*ṭht šmš*).

The Persian system of property grants, indeed, provides a backdrop for understanding a number of instructions in Ecclesiastes. In the first place, there were the grants given outright by the crown to favorites, who had the legal authority during their tenure to reassign portions of their grant to those whom they in turn favored. Those lucky enough to be favored were given the authorization to enjoy the grant, while those who offended the grantor were denied its benefits. Qohelet views life as a portion that one receives from the divine Sovereign, even as one might receive a royal grant in the Persian Empire. Such a grant gives one the right of disposal, including the authorization to enjoy the yields of the lot, but it also invariably entails toil. This gift of enjoyment is issued for no reason other than God's inexplicable *prior* favor (9:7-10). One should, therefore, enjoy life whenever it is possible because the privileges of such a grant do not extend beyond one's lifetime (9:6).

Besides crown grants, the Persian government granted portions to various people on condition of payment of annual dues and military service in the infantry, cavalry, or chariotry. Although initially not alienable, the grantees were soon permitted to sublet their lots or pawn them in whole or in part. As a result, fiefs were sometimes shared by a number of partners, with the rights of proprietorship being transferable in each case by inheritance. This led inevitably to further division of the assets and, consequently, the gradual diminution of the lots. On the one hand, the availability of small lots fostered ambition for people who otherwise might never have had the opportunity to own any property at all. On the other hand, smaller portions meant that the assets could not be efficiently exploited, so that it always seemed necessary to accumulate more and more. In the system's ineluctable pyramid, tenant farmers and workers paid dues to the smallholders whose property they rented, the smallholders in turn paid those above them, and so forth, all the way to the pinnacle of the pyramid, the Great King alone. The delusion of equal opportunity for wealth is, however, extenuated by the harsh reality of the system that inspired ambition but provided no assurances. That environment offered the seduction of success together with the peril of failure, and there were no fail-safe rules that assured results. So the ambitious, while arrogant, were also insecure. Hence, Qohelet describes an unscrupulously exploitative world where "a high one is above a high one, (and) high ones watch over them all" (5:7), and yet people are not satisfied with what they have and even those who have plenty can find no rest (5:8-12).

Apart from the requisite taxes, those who received such grants were expected to render military services as needed. In many cases, however, those who had right of disposal over the lots hired substitutes to fulfill their military obligations. In one instance, a proprietor offered a retainer a certain amount of grain annually for agreeing to take up his duties in the event of a muster.[35] In another case, a slave offered to do substitute service for a coproprietor of a lot according to the standard "going rate."[36] Numerous contracts like these in the Achaemenid period record the payment of such services in goods, cash, a portion of capital assets, or, freedom from detention in prison. The poor were willing to hedge their bets on peace and count on their own survival skills in return for pecuniary benefits, while the relatively rich could purchase exemption from life-threatening obligations. Qohelet, however, argues that in truth no one has any real control over life, and no one can send a substitute to the decisive "battle" that is the day of death (8:8). No one has proprietary rights over the life-breath, as one might have over a poor slave, and one cannot detain (*klʾ*) it, as one might threaten to detain a poor debtor in the *bīt kīli* (literally, "house of detention").

The period that Qohelet observed was one of economic vitality but also volatility. It was a time for heady optimism about hitherto unimaginable opportunities. Yet, that optimism was offset by sociopolitical and economic realities. It was a perplexing new world of rapid political, social, and economic innovations, much of which were initiated and determined in seats of power that the ordinary citizens of the vast empire could hardly grasp.

Beyond Mortal Grasp

No serious study of Qohelet's message can avoid an assessment of the frustratingly elusive meaning of the word *hebel*, traditionally translated as "vanity." The significance of the word for the interpretation of Ecclesiastes lies not so much in its frequency alone, although its thirty-nine occurrences must be regarded as considerable, but in the fact that it appears strategically in summary judgments, not least in the epigram that structurally frames the book (1:2; 12:8).

The conventional interpretation of the word goes back to the Old Latin gloss (*vanitas*) of the word in the Greek version, which almost always translates the word as *mataiotēs* ("nothingness"). The scrupulously literalistic version of Aquila, as well as those of Symmachus and Theodotion, however, prefers the translation *atmos* "vapor." That is the material sense of the term in Hebrew and its cognate languages, where the noun refers to "vapor" or "breath." The literal usage of the term is attested in Isa. 57:3, where one reads of people carried away by wind and snatched by breath (*hebel*). In most of its occurrences in the Bible, however, *hebel* is used as a simile or metaphor for things that are ephemeral, insubstantial, inconsequential, empty, elusive, and illusory. The word in such cases evokes the traits of the material referent, namely, vapor or breath. Thus, Ps. 144:4 refers to the ephemerality of human beings thus: "Mortals are like *hebel*; their days are like a passing shadow." In this case, the material sense of the word *hebel* is obviously intended; human beings are likened to it. Elsewhere, too, the material sense of the word is in view, even when the word is used metaphorically. So Job bemoans the transitory nature of human existence: "I will not live forever; leave me alone, for my days are *hebel*" (Job 7:16). Similarly, one reads in Ps. 62:10 that "mortals are but *hebel*, humans an illusion...less than *hebel*" (Ps. 62:10). Accordingly, then, one should not delude oneself (*hbl*) by relying on plunder to get ahead, for God alone is in control, recompensing all according to their works (Ps. 62:11-13). The poet of Psalm 39 complains about the evanescent nature of life, which is depicted together with all the commotion that life entails as *hebel* (v. 7), concluding that every mortal is but *hebel* (v. 12). Qohelet's usage of the word falls in that semantic range in a few passages, for he, too, recognizes the human lifespan to be limited: "Who knows what is good for humanity in the few days of their *hebel* life; they will spend them like a shadow" (6:12). Human beings should enjoy life whenever they can, for life is *hebel* (9:9; cf. 5:17). They should enjoy themselves because the time to do so is fleeting; everyone who comes into existence is but *hebel*, that is, transient (11:8), and "youth and the dawn of life are *hebel*" (11:10). In this passage, as perhaps in no other in Ecclesiastes, it is indisputable that *hebel* connotes evanescence. Certainly, Qohelet does not mean that youth is vain, futile, or insignificant, for it is youth that makes enjoyment possible, if only for a little while. So a number of scholars have argued for transience as the dominant meaning of the term in the book.[37]

Yet, *hebel* does not connote transience everywhere in the book. In 6:4, for instance, one reads that the stillborn child "comes in *hebel* and goes in darkness." In this case, it would be meaningless to say that the stillborn "comes into transience." Rather, the point is that the fetus has come into the world for naught; it is, like vapor, essentially nothing.[38] Elsewhere, *hebel* is used to convey the fact that the abundance of words adds nothing of substance to reality (5:6; 6:11; cf. Job 21:34). In this sense, *hebel* is something that is, like vapor, insubstantial. A similar range of meaning is evident in other passages, where other traits of vapor are evoked. Thus, reporting on his experiment with pleasure (2:1-3), Qohelet concludes that "it, too, is *hebel*," meaning that pleasure is ultimately inconsequential: "Regarding merriment," I said, '[What] does it boast?' And regarding pleasure: 'What does it really accomplish?'" (2:2).[39] Likewise, human acquisitions and accomplishments all amount to "*hebel* and a pursuit of wind" (2:4-11). It is not that such attainments are of no good whatsoever, for Qohelet says he derived some pleasure from the fruit of his toil (2:10), but such achievements are inconsequential as far as mortality is concerned (2:11). Pleasure and success are, to be sure, desirable, but they are not things that one can count on or hold on to. So, too, wisdom is beneficial (2:13; 7:11-12), but it is, like wealth, ephemeral (7:13). To be sure, it is better to pay attention to the rebuke of the wise rather than to the flattery of fools (7:5). Yet, the relative advantage of wisdom is just that, relative and "it, too, is *hebel;* for oppression turns the wise into fools and a bribe perverts the mind (7:7-6). Thus, even if the wise are generally more trustworthy than fools, they may not always remain wise. There are all kinds of factors that might nullify wisdom's efficacy (cf. 9:13-18).

Qohelet's notion of life as vapor or breath is nothing new. The extension of the metaphor to refer to other things that one cannot apprehend—like pleasure, wealth, wisdom, and youth—because they are ephemeral, inconsequential, elusive, or illusory is also not unique, for there are antecedents and parallels elsewhere.[40] Qohelet, who memorably avows that "there is nothing new under the sun" (1:9), never claims to be saying or doing anything novel. Still, he does not hesitate to employ *hebel* as a metaphor to characterize certain situations that he has observed that utterly perplex or frustrate him.[41]

This is what is different about his usage of *hebel,* not a different meaning of the term altogether but an extension of the metaphor to situations that one encounters. Thus, he speaks of *seeing* a *hebel* (4:7), certainly an ironic imagery in light of the material referent of the term. He describes the case of one who has neither companion nor kin to share his possessions and yet is not satisfied with his bounty. And "this," Qohelet concludes, "is *hebel* and it is a terrible preoccupation" (4:6-8). In the face of the ephemerality of wealth, the endlessness of toil in the case of this solitary individual is simply beyond grasp. In this instance, Fox's contention that *hebel* means "absurd" is compelling.[42] It is not, however, that Qohelet is introducing a new meaning of the term, however. Rather, his reflection on something that is evanescent (wealth) leads him to reflect on the absurdity of obsession with the acquisition of wealth, a situation that makes no sense. Perhaps to signal his unusual nuance on the metaphor of *hebel* in this case, then, he adds that "it is a terrible preoccupation," meaning it is a case that vexes one mightily without possibility of a resolution. One cannot grasp it.

Even more ironic than the imagery of a *hebel* being *seen* is the reference to a *hebel* that is *being done* (8:14). The reference here is to the perversion of justice because of a dragged-out process, the result of which is that the wicked are treated as if they are righteous and the righteous are treated as wicked. This ironic situation Qohelet calls *hebel*. The elusiveness of justice, as illustrated in this particular case of the protraction of the process, may have prompted him to conclude that the situation is *hebel,* a situation that frustrates him. This ungraspable situation is called *hebel,* here meaning an absurdity (Fox) that is brought about by the elusiveness of justice. The rules of life do not seem to hold.

Qohelet's application of the metaphor to various situations does not mean that he disregards the material referent of the term. Indeed, in every case, the characterization of the situation as *hebel* may have been precipitated by his reflection of things that, like vapor, cannot be grasped. So the conclusion about the situation in 8:10-15 (the preposterousness of perverted justice) can hardly be distinguished from the elusiveness of justice. The situation is irksome because justice is not apprehensible. By the same token, Qohelet's judgment in 1:14 that "all is *hebel* and a pursuit of wind" refers to a situation that he cannot grasp, namely, all that he has observed being done under the sun, but it cannot be dissociated from his point about the inefficacy of wisdom. Here the enterprise is described as a "terrible preoccupation," the same phrase used to qualify the *hebel*-judgment of the frustrating situation in 4:8. The effort is also characterized as "a pursuit of wind," an imagery of one trying to grasp something that simply cannot be grasped (see Sir. 34:1-3). This expression is, in fact, used repeatedly with the *hebel*-judgment (1:14; 2:11, 17, 26; 4:4, 16; 6:9) and possibly twice in place of it (1:17; 4:6). The use of the "wind" (*rûaḥ*) is significant because *hebel* in its material sense is viewed as a synonym of wind (Isa. 57:13). It is also tantalizing because "wind" is used in a passage from the Gilgamesh Epic that is widely regarded as a parallel to Ecclesiastes, with its emphasis on human limitations and the evanescent nature of life:

> Only gods live forever with the sun.
> As for humanity, their days are numbered;
> Whatever they do is but wind.[43]

In Qohelet's rhetoric, too, *rûaḥ* ("wind, life-breath, temper") is always unpredictable and uncontrollable. One must not, therefore, overlook the material referent of *hebel* even when the term is used to characterize situations. Indeed, it is often impossible to determine if a *hebel*-judgment refers to an ungraspable entity or an ungraspable situation, for both may be intended. This is the case in 4:4, where Qohelet observes that "every toil and every success of work" is motivated by envy. "This is also *hebel*," he says, "and a pursuit of wind." Here it is impossible to discern if "this" refers to success (which is evanescent) or to the situation (which is absurd). Both may, in fact, be intended: because success is *hebel,* the situation of envy driving people to it is *hebel*. Similarly, the point is made that those who love money will not be satisfied with it, and "that is also *hebel*" (5:9). One must not insist that either money itself or the situation is *hebel*, for both are: because money is *hebel* (evanescent), the case of people wanting more and more of it is *hebel* (absurd). Most clearly, in 3:19-20, one sees that Qohelet does not make any distinction between things and situations. Reflecting on the fate of death that befalls human beings and animal alike, he concludes that there is one breath for them "all" (*kōl)* for "all" (*kōl*) is *hebel* (3:19), "all" (*kōl*) go to one place (Sheol) and "all" (*kōl*) will return to dust (3:20). The *hebel*-judgment points to the ephemerality of all mortals—people and animals alike—but it is, at the same time, a reference to the absurdity of the leveling effect of death for "all." Humans and animals are all *hebel* and that absurd situation, where humans have no advantage over animals, is *hebel;* it is a situation that is imprehensible, utterly beyond grasp.

The same is true with human efforts to grasp wealth (2:18-23). People cannot hold on to the fruit of their toil and wisdom, for the ephemerality of life means that one must leave it all to posterity. The one who toils may not enjoy whatever benefits toil and wisdom may bring. Rather, someone who has not toiled for the benefits may receive them and, even more ironically, that lucky beneficiary may turn out to be an undeserving fool! Qohelet calls this absurd situation *hebel* (vv. 19, 21) and elaborates that it is "a very terrible thing" (v. 21). Human beings strive to satisfy their longings, but far from an assurance of attainment of their desires, they may end up in pain, vexation, and restlessness (2:22-13). "This," says Qohelet, "is also *hebel*" (2:23). Again, one cannot separate his *hebel*-judgments from his emphasis on the transience of life, the insufficiency of toil, and the evanescent nature of wealth. The *hebel* nature of all these things is inevitably associated with the conclusion that the situation as a whole is *hebel.* It is wholly unpredictable and beyond human grasp. For Qohelet, the only control rests in the power of God (2:24), who alone gives the possibility of pleasure, ephemeral though that pleasure may be.

Douglas Miller is no doubt correct that Qohelet is using *hebel* as a symbol throughout the book to convey, among other things, the notions of transience and insubstantiality.[44] I am not persuaded, however, by his argument that the symbol also evokes the idea of "foulness." In fact, all the passages to which Miller has assigned this connotation of *hebel* (2:21; 4:8; 6:2; 9:2 [emended]) depict situations that Fox has more aptly characterized as absurd. In these and, indeed, all other instances where *hebel* is applied to situations, Qohelet's conclusion is inextricably tied with things that cannot be apprehended: success, wisdom, wealth, justice, pleasure, or life itself. Just as these things are beyond human grasp, so are the situations beyond grasp.

So this is what Qohelet means by "all is *hebel*" (1:2, 14; 2:11, 17; 3:19; 11:8; 12:8): all is imprehensible, in every sense beyond mortal grasp. As other scholars have pointed out, however, the word "all" does not refer to all reality,[45] for God and the "fear of God" are certainly not regarded as *hebel*. Rather, "all" refers to all that mortals encounter and seek to grasp in any sense of the term. Thus, the book's opening assertion that "all is *hebel*" (1:2) is immediately explicated through a depiction of a world full of activities, the outcome of which is wearying sameness, with mortals left incapable of grasping all that happens (1:3-11). The abundance of activities—vividly conveyed in the Hebrew through the recurrence of active participles—is illusory, for the final result is entirely negative; the negative participles "no," "not," "none" appear six times in the prose commentary to the poem (1:8-11).

Life Before God

Throughout Ecclesiastes, then, one finds a picture of a world that is in every sense imprehensible. Nothing that human beings accomplish or possess is ultimately reliable, for everything is *hebel*. Any formula for success can only be contingent on countless other factors. Any advice can only be relatively good—better than other alternatives (so the many "better-than" proverbs suggest)—for "there is nothing better for humanity than to eat, drink, and enjoy." Indeed, for all the impression of order in the cosmos, everything is imprehensible. So the tantalizingly rhythmic Catalog of Occasions (3:1-8) leads to the utterly surprising conclusion that mortals are not able to grasp (*mṣ*ˀ) what God has done "from beginning to end." The impression of structure in the poem—intending, perhaps, to mirror the impression of orderliness of the cosmos—is ultimately as imprehensible as vapor. Structure in the cosmos is as elusive as structure in the poem, and neither is graspable. The occasions that humans encounter in life simply come about as and when God determines, and they can only react. The deity's role is utterly perplexing, perhaps even oppressive. God has given humans a "preoccupation" (*ˁinyān*) to "preoccupy them" (*laˁănôt bô*), yet no answer that satisfies their longings to grasp everything (3:10; cf. 1:13). The deity who makes everything appropriate "in its time" (*bĕˁittô*) is, paradoxically, the same who puts "eternity" (*ˁôlām*) in human hearts (3:11). Qohelet thus conveys the absurdity of humanity's plight: people are caught in an ironic situation of having eternity in their heart but they can encounter everything only moment by moment.

God's activity is *lĕʿôlām* "eternal" (3:14) and yet God makes everything appropriate only in time. The transcendence of time that characterizes divine activity and is put in human hearts only accentuates the limitation of human encounter of reality.

Qohelet reiterates a perspective maintained elsewhere in the book, namely, that God is wholly transcendent and free to act, while mortals are limited by their ability to respond only as each situation arises: "God is in heaven but you are on earth" (5:1). In a world where everything is *hebel*, there is nothing good that one can grasp. Even so, one may enjoy whatever good there is at the moment as a gift of the divine Sovereign (3:11-13). Enjoyment is, thus, not an end to be sought. Joy is not something to be pursued. Indeed, nowhere does Qohelet call on people to seek pleasure. Rather, enjoyment is presented as a divine gift (2:26; 3:12-13, 22; 5:19; cf. 9:7). It is a "portion" freely granted by God (3:22; 5:18-19), and that grant implies an accountability for its responsible exploitation: "Follow the ways of your heart and what your eyes see, and know that on account of all these, God will bring you into judgment" (11:9). To Qohelet, then, enjoyment is not a hedonistic ideal but a *responsibility*. It is also viewed as an appropriate *response* to the problem of the imprehensibility of everything (8:15; 11:8). The rightness of this response is, indeed, theologically grounded. The author, who reiterates that "everything is *hebel*" affirms also that God has made "everything appropriate (*yāpeh*) in its time" (3:11). What is *hebel* may, by the free will and sovereign power of God, be appropriate (*yāpeh*), if only ephemerally so. Hence, Qohelet maintains that enjoyment is entirely appropriate (*yāpeh*, 5:17) because God has granted humanity its portion and authorized them to use that privilege (5:17-18). The author never denies that toil is part and parcel of this grant and that human life inevitably comes with uncertainties and miseries. Still, he believes that people may be able to cope with life—with all its miseries and pain—because "God gives a preoccupation through the enjoyment of their heart" (5:20). The word *maʿăneh* ("gives a preoccupation") is a homonym and homograph for the word for "answer" or "response" (*maʿăneh*) found elsewhere in wisdom literature (Prov 15:1, 23; 16:1; 29:19; Job 32:3, 5). It may also be taken to mean "gives a response," that response being *both* God's answer and humanity's possibility.[46] Ironically, the God who gives human beings a vexing preoccupation (*ᶜinyān*) to preoccupy (*laᶜ ănôt*) them (1:13; 3:10) is the God who provides them with an appropriate response and responsibility, namely, the positive preoccupation of joy in their *heart* (5:19)—the same place where God has placed *ᶜôlām* (3:11). The God of eternity is the God of the present; God the problem is God the answer. The deity who vexes is the very One who responds to humanity's plight with an answer: the possibility of enjoyment however fleeting.[47]

This response and responsibility to enjoy the moment is the theological solution to the problem of discontentment that is at issue in this passage (5:7-6:9), which is structured to revolve around the pivotal theological claim of 5:19.[48] Discontentment is caricatured in terms of one whose toil is for his mouth and whose gullet (*nepeš*) is never satisfied (6:7). That is a theologically loaded imagery, for in Canaanite mythology, Death is an insatiable monster whose mouth is wide open and whose gullet (*npš*) is never sated, threatening to swallow up Baal, the god of life.[49] That same imagery is used elsewhere in the Bible to depict the threat of Death (Isa. 5:14; Prov. 27:20; 30:16) and the danger to cosmic order posed by the insatiable consumption of oppressors (Ps. 73:9; Hab. 2:5). By recourse to such language, then, Qohelet effectively equates discontentment with the threat of cosmic chaos. Human discontentment is that pernicious: it is life threatening. And the counterpoint to that threat is in the pivotal theological claim that God has freely given humanity the possibility of enjoyment of the moment. The God who put eternity in the human heart has also put in that same heart the response and responsibility of enjoyment. This is Qohelet's theological ethic in the face of life's imprehensibility.

Qohelet's reflections on enjoyment, then, are not merely the atheological musings of a philosopher. On the contrary, they are profoundly theological. Indeed, his views in this regard constitute not so much a theology of enjoyment as a theology of life before God. Apart from the verb *śmh* ("enjoy") and the related noun *śimhâ,* enjoyment is depicted as living life with full awareness of its imprehensible nature: eating, drinking, donning bright garments, anointing one's head with oil, and being with one's beloved. Synonymous expressions for enjoyment are suggestive; the expressions "see good" (2:24), "do well" (3:12), "be in good" (7:12), and "see life" (9:9) all mean "enjoy." The point is not that one should see only what is good and ignore what is bad. Rather, Qohelet counsels enjoyment of good whenever there is opportunity to do so and acceptance of adversity when it is inevitable: "When times are good, be in good; when times are bad, observe. Yes, God has made the one just like the other so that people cannot grasp anything after them" (7:14). Qohelet's perspective is, thus, not so much fatalistic as it is realistic. He is thoroughly realistic about human limitations in the face of a world subject to *hebel* (cf. Rom 8:20). People must be content with what they have and leave the rest to the inscrutable deity.

The advice here extends beyond the matter of enjoyment of good. Just as mortals have no control over what happens in the world (7:13-14), so they have no control over life and death (7:15). The kind of righteousness and wisdom necessary to allow one to avert death is simply not within mortal grasp (7:16-29). People cannot expect to have only the good, namely, righteousness-wisdom, and escape the hold of the bad (wickedness-folly), "for there is no one on earth so righteous, who does only good and does not err" (7:20). So Qohelet urges recognition of human limitation and the inevitability of the hold that wickedness-folly has on mortals, since "the one who fears God goes forth with both of them" (7:18). Indeed, to Qohelet, this recognition of the inevitability of wickedness is the very opposite of the hubris that believes in the possibility of being so righteous that one can avert death (7:15). Such is the reality of a world where righteousness and wisdom are ultimately beyond grasp, and Qohelet dares to state the case theologically, in terms of the all-important "fear of God." That view of human inability to grasp righteousness and wisdom would later be developed more fully by the Apostle Paul. The apostle observes in the Epistle to the Romans that there are people who have no "fear of God" in them (Rom 3:18), meaning that they believe in themselves and their own ability to grasp what they will, but Paul concurs with the judgment of Qohelet that "there is no one righteous, not even one" (Rom 3:10), "for all have erred and come short of the glory of God" (Rom 3:23). Paul takes the argument of Qohelet to a Christological conclusion—the answer coming through the righteousness of God in Christ—but the seeds of the Gospel have already been sown in "the Preacher's" proclamation of humanity's place amid imprehensibility but before the sovereign and mysterious God.

Qohelet's purpose is admittedly not to present a systematic theological treatise. His reflections concern the practical realities of life and how one may cope with them in an imprehensible world. The sage teaches with constant attention to the mundane socioeconomic realities, but his reflections are finally theological. The intermeshing of context and theology is evident in the passage on enjoyment as the God-given answer to the problem of human discontentment (5:7-6:9), the theological denouement of the first half of the book. It is equally apparent in 11:1-6, which is arguably the theological highpoint of the second half. This passage has been commonly understood to proffer sound economic strategy, an interpretation evident in the translation of the first verse in the New English Bible: "Send your grain across the seas, and in time you will get a return. Divide your merchandise among seven ventures, or eight maybe, since you do not know what disasters may occur on earth." In this view, Qohelet urges the advantages of overseas investment and the diversifying of one's financial portfolio. Yet, such an attempt to ensure desired results would contradict what the book teaches, not least about the imprehensibility of everything. Although it is true that Qohelet probably has in mind the instability of the economic conditions in his generation, his point is not about better planning but about spontaneity in the face of uncertainty. The imagery of releasing "bread upon the waters" is an imagery of liberality, as is suggested by a parallel proverb in an Egyptian wisdom text: "Do a good deed and throw it in the water; when it dries you will find it."[50] As explicated, too, by an Arabic story, the point of the proverb is not foresight, as most contemporary interpreters would have it, but freedom: a boy's spontaneous act of literally casting bread upon the waters of a river results in the salvation downstream of a caliph's son stranded and starving. When asked later by the grateful caliph about his seemingly reckless act upstream, the youngster quoted a proverb that he had learned long ago: "Do good, cast your bread upon the waters; one day you will be rewarded."[51] The theological import of the proverb is conveyed in the Turkish version of the saying: "Do good, cast bread upon the waters; if the fish does not know it, God will."[52] Qohelet affirms that the risk of spontaneity may yield surprising results: "after many days, you may find it." Contrary to the laws of nature, it seems, bread that is released upon the waters may not sink and, even if it floats downstream, may be miraculously retrieved. Thus Qohelet urges liberality despite uncertainties about the future: "Give to seven, or maybe even to eight, even though you do not know what misfortune may come upon the land" (11:2). The point is that the workings of the world are not subject to human control. As in the socioeconomic realm, so in nature one learns about the functioning of the cosmos quite apart from human manipulation: when the clouds are full, it will rain; when a tree falls in one direction or another, there it will be (11:3). These things happen regardless of human determination. Hence, mortals can only live without any pretense of control. Indeed, those who long for perfection and certainty will not be able to function: "One who watches the wind will never sow; one who watches the clouds will never reap" (11:4). Farmers who continually postpone what needs to be done for fear of inclement weather will be incapacitated by their unwillingness to risk; those who look for perfect conditions before they act will never do anything. As Qohelet has intimated elsewhere, the times and seasons are ultimately unpredictable, despite delusive signs to the contrary, for God alone determines them, and any attempt to find certainty is but a "pursuit of wind," a grasping of that which is imprehensible.

As in the first half of the book, where Qohelet uses the metaphor of *hebel* to convey the imprehensibility of things and situations that human beings encounter, he moves readily from reflection on the things that one cannot hold on to materially (bread floating downstream) to what one cannot grasp abstractly. Accordingly, he argues that just as mortals cannot understand how the life-breath enlivens a fetus in a pregnant woman, one cannot know how God acts (11:5). The linkage of this theological point to the preceding materials is indicated by the wordplay in Hebrew: the word for life-giving spirit (*rûaḥ*) in v. 5 and wind (*rûaḥ*) in v. 4 is one and the same, and the word for the pregnant woman (*hammĕlēʾâ*, literally, "the full one") in v. 5 echoes the cloud that becomes full (*yimmālĕʾû*) in v. 3. Qohelet thus moves from the volatility of the socioeconomic context to the unpredictable nature of the weather, to the mystery of a new life by the life-giving spirit and, finally, to the inscrutable work of God in the world, all of which is beyond mortal grasp. Here, as elsewhere in the book, Qohelet's reflection on the plight of humanity in an imprehensible world may, when viewed in isolation from his larger theological argument, be cause for despair. Qohelet persistently points one, however, beyond the imprehensible world to the inscrutability of the sovereign God. Indeed, the theological conclusion on the unpredictable and mysterious activity of God that is analogous to the working of the unpredictable workings of the *rûaḥ* as wind and life-breath provides an impetus for conversations about the mysterious activity of the divine Spirit. And such a conversation about the surprising activity of God in the face of human imprehension has already begun through the words of Jesus that echo the teachings of Qohelet in 11:1-6: "The wind blows where it wills and you hear the sound of it, but you do not know where it comes from or where it goes. So is everyone who is born of the Spirit" (John 3:8).

Conclusion

The ancient rabbis who were concerned about the contradictions in Ecclesiastes eventually affirmed its place in the community of faith because they perceived the book to have been framed by the words of the Torah (*b. Šabb.* 30b). Whether or not the book literally begins and ends with words of the Torah is perhaps less important than the recognition that the book is, for all its tensions and idiosyncrasies, consonant with constitutive elements of Israelite faith. The rabbis took their cues from the book itself, especially the summons at the end to "fear God and keep the commandments" (12:13). The epilogue thus provides one with a final reminder of a motif that may be overlooked for all the attention to the contradictions and vexations that are part and parcel of life under the sun: the fear of God (3:14; 5:6; 8:12-13). The unrelenting emphasis on the imprehensibility of everything may lead one to despair, except when one ponders also the equally persistent insistence of the author that everything is in the hand of a sovereign and mysterious God. And this is the same God of the Torah and, one might indeed add, the same God of all of Scripture. The *deus absconditus* of the book is none other than the *deus revelatus*. The epilogist makes explicit, too, what has been only implicit in the book, namely, that there is a theological-ethical implication in all the talk of imprehensibility: one is to live life before this God who is both *deus absconditus* and *deus revelatus.*

Ancient and medieval interpreters have rightly regarded the author of Ecclesiastes as a "preacher" despite his emphasis on the "vanity" of everything. Christian exegetes, beginning with Gregory Thaumaturgos in the third century C.E., following the lead of the Greek translators who rendered the author's name as *ekklēsiastēs,* took the name to mean that the author was addressing the *ekklēsia*.[53] This was the view held by Jerome and Luther, who viewed Qohelet a "preacher" in some sense (KJV). It has become rather common in recent times, however, to dismiss that interpretation partly on etymological grounds and partly on the assumption that the author is a skeptic. Still, whatever the etymology of the author's pen name, the early interpreters were correct in associating Ecclesiastes with the ecclesia, for the author's message was directed at "the people" (12:9), namely, the people of whom he was a part (that's what Greek *ekklēsiastēs* means). Moreover, his teachings are not presented as timeless philosophical propositions but as the deliberate proddings of a *rōᶜeh* ("shepherd, pastor") based on traditional teachings (12:11). As the epilogue of the book affirms, too, Qohelet did not only draw on the traditions but he tried to find felicitous words and wrote the words of truth rightly (12:10). Like any good preacher, he relied not only on traditions but he observed and reflected upon the contemporary world in which his people lived. They were preoccupied with all sorts of social and economic issues and he readily drew on those concerns and employed idioms that were familiar to his audience in order to subvert their preoccupation. Although they were confronting new economic possibilities and perils, the real issues that they faced were, in fact, nothing new. Others had already wrestled with the realities of life's inconsistencies, contradictions, and absurdities—as is evident in other wisdom traditions. Mortals in every generation and every place had always been and always will be caught in a world that is beyond human control. And amid such an imprehensible world, "the Preacher" proclaims the absolute sovereignty of God, who freely gives and acts. Life for mortals in such a world is necessarily just so for everything is imprehensible, beyond mortal grasp, and all that one possesses must be received only as a gift granted by the sheer grace of the mysterious Sovereign, who is also Spirit.

Endnotes

1. PL XXIII.1172.

2. Gerhard von Rad, *Old Testament Theology*, vol. 2 trans. D. M. G. Stalker (New York: Harper & Row, 1962-65), 458.

3. See F. Delitzsch, "Auslegung des Buches Koheleth," *Bibel und Kirche* (1875): 190.

4. R. K. Johnston, "Confessions of a Workaholic: A Reappraisal of Qoheleth," *Catholic Biblical Quarterly* 38 (1976): 14-28.

5. R. N. Whybray, "Qoheleth, Preacher of Joy," *Journal for the Study of the Old Testament* 23 (1982): 87-98.

6. For psychological explanations of Qohelet's idiosyncrasies, see K. Galling, "Kohelet-Studien," *Zeitschrift für die Alttestamentliche Wissenschatt* 50 (1932): 281; Frank Zimmermann, *The Inner World of Qohelet* (New York: Ktav Publishing House, 1973).

7. William H. U. Anderson, *Qoheleth and Its Pessimistic Theology: Hermeneutical Struggles in Wisdom Literature* (Lewiston: Mellen Biblical Press, 1997), 73.

8. Michael V. Fox, *A Time to Tear Down and A Time to Build Up: A Rereading of Ecclesiastes* (Grand Rapids: W.B. Eerdmans, 1999), 3. See also his *Qohelet and His Contradictions* (Sheffield: Almond Press, 1987; repr. 1989), passim.

9. Michael V. Fox, *Qohelet and His Contradictions*, 143.

10. So Elias J. Bickerman, "Koheleth (Ecclesiastes) or the Philosophy of an Acquisitive Society," in *Four Strange Books of the Bible: Jonah, Daniel, Koheleth, Esther* (New York: Schocken Books, 1967; repr. 1984), 139-67; F. Crüsemann, "The Unchangeable World: The 'Crisis of Wisdom' in Koheleth," in *The God of the Lowly: Sociohistorical Interpretations of the Bible* , ed. Willy Schotroff and Wolfgang Stegemann, trans. Matthew J. O'Connell (Maryknoll: Orbis, 1984 [German original, 1979]), 57-77; C. R. Harrison, *Qoheleth in Socio-Historical Perspective* (Unpublished Dissertation, Duke University, 1991), *idem*, "Qoheleth Among the Sociologists," *Biblical Interpretation* 5 (1997): 160-80; Choon-Leong Seow, "The Socioeconomic Context of 'The Preacher's' Hermeneutic," *The Princeton Seminary Bulletin* 17 (1996): 168-95.

11. "The Book of Ecclesiastes," in *New Interpreter's Bible* vol. 5 (Nashville: Abingdon Press, 1994-), v.283.

12. *Proverbs, Ecclesiastes*, vol. 18, *The Anchor Bible* intro. and trans. Robert B. Y. Scott (Garden City, New York: Doubleday, 1965), 196.

13. Still, R. N. Whybray would portray the author as "a theologian for his time." See his "Qoheleth as a Theologian," in *Qohelet in the Context of Wisdom*, *Bibliotheca Ephemeridum Theologicarum Lovaniensium* 136, ed. A. Schoors (Leuven: Leuven University Press, 1998) 239-65.

14. Apart from the grammatical particles, the most common words in the book are, in order, "all," "good," "humanity," "see," "be/happen," "do/act," "mind/heart," "time," "God," and "vanity."

15. 1:14, 16; 2:1, 3, 12, 13, 24; 3:10, 16, 22; 4:1, 4, 7, 15; 5:12, 17; 6:1; 7:15; 8:9, 10, 16, 17; 9:11, 13; 10:5, 7.

16. As Fox has observed, the verb *hyh* very often refers to what is happening rather than to "the static fact of existence" (*A Time to Build*, 107). This is particularly true in the expression *mh šhyh* "whatever has happened" (1:9; 3:15; 6:10; 7:24).

17. M.J. Dahood, "Canaanite-Phoenician Influence in Qohelet," *Biblica* 33 (1952): 220-21.

18. On these and other ancient Near Eastern parallels, see Choon-Leong Seow, *Ecclesiastes: A New Translation with Introduction and Commentary*, vol. 18 *The Anchor Bible* (New York: Doubleday, 1997), 60-65.

19. *Contra* Mark Sneed "The Social Location of the Book of Qoheleth," *Hebrew Studies* 39 (1998): 41-51. Sneed is entirely skeptical about locating Qohelet's work in a sociohistorical context, concluding without argumentation that the author was a "filthy rich" intellectual and that "intellectual are known for becoming cynical dissidents who sometimes even 'bite the hand that feeds them.'"

20. I hope to return to this issue in another forum. For now, see my "Linguistic Evidence and the Dating of Ecclesiastes," *Journal of Biblical Literature* 115 (1996): 657-60 and *Ecclesiastes,* passim.

21. See F. Bianchi, "The Language of Qohelet: A Bibliographical Survey," *Zeitschrift für die Alttestamentliche Wissenschatt* 105 (1993): 210-23.

22. Choon-Leong Seow, "Linguistic Evidence," 643-666.

23. See H. Z. Szubin and B. Porten, "Royal Grants in Egypt: A New Interpretation of Driver 2," *Journal of Near Eastern Studies* 46 (1987): 39-48.

24. Contrary to the interpretation of some commentators and reflected in a number of English translations, the "shepherd" refers, strictly speaking, to the sage rather than to God.

25. See George G. Cameron, *Persepolis Treasury Tablets*, vol. 65, *Oriental Institute Publications* (Chicago: University of Chicago Press, 1948), 1-4.

26. Cameron, *Persepolis Treasury Tablets*, 137 (Tablet 32).

27. Persian-period hoards have been found at Tell Abu Hawam, Abu-Shusheh, Tell el-Fukhar (Akko), Askelon, Atlit, Wadi ed-Daliyeh, Moshav Dalton, Gaza, Khirbet el Kerak, Safed, Samaria-Sebaste, and Nablus (Shechem).

28. For a recent assessment of the socioeconomic situation of Persian-period Yehud, see Charles E. Carter, *The Emergence of Yehud in the Persian Period: A Social and Demographic Study*, vol. 294, *Journal for the Study of the Old Testament, Supplement Series* (Sheffield: Sheffield Academic Press, 1999).

29. See Seow, "Socioeconomic Context," 174-76.

30. See Muhammad A. Dandamaev, *Slavery in Babylonia: from Nabopolassar to Alexander the Great (626 - 331 B.C.)* trans. Victoria A. Powell (DeKalb: Northern Illinois University Press, 1984), 327-30.

31. "Kohelet und die Banken: zur Übersetzung von Kohelet V 12-16," *Vetus Testamentum* 39 (1989): 488-95.

32. So Roland E. Murphy, *Ecclesiastes* , vol. 23A *World Biblical Commentary* (Dallas: Word Books, 1992), 101. Murphy cites Prov. 19:10 and 30:21-23, but those passages lack the specificity and intensity of the passage in Ecclesiastes. More to the point are parallels from Egyptian wisdom literature that probably reflect societal turmoil. See "The Complaint of Khakheperre-Sonb," "The Admonitions of Ipuwer," and "The Prophecies of Nerferti" in Miriam Lichtheim, *Ancient Egyptian Literature*, vol. 1 (Berkeley: University of California Press, 1971-80), 135-62.

33. See Seow, "Socioeconomic Context," 187.

34. *KAI* 14.17-19.

35. Guillaume Cardascia, *Les archives des Murašû, une famille d'hommes d'affaires babyloniens à l'époque perse (455-403 av. J.-C.)* (Paris: Imprimerie Nationale, 1951), 165-66.

36. *UET* IV, 109.

37. Thus, for example, Daniel C. Fredericks, *Coping with Transience: Ecclesiastes on the Brevity in Life* (Sheffield: Journal for the Study of the Old Testament Press, 1993), 11-32.

38. One may perhaps compare the usage here to a midrashic passage where fetus is called *hebel*, meaning something that is still insubstantial (*Lev. Rabb.* 29.8).

39. For this reading of the verse, see Seow, *Ecclesiastes*, 126.

40. See K. Seybold, "*hebhel*," *Theological Dictionary of the Old Testament*, vol. 3 313-20; Oswald Loretz, *Qohelet und der alte Orient: Untersuchungen zu Stil und theologischer Thematik des Buches Qohelet* (Freiburg: Herder, 1964), 218-25.

41. See Bruno Pennacchini, "Qohelet ovvero il libro degli assurdi," *Euntes Docete* 30 (1977): 491-510.

42. Michael V. Fox, "The Meaning of *Hebel* for Qohelet," *Journal of Biblical Literature* 105 (1986): 409-27.

43. Gilg. Y. iv.5-8. Translation mine.

44. "Qohelet's Symbolic Use of הבל," *Journal of Biblical Literature* 117 (1998): 437-54.

45. For instance, Norbert Lohfink, "Koh 1,2 'Alles ist Windhauch'—universale oder anthropologische Aussage?" in *Der Weg zum Menschen (Fs. A. Deissler)*, ed. R. Mosis and L. Ruppert (Freiberg: Herder, 1989), 201-16.

46. The root *ᶜnh* is multivalent and the word *maᶜăneh* has, in fact, been interpreted variously to suggest preoccupation (most ancient versions), answer (Ibn Ezra), song (Rashbam). One may also consider the meaning "to humble, make wretched."

47. N. Lohfink ("Qoheleth 5:17-19—Revelation by Joy," *Catholic Biblical Quarterly* 52 [1990] 625-35) contends that we come close to a sense of revelation at this, the theological highpoint of the book. In this view, then, God is known not just in history nor in nature, but in the encounter of joy in the present.

48. On the chiastic structure of 5:7-6:9 and the pivotal place of 5:19, see Seow, *Ecclesiastes*, 215-18.

49. *KTU* I.5.2.2-4; 1.23.61-62.

50. Lichtheim, *Ancient Egyptian Literature*, vol.3, 174.

51. See Heinrich F. von Diez, *Denkwürdigkeiten von Asien* (Berlin: Nicolaischen Buchhandlung, 1811), 106-116.

52. Quoted in von Diez, *Denkwürdigkeiten*, 115.

53. See John Jarick, *Gregory Thaumaturgos' Paraphrase of Ecclesiastes*, vol. 29, *Septuagint and Cognate Studies* (Atlanta: Scholars Press, 1990), 18-19, 300-301.

Protestant Christianity and the Conundrum of Islam

Jane I. Smith
HARTFORD SEMINARY
HARTFORD, CONNECTICUT

Christians and Muslims have been squaring off against each other theologically as well as militarily since the emergence of Islam in the seventh century C.E. Western Christendom found Islam threatening not only because of its rapid territorial expansion, but because it preached a message ostensibly similar to Christianity in its avowal of one God, yet denied the essential Christian doctrines of the incarnation, the Trinity, and the crucifixion of Jesus. While on the theological level Christians tried to relegate Islam to the status of Christian heresy, Christians in the Middle East, North Africa, and Spain were struggling under varying conditions to accept their new status as Dhimmi or protected communities in the Islamic empire. Interfaith relations "on the ground" were often harmonious and Christians served in respected positions in caliphal courts, while theologians, in alarmed recognition that Islam was not going to disappear, resorted to increasingly vituperative descriptions of the religion and especially of its founder Muhammad.

The details of this kind of interaction, sharpened by the tragic encounters of the Crusades, form the background and legacy for Christian reflection on Islam in the nineteenth and twentieth centuries. This project focuses on Protestant theology in relation to Islam as it has developed over the past several hundred years in a number of different contexts. The literature from which the findings of this study have been gleaned includes missiological texts, the growing body of Christian theological reflection on pluralism and (in some cases) specifically on the relationship of Christianity and Islam, and the occasional theological speculations and proposals of scholars whose primary vocation is the academic presentation of various aspects of the religion of Islam. The task of this project has been to order this material, to consider the reasons for its presentation and the contexts in which different interpretations have been proposed, and to highlight some of the dominant themes that have emerged in the last several decades.

One other broad category of writings that were part of the subject material of this study is the fairly recent body of literature prepared by Protestant denominations on new relationships with Muslims and ways in which to present Islam to member churches. While the effort is to be applauded, and the fact that more denominations are sensing the urgency of acknowledging the presence of Islam as a growing religious element in the West, the fact is that on the whole there is little that is innovative or even substantially very helpful about most of this material. Much of what is written specifically for churches is quite uninspired, suggesting "niceness" as an antidote to centuries of ill will but not giving much significant content as to how Christians might actually think theologically about Islam. An analysis of syllabi used by persons teaching courses in ATS theological schools on Christianity and Islam, religious pluralism, and trends of contemporary theology revealed that there is a clear need for more creative theological reflection on how people preparing for Christian ministry can help their congregations think about other religions in general and Islam in particular.[1]

Protestant Missionary Responses to Islam

The modern missionary movement, which began two centuries ago, has engendered a number of different kinds of theological responses to Islam. Theologians of the nineteenth century for the most part believed the adherents of non-Christian religions in general, and Islam in particular, to be outside the possibility of salvation,[2] although there were a few significant exceptions.[3] In many cases they found it difficult to move past the ancient repertoire of accusations against the Prophet Muhammad of charlatan, knave, and agent of the devil. The twentieth century has seen a number of world mission conferences in the context of which Christian relations with Islam, and theological response to that faith, have been discussed. Early twentieth-century missiological writing stressed such themes as the questionable morality of the Prophet Muhammad, the overly aggressive characteristics of the faith, and the inevitability of the decline of Islam.[4] Over the succeeding decades missionaries came to study Islam much more deeply, both to be able better to understand the nature of the problem and to avoid offending those with whom they were sent to work. Still the theological conundrum which has faced Christians from the earliest days of Islam—how to reconcile it theologically with Christian proclamation—remained.

By the mid-twentieth century many Christians began to challenge the right of the church to exercise its missionary mandate in the traditional way.[5] This was accompanied by the serious beginnings of a number of attempts to find some kind of reconciliation between Islam and Christianity, either through the emphasis on a common monotheism or in finding similar ethical imperatives. The period of the mid-1960s was characterized by increased openness to Islam as a true faith whose adherents are genuine seekers after God and, for many, by the impetus toward dialogue as an essential means of communication. The formation of the World Council of Churches (WCC) in 1948 signaled the beginning of what has become a continuing debate about the relationship between mission and dialogue. Evangelicals were and continue to be concerned about movements that seem to them to downplay the uniqueness of Christ in the attempt to reach out to people of other faiths. Throughout the succeeding decades of this century, the WCC has continued to pursue the agenda of dialogue with Islam as with other world faiths, encouraged also by the new mood of openness engendered by Vatican II. Many Christian theologians have continued to justify dialogue as a necessary part of the mission enterprise.[6]

In the last several decades the quantity of mission literature in relation to Islam has grown significantly, not unrelated to the rise of Islam as an increasingly important world force. Many missiologists again have struggled to reconsider their approach to Islam. Much of the more conservative response has been characterized by the frequently articulated question of why the "harvest" of Muslim converts has been so small. Urging a redoubling of effort, some have suggested that evangelization of Muslims is the special challenge for the end of the twentieth century.[7] Conservative organizations such as the U.S. Center for World Mission and the Samuel Zwemer Institute keep the church aware of the ongoing challenge of Islam for Christians.[8] Since the 1970s, the theme of "contextualization" has been the focus of much Protestant writing about mission to Islam. The goal is no less than conversion of Muslims to Christianity, but the tactics are based on the understanding that the church needs to become indigenous so that a convert to Islam, while changing faith, need not give up his or her culture.[9]

A somewhat different genre of Protestant missiological literature, distinct from that which discusses tactics and techniques, attempts to help Christians think theologically about Islam. Much of this is written by persons who have themselves been missionaries to Muslim countries and have returned to the West to become professors in theological schools. They make a particularly important contribution to the theological conversation about Christianity in relation to Islam precisely because they have spent time in Muslim countries, generally have befriended many Muslims, and speak with a kind of immediacy of personal knowledge that often is not the case for Western scholars and theologians.

Methodological and Categorical Considerations

One of the issues for consideration in examining the themes that contemporary thinkers are emphasizing in looking theologically at Christianity and Islam, then, is how to balance the reflections of these respective contributors to the conversation. Those who know the most about Islam in its more formal sense (scripture, texts, doctrines, laws, theological developments) are often scholars who may or may not have actually lived among Muslims. For the most part they are persuaded by the necessity of *epoche* or bracketing of personal judgments, and therefore are unlikely to offer the kind of theological reflection on Islam for which this project calls (although insistence on such reserve is being seriously challenged). In fact, some prominent scholars of Islam have indeed offered important assessments of how taking Islam seriously should mean significant rethinking about the claims of Christianity (although for the most part these are the reflections of thinkers who are nearing the end of their academic careers). Persons who know the most about Islam in its more informal sense (how Muslims live on a daily basis, their actual beliefs and practices (despite whether these conflict with "orthodox" pronouncements), what living Islam means to the ordinary Muslim) are usually either: (a) anthropologists or ethnologists who, also functioning as scholars, generally refrain from personal or theological reflection on Islam, or (b) missionaries or persons who have worked (or are working) in a service capacity in a primarily Muslim country, and whose theological response to Islam is naturally colored by the religious impetus that took them there in the first place.

Other concerns arise in thinking about the different kinds of experiences of those who engage this issue, as well as the different motivations for their reflections. Some of the thinkers under consideration for this project, for example, have written very little on the subject, while others have spent much of their lifetime in its pursuit. Among the latter are, most obviously, Bishop Kenneth Cragg whose works on Islam and Christianity are voluminous, and Wilfred Cantwell Smith, whose major area of study as historian of religion has been Islam and who is one of those scholars whose writings do reflect a clear theological interest. Should persons who have struggled deeply with these theological concerns be given priority of place in this study over those whose references are much more brief? And should those whose reflections are based at least to some degree on personal interaction with Muslims have priority over those for whom this is not the case? One might also ask how reasonable, or helpful, it is to extrapolate what is specifically applicable to the case of Islam from the more general comments of theologians considering possible Christian responses to religious plurality. There is increasing recognition across the board of the importance of the context in which new theological reflection takes place. It can be a very different matter for a Christian to think "courageously and boldly" in the freedom of a Western setting, than for a Christian to reflect on Islam in a context in which Christianity is a minority religion and he or she may be subject to discrimination and even persecution, to say nothing of the obvious fact that the potential of persecution will doubtless color one's responses to the other faith, theological or otherwise.

When one examines most of the current writing on theological pluralism, or more specifically on the ways in which Christians might think about other faiths (here specifically Islam), it is difficult to avoid the use of the categories "exclusivist," "inclusivist," and "pluralist." While initially somewhat illuminating, such a tripartite categorization is now generally acknowledged to be restrictive, outdated, based on a rather narrow Christian theological perspective, and often distracting rather than helpful.[10] Unfortunately these categories are so universally acknowledged that even scholars who dislike them find themselves falling to their use. Also, no one has come up with other categories that seem quite so tidy. (The problem actually may be resolved with a better clarification, or formulation, of the questions.) The material of this study strongly suggests that rather than falling into such graded categories, Protestant thinkers who take a theological position *vis-à-vis* Islam fall on one side or another of a significant watershed, no matter how they may try to qualify their conclusions. Either one considers that Christianity is "unique" and is the only truly salvific faith, or one holds that despite Christianity's uniqueness (all religion, one supposes, could make a claim to uniqueness) it ultimately has no greater claim on salvation (or saintliness, etc.) than any other religion. Those in the second camp have the theoretical opportunity to value Islam as highly as their own faith. Among John Hick's assertions, for example, is that all of the three religions of Judaism, Christianity, and Islam are responses to divine revelation, and that "salvific transformation seems to occur to about the same extent within each. . . . [S]o far as we can tell none of them, taken as a totality, has been markedly more . . . or less successful than others in bringing about the redemption of human life in self-giving to God."[11] For those in the first camp, despite all the caveats and apparent compromises, Islam falls [either somewhat or woefully] short of Christianity and in general it is felt that Christians have little to learn from it. (Variations on these alternatives, of course, are many and subtle.) The distinction has often turned on the issue of general vs. special revelation, and posed first in terms of whether the New Testament allows salvation in any other way, and second in terms of whether there is hope specifically for Islam.

Major Themes in Theological Reflection on Islam

Taking into consideration, then, the several genres of writing that relate to the response of Christianity to the reality of Islam, and the problems encountered in determining the nature of their contributions, let me suggest some of the themes that emerge as important to Protestant Christians who are engaging in theological reflection on Islam. They are only suggestive, of course, of the great range of issues that have long been addressed and continue to be worthy of attention, as well as of others that are newly emerging as theological reflection on Islam becomes more imaginative and more sophisticated.

Questions of Method and Approach

For most of the history of Christian thought about Islam, little if any consideration was given to the question of whether the categories Christians automatically used in assessing the faith of Muslims were adequate and appropriate. More recently that has become a very important issue for many thinkers, and the question is being raised about what one does when it is quite clear that categories of comparison are formed by Christian theological presuppositions and really do not fit Islam. While some advocate stopping the comparison at that point, others continue the struggle to "make" them fit. A few of the most bold spirits argue that we should throw out all our preconceived categories altogether, with the proposed aim of working together with Muslims to devise new ones that would be mutually acceptable; others propose slightly less radical changes.[12]

Some of the theologians who have struggled to "make categories fit" have been accused of "Christianizing" Islam. To say that Christianity and Islam can be, and are, mutually enriching may really mean that it is Christianity that can enrich Islam as Muslims are invited to see things more "Christian-ly." Byron Haines at the 1979 conference on Christian witness to Islam in Mombasa, Kenya, said, "We must be careful not to impose our theological data upon other systems lest the integrity of those religions and the people who constitute them be denied or distorted."[13] A good idea, many have noted, but is it really possible? Andreas D'Souza, director of the Henry Martyn Institute in Hyderabad, India, seriously challenges the notion that people with an explicit Christian faith commitment can ever adequately understand and interpret Islam, precisely because wittingly or not they force upon it their own preconceptions.[14]

An occasional voice is being raised calling for a "justice" approach to Islam rather than a "theological" approach. (This may actually mean, rather, understanding the scope of theology to be much broader than doctrine, which some Roman Catholics and a few Protestants are already doing). Protestantism from its inception has been a protest against injustice, they note, initially as that was perceived in the Roman Catholic church. There might be Protestant reasons for consciously preferring to deal with those Muslims who are at the center of protest and are looking for a way to develop an understanding of Islam in cultures of repression. Such advocates are asking why we do not simply choose justice to be the criterion by which we look for conversation partners in Islam *and* by which we develop some measures of assessment to replace the old theological criteria.[15]

The Use of Scripture

One can argue, and many have, that the beginning and ending point of Christian theological reflection on Islam is Scripture: biblical affirmations about the nature of Christ and the possibility of salvation only through him, and the Qur'anic insistence on their denial. Both Islam and Christianity define themselves finally in terms of a revealed text. (Some are persuaded that the textual argument is particular to Protestant thought and is not normative in the same way for Roman Catholics, and even that the emphasis in Protestant Christianity on the importance of the text actually amounts to a "Protestantizing" of Islam.) Throughout history both Muslims and Christians have used their own Scriptures as the starting point for assessing the faith of the other. Conservative Protestants tend to remain in this position, finding whatever flexibility they may feel is appropriate in their approach to Islam and to Muslims—certainly not in a radical reinterpretation of the New Testament message. Others, however, are searching for ways out of this apparent impasse. How can we avoid falling into the trap, they ask, of using our own Scriptures to "prove" the inaccuracy or invalidity of the other? Biblical scholars are putting forth fairly complicated arguments about whether or not Jesus can be understood by Christians to have been a prophet; from there the question is raised whether such an approach by Christians might actually help them better understand both who Muslims believe Muhammad really was, and how Muslims view Jesus.[16]

Another tack taken by biblical scholars is to cull for consideration all the passages that suggest Jesus' openness to those who were considered "other." How was the event of Christ an example of the "other" coming into the Jewish world and can this be a model for our understanding of Islam? Such an approach may be open to question, however, on the grounds that the situation of New Testament interfaith encounter was significantly different from that which pertained at the time and place in which Muhammad received his revelations. Some Christians are urging that we look on the Qur'an as occupying a special status in relation to Christian Scripture. Peter Ford, a United Church of Christ missionary in Sudan, has proposed that as the Reformers recognized that the Apocrypha deserved a special reverence even if not equated with canonical Scripture, this may well provide a model for individual Christians to respond to the Qur'an, i.e. "as a kind of scriptural supplement for spiritual and theological reflection."[17]

Students of comparative religion, of course, have been familiar for decades with Wilfred Cantwell Smith's famous query, "Is the Qur'an the Word of God?" He observes that both answers to the question, yes and no, are based on pre-convictions that prove to be self-fulfilling prophesies. Speaking boldly, as usual, Smith argues that as the text *becomes* the word of God for the Muslim because he believes it to be so, by implication it has the same potential for the Christian, at least in part. His conviction of the essential unity of knowledge, and of humankind—insofar as we share a common world history—leads him to conclude that finally the answer to the question must be equally satisfying to both Christian and Muslim.[18] Smith's position continues to intrigue both his students and his detractors, but thus far few have taken up his argument with similar conviction.

The Nature of God and of Humankind

Can God be known? What is the function of revelation? Does God "participate" in human affairs and what does that say about the nature and being of God? Are humans by nature sinful? Can wrongdoing be redeemed by human endeavor alone? What is the relationship between divine forgiveness and salvation? Because of the Qur'anic denial of some of the basic tenets of the Christian faith such as the incarnation, the Trinity, and the crucifixion, Christians have tended to focus their theological responses on these matters specifically. Many, however, are acknowledging that the real issue is not whether these particular articles of Christian faith are affirmed or denied in Islam, but what their denial has to say about divine and human characteristics and qualities. Therefore the ground of discussion has shifted significantly from the earlier and dominant question—Is there salvation in Islam?—although the issue of the distinction between general (usually affirmed) and special (usually denied) revelation as implicit in that question is still addressed in some literature.

Whether Muslims and Christians believe in the same God is a favorite question. For some the answer is an obvious *yes*[19] (often those trying to ground the conversation on the commonality of the most basic belief for both faiths, and sometimes for the Abrahamic faiths over against all others), or an obvious *no* (often those who see Allah as more vengeful or arbitrary than just or loving, or who feel insisting on such commonality is finally not helpful in furthering dialogue). Others conclude that it is not that we believe in a different God, but that we believe in one God differently.[20] The question then becomes, as Colin Chapman formulates it, "Is there *enough in common* between the Christian's idea of God and the Muslim's idea of God to be able to use the same word?"[21] Or put another way, are the commonalities basic enough to warrant overlooking the differences? And in a very few cases the question is put thus: Are the differences themselves so valuable in enhancing our own understanding of God that they should be the stuff of our consideration rather than the similarities? One interesting way in which some contemporary writers are engaging the issue of divine oneness and Muslim insistence on denial of the Trinity is to look creatively at the Muslim notion of the ninety names of God. Could these be seen, they ask, as alternative expressions of the ways in which the one God makes God's self known to humans?[22] It may not matter, in effect, whether these ways are seen as three, or ninety, or any other number.

Christian Recognition (or lack thereof) of Muhammad as a Prophet

Is Muhammad "enough" of a prophet to have revealed something of God in the Qur'an? David Kerr, among others, notes that the oldest question the Muslim has asked the Christian is, "Do you accept Muhammad as a prophet of God?"[23] Answered resoundingly in the negative over most of the centuries since the rise of Islam, it has never—until fairly recently—been taken with any real seriousness by Christians. Criticism and even ridicule of Islam as a religion have been sharpest and most bigoted when focused on Muhammad, who was considered a liar, a charlatan, sexually licentious, and driven by a lust for violence. Only in the rarest of exceptions was the possibility of his prophethood seriously considered. More recently, however, the question is being raised among theologians and others thinking about Christianity in relation to Islam, including some missiologists.

Some theologians are proposing that perhaps the best way to see Muhammad as a prophet is to equate him with those of the Old Testament. This idea is certainly not new, and it reflects the above-mentioned distinction between the general revelation available to many people, and the specific revelation only through God's saving act in Jesus Christ. It has been suggested in one form or another over the centuries, and it received considerable support in the writings of Samuel Zwemer, Temple Gairdner, and others at the early part of this century. More lately the notion has been interpreted as meaning that Muhammad should be lifted out of historical sequence, so to speak, and seen in a theological sense to be *pre-* rather than *post*-Christian.[24] R. H. Drummond, for example, says that just as we consider the prophets of the Old Testament to be authentic, even though their messages sometimes differed from the New Testament witness, so we should see Muhammad and his message as authentic even if not infallible.[25] Such apparently charitable attempts to include Muhammad in the chain of those considered by Christians to have received messages from God are not, however, viewed by all as really so charitable. Dating Muhammad in such a way, insists Willem Bijlefeld, " . . . is not a halfway affirmation of the Qur'anic proclamation but a rejection of it. . . . These and similar well-intended 'positive' statements about Islam are sharply resented by many Muslims and seldom, if ever, serve as bridge builders."[26]

Other theologians are seemingly more bold in their assessments. "True openness to other traditions will require that we make their history our own," says process theologian John Cobb, whose own interfaith engagement has been more with Buddhism than with Islam. Arguing his "transformationist" theological perspective, he insists that this sharing of history means that, "We Christians will view Mohammed as our prophet as well. . . ."[27] This position is gaining more adherents, both in terms of history and of theology. Many feel that while this is fine to say, its implications are too serious not to be radically examined. Kenneth Cragg, who has struggled as deeply and personally as anyone with the attempt to bring Islam and Christianity into more mutual agreement, asks poignantly, "How is the Christian to contemplate positive acknowledgment of Muhammad when his prophetic significance involves such crucial disavowal of truths Christian? Is God the author of confusion?"[28]

Many Christians, of course, simply acknowledge that they find recognition of Muhammad's prophethood theologically impossible. ". . . [A] Christian can subscribe wholeheartedly to the first part of the Islam creed [There is no God but God]," says Chawkat Moucarry, ". . . but cannot, without denying his own faith, endorse the second part [and Muhammad is the Messenger of God]."[29] Colin Chapman, long-time missionary to Muslim lands and one dedicated to clarifying a sympathetic evangelical approach to Islam says that on the subject of Muhammad he cannot bring himself to say that he was a prophet, even a "post-Christian" one, because his message as a whole does seem to deny elements of the Christian Gospel that are absolutely fundamental.[30] There is little question but that the issues involved for Christians in trying to determine whether to accord to the Prophet of Islam status as a prophet in their own understanding are only beginning to be aired.

What Islam Are We Talking About?

Some scholars are now asking whether it is not time to acknowledge that Islam has taken so many forms, as indeed has Christianity, that traditional modes of theological response to the religion as if it were monolithic are outdated and unhelpful. ". . . [T]he bewildering variety of opinions within each community," notes Hugh Goddard, "has given rise to the suggestion that perhaps we no longer speak of Islam and Christianity, but of Islams and of Christianities," with each faith represented as a spectrum.[31] While few have risen to accept this challenge directly, there certainly is considerable discussion about the differences between "normative" Islam, that of the Qur'an and practiced by the Prophet, and the multitude of ways in which Islam has been lived and believed in. How, then, do we move from seeing a religious tradition only in its essential form to consideration of the personalized religious experiences of each (or any) of its members, some are beginning to ask, and what does that do to our efforts to understand Islam theologically? Perhaps influenced by Wilfred Smith's classic *The Meaning and End of Religion*,[32] some are questioning if either Islam or Christianity is anything more than the accumulation of the individual perceptions and practices of its adherents. What is the Islam, then, about which we want to think theologically?

One of the very important issues currently being engaged relates to whether or not a Christian has any responsibility (or, of course, any right) to challenge Muslims when it appears that they have deviated significantly from what the Qur'an or the Prophet has advocated. If the non-Muslim observer of Islam is able to demonstrate clearly that Islamic practice has diverged from Qur'anic perspective, does that mean that the practice is somehow "un-Islamic" and should be identified as such? And should such perceived deviations play a role in the way one responds theologically to Islam? This is not merely a theoretical discussion, but one grounded in the reality of Muslim practices such as execution for apostasy, or terrorist activities against Christian minorities, that are part of the reality of some Christians living and working in Muslim contexts. Arm-chair theologizing is increasingly identified with those whose daily lives involve encounter with Muslims as the luxury of a predominantly white, Western, and male elite whose determinations should no longer be allowed to dominate the Christian theological scene. This critique is being levied whether the theological conclusions of those who deal with texts and doctrines result in a denial of truth to Islam or an open-armed acceptance.

What Is the Relationship Between Dialogue and Witness (Evangelism)?

Since the formation of the World Council of Churches in 1948, as noted above, a great deal of attention has been given to distinguishing between, or arguing for the essential integrity of, proclamation (evangelism, mission, witness) and dialogue. In 1975 several evangelicals wrote to the general secretary of the WCC warning of the prospect of a division among confessing Christians as deep as that which occurred at the time of the Protestant reformation, i.e., a division between "ecumenical" Christianity and "evangelical" Christianity.[33] While there has been much rhetoric about the importance of dialogue for mission, and of mission as a continuing emphasis of the Christian WCC, there is no question that the distinction in emphasis is significant. Much of the current theological literature, coming out of both the evangelical wing and on the part of those who are committed to the enterprise of dialogue, has focused on the relationship of these two tasks of the church. The issue can be stated thus: "Is witness to one's understanding of 'truth' integral to or essentially an enterprise distinguishable from, or even incompatible with, dialogical encounter?"

Many argue that dialogue is actually a creative form of witness, and that true dialogue cannot take place without each side proclaiming as clearly as possible what it believes to be the truth of its own revelation or experience. "Our responsibility in mission," insisted Byron Haines in 1979, "is not to make converts, but to conduct ourselves in such a way that we allow for the divine possibility of conversion in our lives and in that of others. . . . To a great extent, the concerns articulated under the rubric 'dialogue' represent an attempt to address all these issues in mission, including the hermeneutical task, in a more relevant way."[34] The differing perspectives on dialogue and witness are slowly coming to some resolution in the recognition on the part of many that witnessing to our own faith is essential to the dialogue, and that real interfaith exchange cannot take place without it. But the question is far from fully resolved, and continues to be one of the most important points of discussion in Christian reflection on Islam and encounter with Muslims.

Theological Enrichment through Exposure to Islam

Through reading, correspondence, and personal conversations, I have tried to determine how exposure to Islam, either through texts or through personal contacts with Muslims, has changed, enhanced, and broadened the understanding individual Christians have of Christianity (or of God, themselves, etc.). Many profess that indeed it has, but they do not seem able to articulate quite how, on the one hand, this may reflect a kind of theoretical conviction that such change ought to take place, rather than acknowledgment of whether or not it actually has. On the other hand, many conservative Christians are still repeating old themes, arguing that such change is exactly what must *not* happen and insisting that he or she who is not firm in the faith should be wary of interfaith exposure.[35] Nonetheless, across the theological spectrum, there are some who (in a few instances through specific prodding from me) do indicate that they acknowledge such enrichment to have taken place. Among the many qualities that they find admirable in Islam and in Muslims, and which they somewhat implicitly seem to say could benefit Christian attitudes, are the constant awareness that Muslims have of the majesty of God, the importance of Scripture, the connection between religion and community over against Western individualism (one expressed it in terms of a cultural hermeneutic that is more group-oriented *and* vertical[36]), the rigor of disciplined devotion, the integrity and quality of Muslim lives, a keen sense of the "unfathomable mercy of God,"[37] a sense of divine love as both intimate and distant, and the ways in which Muslim virtues of honor and loyalty can both enrich Christian lives and provide links for common conversation.[38] For the most part, it is clear that these insights provide clues for the enhancement of Christian thinking about God and about community rather than suggesting dramatic changes in basic theological affirmations. It also seems clear that those who do propose some radical reinterpretations of Christian doctrine, with implications for the understanding of Islam, do so in the broader context of philosophical/theological reflection, rather than specifically out of an experience with Islam.

The twentieth century, someone has remarked, has been a kind of "fast-forward" in history, a time in which truly amazing changes have taken place in a great range of areas. While Christian theology is under attack by many for not keeping up, for slipping into irrelevance, I think it must be said that from another perspective it has also made remarkable strides over the course of this century, particularly in relation to the fact of religious plurality. Although the range of current theological responses to other religions in general and to Islam in particular is great, there are few who now would seriously question the urgency of interfaith engagement and theological response. In relation to Islam, a somewhat vacillating but still clear movement on the part of most Protestant Christian thinkers can be seen from condemnation, to ignoring, to timid openness, to new thinking about ways to approach and enter into conversation with our Muslim neighbors. Perhaps the next step in the theological process will be to continue the tentative efforts being made by a few across the spectrum of Protestant theological reflection to think not only *about* Islam, but *with* Muslims about questions of religious truth. Early in this decade, Willem Bijlefeld put the issue clearly when he asked, "Can we, as Muslims and Christians, begin to think in different terms than that of an approach to each other, and rather understand our relationship in terms of a common pilgrimage to God, a pilgrimage not *out* of this world, but, *for God's sake*, into this world?"[39] In this, I think, lies the real challenge for Christian theology.

Endnotes

1. Two major projects described as part of the original intention of this study remain in process. One is a monograph of the history and current state of Protestant theological reflection on Islam. The second is a much smaller booklet intended for use by churches and church-affiliated study groups to suggest the issues at stake and some of the possible approaches that members of congregations may take in thinking about Islam.

2. See, e.g., Cyrus Hamlin, *The Oriental Churches and Mohemmedans* (Boston: American Board of Commissioners for Foreign Missions, 1853), 2.

3. Clinton Bennett provides an interesting discussion of some of the contrasts in nineteenth-century theological reflection on Islam in *Victorian Images of Islam* (London: Grey Seal, 1992).

4. Among many works detailing this theme, see W.H. Temple Gairdner, *The Reproach of Islam* (London: United Council for Missionary Education, 1920) and Samuel Zwemer, *The Cross Above the Crescent: The Validity, Necessity, and Urgency of Missions to Moslems* (Grand Rapids: Zondervan Publishing House, 1941).

5. James Thayer Addison, *The Christian Approach to the Moslem: A Historical Study* (New York: Columbia University Press, 1943).

6. "The spirit of dialogue has great value in preparing the way for the apologetic message and must pervade all forms of encounter in mission." Marston Speight, "Some Bases for a Christian Apologetic to Islam," *International Review of Missions* 54 (1965): 195.

7. See, for example, James F. Engel *et al*, "What's Gone Wrong With Our Harvesting?" *Missiology* vol. 2, no. 3 (July 1974): 349-358.

8. Sharon E. Mumper, "New Strategies to Evangelize Muslims Gain Effectiveness," *Christianity Today* 29 (May 1, 1985): 75.

9. Dudley Woodberry, "Contextualization among Muslims: Reusing Common Pillars," in *The Word Among Us. Contextualizing Theology for Mission Today*, ed. Dean S. Gilliland (Dallas: Word Publishing, 1989), 282-308; Phil Parshall, *New Paths in Muslim Evangelism: Evangelical Approaches to Contextualization* (Grand Rapids: Baker Book House, 1980). Missionaries have been encouraged to "go native" in their dress, to hold worship services in churches bare of any seating, and even to fast in the style of Muslims.

10. Credit is generally given to Alan Race who articulated these categories in *Christians and Religious Pluralism: Patterns in the Christian Theology of Religions* (Maryknoll: Orbis Books, 1982).

11. John Hick, "Trinity and Incarnation in the Light of Religious Pluralism," in *Three Faiths—One God: A Jewish, Christian, Muslim Encounter*, eds. John Hick and Edmund S. Meltzer (London: Macmillan, 1989), 197.

12. Says British theologian Christopher Lamb: "It is not a matter of moving beyond the old questions, but of coming at them in new ways prompted by the new social political context in which we are working in the West on the one hand, and on the other the post-colonial, post-modern discussion. It is not a question of dismissing the old questions, but of dismantling them and looking at them in new ways." Remarks made during a May 21-23, 1998, conference in Edinburgh, Scotland, held to give continental Protestant theologians an opportunity to respond to some of the issues raised in the project "Protestant Theology and the Conundrum of Islam."

13. Byron Haines, "Mission and the Muslim World: Some Theological Reflections," *Christian Presence and Witness in Relation to Muslim Neighbors* (Geneva: WCC Dialogue with People of Living Faiths and Ideologies, 1981), 53.

14. Andreas D'Souza, "Christian Approaches to the Study of Islam: An Analysis of the Writings of Watt and Cragg," *Bulletin of the Henry Martyn Institute* (July-December 1992): 33-80.

15. This was a major theme of a May 1998 Edinburgh conference (see note 12).

16. See Mark W. Thomsen, *The Word and the Way of the Cross: Christian Witness Among Muslim and Buddhist Peoples* (Chicago: Division for Global Mission, ELCA, 1993); Stuart Brown, trans., *The Challenge of the Scriptures: The Bible and the Qur'an* (Maryknoll: Orbis Books, 1989).

17. Peter Ford, "The Qur'an as Sacred Scripture: An Assessment of Contemporary Christian Perspectives," *The Muslim World* vol. 83, no. 1 (1993):163. I asked Ford what kind of response he received to this proposal from either Christians or Muslims; his answer was "very little."

18. W. C. Smith, "Is the Qur'an the Word of God?" in *Religious Diversity*, Willard G. Oxtoby (New York: Harper & Row, 1976), 39-62.

19. ". . . [A]lready we recognize that the God whom Jesus called Father is the one they call Allah." John B. Cobb, Jr., "Toward a Christocentric Catholic Theology," in *Toward a Universal Theology of Religion*, ed. Leonard Swidler (Maryknoll: Orbis Books, 1987), 86-100.

20. See, for example, Paul V. Martinson, "Christian-Muslim Problematics," in *God and Jesus: Theological Reflection for Christian-Muslim Dialogue* (Minneapolis: The Division for World Mission and Inter-Church Cooperation, 1986), 22-24.

21. Colin Chapman, "Going Soft on Islam? Reflections on Some Evangelical Responses to Islam," *Vox Evangelica* (1987): 15.

22. Douglas Pratt, "Christian-Muslim Theological Encounter: the Priority of *tawhid*," *Islam and Christian-Muslim Relations* vol. 7, no. 3 (1996): 271-84.

23. David Kerr, "He Walked in the Path of the Prophets: Toward Christian Theological Recognition of the Prophethood of Muhammad," in *Christian-Muslim Encounters*, eds. W.Z. Haddad and Y.Y. Haddad (Gainesville: University of Florida Press, 1990), 426.

24. This idea is generally credited to Charles Kraft, *Christianity in Culture: A Study in Dynamic Biblical Theologizing in Cross-Cultural Perspective* (Maryknoll: Orbis Book, 1979), 252.

25. R.H. Drummond, "Toward a Theological Understanding of Islam," in *Muslims in Dialogue*, ed. Leonard Swidler (Lewiston: Mellen Press, 1992), 193.

26. Willem Bijlefeld, "Approaches to Islam," *Chicago Theological Seminary Register* 80 (Fall 1990): 20.

27. John B. Cobb, Jr., "Global Theology in a Pluralist Age," *Unitarian Universalist Christian* vol. 43, no. 1 (1988): 84.

28. Kenneth Cragg, *Muhammad and the Christian. A Question of Response* (Maryknoll: Orbis Books, 1984), 11.

29. Chawkat Moucarry, *Islam and Christianity at the Crossroads* (Tring: Lion, 1988), 43.

30. Private communication to the author, October 17, 1998.

31. Hugh Goddard, *Christians and Muslims. From Double Standards to Mutual Understanding* (Surrey: Curzon Press, 1995), 169-170.

32. Wilfred C. Smith, *The Meaning and End of Religion* (Minneapolis: Fortress Press, 1991).

33. See Alan J. Baiyles, "Evangelical and Ecumenical Understandings of Mission," *International Review of Mission* 35/339 (Oct. 1996).

34. Byron Haines, "Mission and the Muslim World," 56-57.

35. Evertt Huffard, *Thematic Dissonance in the Muslim-Christian Encounter: A Contextual Theology of Honor* (Ph.D. Dissertation, Fuller Theological Seminary, June 1995), 321.

36. Phil Parshall, *Bridges to Islam. A Christian Perspective on Folk Islam* (Grand Rapids: Baker Book House, 1983), 19-20.

37. Bill Musk, "Honor and Shame," *Evangelical Review of Theology* vol. 20, no. 2 (1996): 156-67.

38. German theologian Klaus Hock in a private communication to the author, June 1998, said: "Today I would prefer to look more into possibilities of an (inductive) interreligious dialogical theology instead of spending too much time on theological self-reflection."

39. Willem Bijlefeld, "Approaches to Islam," 22.

The Gap Between Liberty and Equality: Christian Faith and the Civil Rights Movement

Mark G. Toulouse
**BRITE DIVINITY SCHOOL
OF TEXAS CHRISTIAN UNIVERSITY
FORT WORTH, TEXAS**

The problem of racial prejudice has always reached much deeper into church and, for that matter, cultural life, than only the way it has affected the rights of individuals. The problem facing African Americans in 1955, at the beginning of the Civil Rights Movement, was systemic, deeply woven into the cultural fabric of the nation. One might say today that racism had always been an essential ingredient of the American Civil Religion. It ran through the whole religious, economic, and political structure of American life. Therefore, racism was not merely a problem of rights. If it was to be truly eradicated, it would take more than the simple act of excommunicating (or imprisoning) the offending parties who kept minority Americans from exercising their ecclesial (or civil) rights; every aspect of American life would have to be addressed. The white church, as one black church leader put it in 1963, would need to become "a revolutionary force committed to distinguishing and separating the Christian understanding of life from the idealizations and norms of middle class white society."[1]

The white American church leadership had difficulty grasping this point. As long as the movement emphasized the individual rights possessed by every American citizen, the mainline church in America, eventually, mostly offered its unqualified support. As the movement matured and began to develop a sense of the connections between racism and economic life in America, for example, the churches balked, at least in terms of activist support. Possessing rights and gaining equality were really two different things. Such connections, especially as they developed in the last half of the 1960s, most often lay beyond the experience of white church leaders. And when they were confronted by them, they were, as white middle-class Americans, too threatened by the possible solutions to be in much of an activist mood to support them.

As it was, organized and activist support of the Civil Rights Movement among the white churches in America was primarily limited to the period between the summer of 1963 and the summer of 1965, marked conveniently on either side by the dramatic actions of Bull Connor and Martin Luther King Jr. in Birmingham and the fiery riots in Watts. The sympathies of the white church, of course, clearly were present and accounted for prior to 1963. But the character of church support varied throughout the movement. This variety can most effectively be divided into three periods: the sympathetic period (1954 to mid-1963), the activist period (mid-1963 to mid-1965), and the muddled and threatened period (mid-1965 to 1970).

The Sympathetic Period (1954 to mid-1963)

White Christian leadership in the mainline Protestant and Catholic churches supported the idea of desegregation from the time serious discussion about it entered the public domain in American life. This was in keeping with the rising consciousness among white Christians throughout the early twentieth century about the problems associated with racial prejudice. The Federal Council of Churches of Christ in America (FCC) had announced a non-discrimination racial policy as early as 1946. Most of the Protestant denominations affiliated with the FCC passed their own versions in succeeding years. Shortly after the National Council of Churches (NCC) formed and absorbed the FCC in 1950, it passed a more extensive resolution admitting church culpability in the racial discrimination and segregation that plagued the nation and indicating its intention to stand squarely against them in the future. The NCC expressed its approval of the 1954 *Brown v. Board of Education* decision within days.[2] Most mainline denominations followed suit as quickly as their processes allowed, including the majority of the so-called mainline denominations in the South.

Individual Protestant ministers acted courageously in local contexts only to be fired or, worse, run out of town by their congregations. This happened more than a few times in the South. Most of the Protestant denominations were powerless to keep it from happening. As Reinhold Niebuhr put it in 1955, in cases like these, "one might well regret the extreme congregationalism of Protestantism and envy the Roman Church." At least the Catholic hierarchy, Niebuhr mused, had some true authority to exercise at local levels.[3]

As might be expected, the American Catholic Church possessed a sterling record of sympathetic support for the 1954 decision. Individual Catholic bishops, in the wake of the Court decision, issued pronouncements of their own. Jointly, the American bishops issued a statement in 1958 that condemned "enforced segregation" as incompatible with Christian faith. The adjective "enforced," preceding the word "segregation" in the Catholic bishop's statement, was, no doubt, carefully chosen. Mainline Christian leaders who supported the 1954 decision were certain that *de jure* segregation, segregation supported by the force of law, was unacceptable. This is what the civil rights battle in the beginning years was all about. However, many lay Christians believed if whites or blacks wanted to worship by themselves, due to cultural or stylistic differences, or voluntarily choose to live in their own communities, they should be able to do so. Awareness of the implications of *de facto* discrimination were slow to develop among most white Christians.[4]

The bishops' statement clearly raised concerns of both "love of neighbor and respect for his rights." The nation would face a "grave internal crisis," the bishops warned, "if our hearts are poisoned by hatred, or even by indifference toward the welfare and rights of our fellow men." But, like most Americans, Catholics understood love of neighbor as mostly synonymous with respect for individual rights. Most Americans believed a person's welfare was protected if that person's individual rights were honored. Language arguing the protection of individual rights pervades all the church literature of these early years. Later, some black leaders began to separate individual rights from issues related to the corporate welfare of black people in particular. Most church leaders did not want to follow the implications of that logic. But leaders of the American mainline church, both Protestant and Catholic, found "individual rights" language compelling and, institutionally at least, continually offered words of sympathetic support for the movement as a whole.[5]

Leaders in both churches regularly praised the nonviolent techniques of the early movement. Their independent journals offered unqualified support for Martin Luther King Jr., the Southern Christian Leadership Conference (SCLC), and the National Association for the Advancement of Colored People (NAACP). *The Christian Century* began publishing King's essays in February of 1957 and named him to its staff as an editor-at-large in October of 1958. In this way, editors at the *Century* promoted very early on King's role as a teacher of the broader church, a stark contrast to *Christianity Today's* complete neglect of King during these years.[6] Editors of the mainline journals supported virtually every non-violent activity of the early Civil Rights Movement. They reported on, analyzed, and theologized about all the events of these years, from Montgomery to Little Rock to the sit-ins to the freedom riders, with considerable interest and always accompanied by profound expressions of respect and human sympathy.[7]

What is missing during these years is much mention of courageous and activist involvement of the institutional church itself. The paucity of such literature stems from the fact that such activity did not much exist. Localized and individual acts of the church were not very frequent. Editors and authors lamented the fact that local congregations in crisis areas were not more involved. Future Senator Paul Simon, a member of the House in 1958, quoted a black minister who condemned the "silence of the good people," who are so "objectively analytical that they never get subjectively committed." As for denominational groups, this young black minister reported, there was "a high blood pressure of creeds and an anemia of deeds." Andrew Greeley questioned whether justice was alive on Catholic campuses because Catholic students were largely absent from any forms of activism. One southern minister, after looking in vain for news indicating an active white Christian protest of the Emmett Till murder or the atrocities at Koinonia, intoned, "God has been forced to call impromptu prophets in judicial robes and baseball uniforms to summon the sinful to repentance." Meanwhile, Reinhold Niebuhr hoped the church could "prove it is at least as good as sports in establishing brotherhood between the races." The fact that the institutional church failed in these matters is why Gayraud Wilmore was probably justified in 1963 in describing the "New Negro's" image of the white Protestant as "at best a condescending, paternalistic gradualist and at worst a vicious wielder of power who in the south opens White Citizens Council meetings with prayer and who in the north champions conservative Republicanism."[8]

Few Protestants or Catholics questioned why forms of the institutional church were not more heavily invested in the actual work of civil rights. In the Protestant case, most of them knew that the national bureaucracies were unable to commit resources and personnel to areas of controversy unless the local churches were equally committed. Catholics generally acted through the Catholic Interracial Councils or through bishops who issued orders of integration for parochial education. The Catholic record of accomplishment was a bit better, but none of the local parishes or other institutional arms of the church distinguished themselves through radical activism during these years either. Both Protestant and Catholic leaders understood and generally honored the limited tolerance most American Christians had for organized institutional activism in political matters.

They did, however, regularly stress the moral failure represented by segregation and consistently urged American Christians to support integration because it was the Christian thing to do. As Cardinal Cushing once put it, "[T]he racist Christian is a contradiction." During this first period of the movement, both Catholic and Protestant church leaders seemed genuinely optimistic that things would work themselves out over time, especially if the "Negroes" could continue to use nonviolent techniques effectively. Such feelings helped to reduce any sense of urgency to become actively involved themselves. After the first few years of the movement, they possessed increased confidence that the self-interest motives operating against segregation would eventually carry the day. Southern cities and states where segregation remained most prominent, by 1961, had begun to experience economic difficulties directly attributable to their stance on segregation. As one Protestant minister put it, "[I]n the end, the almighty dollar will determine the outcome."[9]

Occasionally, these Christian leaders also discussed realities that, in their view, limited white Christian leadership in its ability to push the institutional church toward an activist involvement in the quest for civil rights. As previously mentioned, Reinhold Niebuhr and Waldo Beach liked to emphasize the congregational realities of Protestant life. Protestants simply did not possess the kind of authority that could enable a massive and activist response. Niebuhr also stressed the nature of sin, particularly the difference between individual sins and collective sins. When one has "a religious experience of repentance and conversion," that person is more likely to recognize the need to repent "individual sins which defy common standards of decency than collective sins that are imbedded in these common standards." For Niebuhr, the ability of the church to deal with "collective sins" offered "the real test of the redeeming efficacy of our Christian faith."[10] The church always has trouble dealing honestly and forthrightly with the notion (and the implications) of corporate sin.

Niebuhr here made a distinction that not too many Christian leaders would make clearly when they struggled with the nature of Black Power after 1965. The collective sin embodied in "our peculiar cultural values, our 'Southern way of life,' or 'our American way of life,'" as Niebuhr variously phrased it, most often escaped the white line of sight. American Christians in white churches, both South and North, usually repented their own sins when they violated "common standards of decency" but few questioned whether those common standards themselves might be sinful. As Niebuhr put it elsewhere, this constitutes the very nature of the power of culture over faith.[11]

Protestants and Catholics also had to deal with significant differences in attitudes between clergy and laity, affecting the church's willingness to act. Clergy were mostly well-educated, trained in seminaries where questions related to ethics and justice were built into the curriculum. Lay people, on the other hand, rarely had the opportunity to discuss or analyze serious ethical questions. Attitudes differed considerably. An early poll showed that southern Protestant ministers overwhelmingly favored integration. Not so among lay people. In 1964, Catholic leaders were shocked to discover that 55.5% of Catholic ballots in a Maryland preferential election were cast for George Wallace in spite of the consistent teachings of Catholic leaders in that state dealing with race. As late as November 1966, a majority of lay people in one of the most socially active and liberal Protestant denominations, the United Church of Christ, expressed the belief that blacks were moving too quickly. Less than half of the respondents were willing to accept blacks as neighbors. This was true in spite of a consistent educational campaign about the merits of the Civil Rights Movement being conducted within the denomination during these years.[12]

During these earlier years, mainline Christian editors stressed the successes of the movement, including celebrating tokenism because it at least opened the door to further integration. In good liberal fashion, they believed educational programs would help solve racial problems and had confidence in the law's power to effect change, even though they recognized it would take years of struggle to do so. Mainline Protestants and Catholics alike supported early attempts to pass civil rights legislation, though not all of them agreed about granting government particularly strong enforcement powers. Most recognized the importance of the political side of the battle and were realistic about the give-and-take one finds in such an arena. Some stressed the ethical realism that emphasized "the social responsibility to seek through political action the largest possible net gain in terms of accepted values." Most were not too critical in analyzing the foundation of these "accepted values." They were realistic enough to recognize they did not have forever to make substantial changes.[13]

By 1961, when white mainline leaders complained about gradualism, or groused that progress came much too slowly, they most often did so because they understood the potential of black militancy. An acute fear of violence, sometimes veiled, sometimes not, usually accompanied their strong support for King's program of nonviolence after this time. White Christians worried about the outbreak of racial violence and, when black nationalism and the Black Muslim movement caught their attention in 1960-1961, that fear found regular expression. Black nationalism offered something tangible that could speak to their despair. Black militancy, once it appeared, loomed larger and larger in the white perspective with every passing year.[14]

Malcolm X spoke the language of black nationalism better than anyone. He frankly scared white Christian liberals. They appreciated the fact that King and other moderate middle-class African-Americans shared their perception of him as dangerous, racist, and an advocate of black supremacy. But by 1963, James O'Gara of *Commonweal*, incisively noted that "the position of these [responsible] Negro leaders becomes more and more difficult precisely to the extent that Black Muslim charges against white society seem to be true."[15] When Malcolm X appeared in the viewfinder of white Americans (late 1959-1960), neither King nor most of the white liberals understood just how different the experience of racism was for blacks living in the urban ghettos of the northern cities from that experienced by blacks in the South.

It would be a few years before King even possessed an inkling of understanding about the situation in northern ghettos, and most white Christian liberals were slow to catch on as well. One of the rare, discerning white liberals, William Stringfellow, predicted in early 1962 that the racial "exploitation" and its accompanying "alienation" and "estrangement" of the races evident in Harlem, could lead to a northern explosion of revenge: "To Negroes in the north, revenge may seem sweeter than equality and certainly seems more honorable than acceptance of further appeasements."[16] Beginning especially with the summer of 1965, the ramifications of black experiences in the North would be virtually impossible to ignore. Eventually, they represented a shift in focus for the Civil Rights Movement, from the South to the North. Mainline Christian support ultimately disintegrated due to the seismic nature of that shift. The shift recorded a movement from an emphasis on "rights" to a severe questioning of the core values of the American culture itself. During the period under current consideration, however, ecumenical mainline leadership, among both Catholics and Protestants, strongly sympathized with the Civil Rights Movement, offering educational materials, church resolutions, and other forms of vocal support for its objectives.[17]

There was also a very evident fear among these white leaders that African-American patience was nearing its end. The grave possibility of black violence grew more likely with each Birmingham-kind of event. Reinhold Niebuhr, noting declining patience among blacks, pronounced the "record of the white Protestant Church . . . shameful." When he wrote these words, he was aware that many national leaders were taking steps to enter the Civil Rights Movement more intentionally and with a commitment to act more directly. "We Protestants," he wrote, "might begin the new chapter in our national life by contritely confessing that [mainline] Christianity has failed to contribute significantly to the solution of the gravest social issue and evil that our nation has confronted since slavery."[18] Many church leaders, Niebuhr among them, hoped that things were about to change.

The Activist Period (Mid-1963-Summer 1965)

The first step toward a more activist role, one could argue, appeared with the convening of a national and ecumenical Conference on Religion and Race, held in Chicago on January 14-17, 1963, one hundred years after the Emancipation Proclamation. Sponsored by the National Council of Churches (Protestant and Orthodox), the National Catholic Welfare Conference (Catholic), and the Synagogue Council of America (Jewish), the conference attracted somewhere between 650 and 800 delegates. About twenty-five percent of the delegates were black, but among blacks only the chair of the conference, Benjamin E. Mays of Morehouse College, and the closing speaker, Martin Luther King Jr., participated in major ways. Essentially, white church leaders controlled the event.

Nothing significant resulted from the conference, perhaps because of the unwieldy attempt to put together yet another social agency, this one representing the social departments that already existed within the three major religious organizations. But the conference did demonstrate an increasing will to act on the part of the white religious establishment. For the most part, these religious leaders wanted to stop standing on the sideline; they remained unsure how best to get in the game. Why, suddenly, did they feel that way? Events in Birmingham appear to have acted as a turning point.

Most local pastors in Birmingham stood on the side of the *status quo*. Eight of Birmingham's most prestigious religious leaders, including the Auxiliary Bishop of the Catholic diocese, urged King and his demonstrators to disperse, at the same time praising law enforcement officers for their restraint.[19] An interracial mix of nine pastors spoke out otherwise, but even after an agreement between King and the city's leaders was reached, the executive committee of the city's ministerial association refused to endorse it.

While King was jailed in Birmingham during these events in 1963, he wrote one of the most significant documents to emerge from the Civil Rights Movement. His "Letter from Birmingham Jail" received its first national exposure through publication in the June 12, 1963 issue of *The Christian Century*, though it had already been distributed among most white Christian national leadership by the end of May. Addressed to the eight members of the clergy in the city who had advised him to stop his demonstrations, but accompanied by the strong implication that it also meant to address the clergy of the nation, King's letter returned a powerful indictment of the inaction of the white church leadership during the Civil Rights Movement:

> Though there are some notable exceptions, I have also been disappointed with the white church and its leadership. . . . In the midst of blatant injustices inflicted upon the Negro I have watched white churchmen stand on the sideline and mouth pious irrelevancies and sanctimonious trivialities. . . . The judgment of God is upon the church as never before. If today's church does not recapture the sacrificial spirit of the early church, it will lose its authenticity, forfeit the loyalty of millions, and be dismissed as an irrelevant social club with no meaning for the 20th century.[20]

King's letter, widely read in the white religious community, contributed to the creation of what James F. Findlay has aptly described as the *kairos*, the development of that moment in time demanding activism from the white church. King had fired an arrow directly into the heart of liberal guilt.

On June 7, within weeks after King issued his letter from Birmingham, and shortly after their meeting in New York with some of the city's key African Americans, the NCC General Board made an announcement. Effective immediately, a new Commission on Religion and Race had the mandate from the General Board to become involved directly in the daily activities of the Civil Rights Movement. The commission was exempt from the normal bureaucratic functioning of other units within the NCC, and would report directly to the General Board. Further, it received $175,000 for the remaining months of 1963, with a commitment of $275,000 for 1964. In addition, General Board members themselves promised to engage personally in direct action. Among other activities, the new commission, with help from the United Church of Christ and other member denominations, began providing money for bail bonds. This activity proved to be of immediate benefit to some ninety African-American demonstrators, from teenagers to people in their seventies, who were wasting away under threatening conditions in prisons located in the South.[21]

These actions from the NCC followed the action of the United Presbyterian Church, U.S.A., which on May 20th had established its own Commission on Religion and Race, and funded it with $150,000 for the remainder of the year. Presbyterians chose African American Gayraud Wilmore to head their commission, while the NCC chose a white minister, Robert Spike, from the United Church of Christ. At about the same time, the Protestant Episcopal Church committed itself to active involvement in the struggle through its interracial unit, the Episcopal Society for Racial and Cultural Unity. The Catholic Theological Society unanimously passed its own resolution dealing with the moral issues, urging everyone to cooperate through action to solve the problem. The American bishops issued a pastoral letter on interracial justice in August, and on July 4th in Baltimore, nine Catholic priests joined picket lines to protest segregation at the local amusement park.[22] Clearly, the mood of white church leaders had shifted toward a more activist mode. The idea that history might view it as too-little-too-late did not escape all of them. Robert McAfee Brown wrote in August 1963, that:

> Until the summer of 1963, one did not have much sense that the white churches had really thrown in their lot with the Negro. . . . So it is not particularly to the credit of the churches that the date of their active involvement will be read by future historians as 1963. . . . It may be that it will be too late to redeem the church's bad record, and too late to convince the secular fighters for civil rights that Christians now mean business; eleventh-hour aid is not always appreciated by those who have had to fight alone in the heat of the day . . . Nevertheless, the churches, who must care more about being right than being victorious, are now committed to acting and not merely speaking.[23]

The first major initiative of this new activism surrounded the efforts to secure new legislation enforcing civil rights. On June 17, approximately 250 church leaders met with President Kennedy who had already been at work trying to garner support for his bid to introduce new legislation to Congress. Church leaders pledged national and local activity on behalf of new legislation.[24] On June 19, Kennedy submitted his legislation to Congress, the foundation for what would, in due time, become the Civil Rights Act of 1964. The

NCC orchestrated a massive lobbying effort with a two-pronged focus: one arm concentrated on both houses of Congress, while the other sought "to educate and to energize people at the grass roots."[25]

Part of this lobbying effort included church participation in the scheduled March on Washington, planned for August 28, 1963. The march focused its concern on offering support for securing both jobs and vote for African Americans. White church leaders were latecomers to the march and some wrung their hands, fearful that the event could turn to violence. Aided by the extensive efforts of the NCC, churches were able to contribute an estimated 40,000 church leaders who marched alongside some 200,000 other people. By one person's count, there were forty-nine Catholic groups involved in the march, twenty-three of them connected to local Catholic Interracial Councils. Evangelical church leadership was largely absent from the event, a fact noted and challenged by one evangelical pastor:

> Evangelical leadership completely missed the point of the March on Washington and was not represented. . . . Actions are needed. . . . The conservative Protestant church had better get involved in this Negro revolution or face inevitable judgment by the Negroes and youth of today and the historians of tomorrow.[26]

As summer gave way to fall, Robert Kennedy began to back off of a strong bill in order to get something passed successfully. The NCC pulled out all the stops to secure the strongest possible bill, insisting that the bill not be watered down in any way whatsoever. Mainline Catholics and Protestants supported limiting individual private rights to enrich the public good and represent the interdependence of life in a complex and pluralistic society. Many evangelical leaders, though they supported passage of the civil rights bill, took the opposite view, interpreting this part of the legislation as a menacing example of the growth of federal power intruding on the sacred territory of individual rights.[27] The major lobbying efforts of the NCC were so successful at garnering attention that Senator Strom Thurmond suggested the church organization should have its tax-exempt status removed because of its involvement.[28]

Thurmond's criticism raised the question whether these mainline Christians violated the norms of church and state through their lobbying efforts. It is a legitimate question to ask whether funds raised under tax-exempt auspices should be used to ply legislators to vote this way or that way on a particular piece of legislation. Lobbyists for the NCC, on the one hand, understood their tasks in Washington as part of the fulfillment of the gospel; on the other hand, they lobbied members of Congress because, wholeheartedly, as citizens, they believed this civil rights legislation was the best thing for the country. Realistically, that is not too much different from the motives that drove the political activities of the radical right during the 1980s.[29]

The one difference might be that most of these earlier lobbyists did not live under the illusion of the priestly perspective that this country had ever been Christian, or that any amount of legislation could ever make it so. On the latter point, at least in 1963-1964, evangelicals and mainliners agreed, whether they realized it or not.

As the summer of 1964 approached, the tension in the country rose appreciably. Christian leaders of all persuasions urged quick passage of the legislation, believing that a new law would help to keep the pot of racial tension from boiling over in the heat of the summer. They knew passage would not solve all the problems facing the country in this area, but they believed it could help to ward off the violence everyone expected to come if it did not pass.

On June 10, for the first time in American history, the Senate voted cloture against a civil rights filibuster (seventy-five days long) by a vote of seventy-one to twenty-nine, four votes more than were actually needed. The civil rights bill was passed shortly thereafter. Hubert Humphrey, speaking before the American Baptist Convention in May, warned Christians that the bill would not be the answer to racial problems in America. Christians, he declared, needed to be in it for the long haul. With considerable insight, Reinhold Niebuhr, after the bill passed, spoke realistically about its effects and addressed the difference between basic rights and full equality. Many Christian leaders missed this distinction.

> The real paradox of our racial crisis, which we must understand in order to appreciate its frightening dimensions, is that, despite the fact that the laws guarantee the Negro his basic rights, his status is still inferior. The civil rights bill offers him no hope. . . . And their economic ills will not be cured by any

> fair employment provision in the new bill. The situation is desperate because of the heritage of decades of inadequate education, on the one hand, and the rapidly developing technical efficiency of our industries, on the other. The desperate hopelessness of young Negroes—the product of the growing sense of uselessness, the unemployed days and the sheer resentment born of years of accumulated frustration—partly explains the "crime wave" that has disturbed the authorities and the "white liberals" in the Northern cities. . . . But the white majority must stretch its imagination and empathy radically to understand the roots of this unrest.[30]

With all its strengths, the new law remained basically a moderate law. It failed to put any teeth in the federal government's ability to deal with voting rights for African Americans in the South. King believed the new law provided dignity, but without the vote, it was "dignity without strength."[31]

The NCC, in its new activist mode, took a particular interest in the need to do something about both voting rights and the condition of black poverty in the South. During the events of the summer and fall of 1963, the Commission on Religion and Race (CRC) found itself drawn more and more into work in Mississippi. Within a week after the NCC created the commission, Medgar Evers, the Mississippi director of the NAACP, was shot to death in front of his home. Representatives from the NCC attended the funeral.

Through a variety of activities, commission leaders came into closer contact with the Student Nonviolent Coordinating Committee (SNCC) and the Council of Federated Organizations (COFO), the organization representing all civil rights groups in Mississippi. The Presbyterian and Episcopalian denominations also maintained a significant and activist presence in Mississippi. Together, the churches worked in Hattiesburg, and to some degree in Canton and Greenwood, on voter registration and voter education. Presbyterians provided most of the ministers who participated in these drives.

Leading into the summer of 1964, Robert Spike, of the NCC, and Robert Moses, of the SNCC, had conversations about how the commission might help with voter registration over the summer. With Spike's enthusiastic support, the commission became involved in what became "Freedom Summer." About 800 students from across the country came to spend the summer in Mississippi to help with voter registration drives. Another objective of the summer included the efforts to offer remedial education to young and disadvantaged black youth in so-called "Freedom Schools." These college students also were sent to staff community centers to help teach adults to read and write, and to teach job skills of various sorts. The Commission helped to coordinate the planning of the event and provided supervisory and administrative support during the training sessions for the students in Oxford, Ohio.

The tragedy that befell three of the movement's workers, James Chaney, Andrew Goodman, and Mickey Schwerner, fulfilled some of the fears surrounding these efforts. As one could have predicted, the deaths brought unwarranted criticism of the NCC efforts from evangelical sources claiming that "neither the commission nor its idealistic participants are fully prepared" for the complexities involved in this work. A month later, they came close to blaming the NCC for the deaths: "The loud voices of ecclesiastical programming may some day discover that the tragic murders in Mississippi may possibly have stemmed in part from the shift of the Church's mission from persuasion to compulsion." Evangelicals were not alone in their opposition. A Louis Harris Poll taken at the time showed that sixty-five percent of Americans opposed the activities of the college students in Mississippi.[32]

Over the course of the summer, no college students were involved in serious incidents of violence. The churches provided "minister-counselors" to accompany students in their work in the hope that their presence might keep the threat of violence to a minimum. Some 275 ministers and lay people from across the country spent from ten days to two weeks as counselors in Mississippi during the summer. As one source reported the figures at the beginning of the summer, of some 915,722 blacks in the state, only about 28,000 (about three percent) were registered to vote. A second source reported the percentage in early September, three months later, to be 6.7%. If these statistics are accurate, the summer's voting drives across the state registered some 33,350 blacks. The statistics also reveal how large a task remained to be done in this area.[33]

After the summer of 1964, the commission remained active in Mississippi, working closely with SNCC, in addressing black economic and social problems, voter registration, and political education in the Delta area of the state. In mid-1966, the executive leadership in this ministry shifted from white to black, and the financial support broadened temporarily to include Methodists. From 1964-1974, the NCC carried on this significant and effective "community building" ministry known as the Delta Ministry. Its strongest work included the period from 1964-1971, the latter date being the year it lost the lease on its home headquarters, the old Mt. Beulah college campus near Edwards, Mississippi. Financial struggles and the lack of a home operating base restricted activities during the final three years. For nearly a decade, however, the ministry demonstrated one slice of the church's response to the race crisis in America. On the one hand, it revealed the serious dedication of numerous church people to the struggle and what the efforts of a few could accomplish; on the other, it illustrated that problems were so vast that any form of the church's ministry during these years seemed barely to scratch the surface.[34]

In January 1965, King decided to focus nationwide attention on Selma, Alabama. SNCC had been hard at work in Selma for a couple of years. In Dallas County, about 32,700 people were black, of which only about 400 were registered voters. One lawsuit noted that only fourteen blacks had registered successfully in Selma between 1954 and 1960; among those turned down because they did not meet voter registration requirements were black school teachers with college and advanced degrees. Civil rights activity came to a head in early March. On Saturday, March 6, sixty to seventy white marchers, under the leadership of Joseph Ellwanger, marched to the Dallas County Courthouse in an "act of identification" with blacks in Selma. This was perhaps the only all-white march on behalf of black civil rights in the South. On Sunday, a large contingent of black demonstrators and a few whites headed out of Selma toward Highway 80, intending to march to the capital. Alabama state police brutally broke up the peaceful march at the Edmund Pettus Bridge. Television news captured enough of the violence to shame Alabama. King issued a call to all white churches and synagogues to send help to Selma. More than 400 white clergy, joined by other whites from across the country, arrived in Selma on a moment's notice.[35]

On Tuesday, gathered at Browns Chapel A.M.E. Church, the waiting demonstrators heard that a federal judge had issued an injunction against the march. SNCC leader, John Lewis, told those gathered that they must march anyway. King, though he had never acted in contradiction to a federal court injunction, stood before the crowd and told them he intended to march. What SNCC leadership and whites and blacks in attendance did not know is that King had already arranged an agreement with authorities to turn back at the bridge after a peaceful confrontation with state troopers. Popular media began to pick up on serious tensions that had developed between King's SCLC and the younger, more militant SNCC.[36]

That night, three white ministers were eating dinner at a restaurant in the black neighborhood of Selma. When they left the restaurant, they walked past a blue collar whites-only restaurant named the Silver Moon. They were set upon by at least four white men who beat them. James Reeb, a Unitarian minister, took a blow to the temple. The three men stumbled for a few blocks until they found help. Reeb died a few days later. Whites and blacks together carried on several peaceful demonstrations through the days after Reeb was attacked. At a memorial service in Brown's Chapel, a huge crowd gathered, about equally black and white. By the end of the next week, President Johnson had promised to send a strong voting rights bill, guaranteeing the vote to all citizens, to Congress. He invited Robert Spikes and Eugene Carson Blake of the NCC to sit in the family box on March 15 when he proposed the Voting Rights Act before Congress.[37]

Six days later, somewhere between 4,000 and 8,000 marchers (depending on who was counting), and including large numbers of white ministers and rabbis, lay people, and secular sympathizers, finally made the march of fifty miles from Selma to the capitol at Montgomery, under protection of a federalized Alabama National Guard. Evangelical church leaders "shared sympathy" for black voting rights, but "hesitated to identify themselves with clergy social-action pressure." They expressed a preference for "judicial process" over "mob pressure." When demonstrators arrived in Montgomery, an aide of Governor Wallace informed them, "The capitol is closed today." But, in front of a crowd that had grown to some 25,000, an exhausted King delivered an impassioned speech laced with optimism that the great battle for civil rights was nearly won. But was it?

Watts was on the horizon. And shortly after Watts, in August, Jon Daniels, an Episcopalian seminary student who had stayed on to work in Selma for the Episcopal Society for Cultural and Racial Unity, was shot by a cursing deputy sheriff. A Roman Catholic priest from Chicago was also critically wounded. In the months after Selma, though voting rights were won, King's optimism would wane and, as James Cone has described the change, a more militant King would emerge.[38]

The white church's very visible presence at Selma served as symbolic of its more activist involvement of the last two years. But, after the president introduced the Voting Rights Act of 1965, many church leaders began to conclude that the long fight for civil rights was all but over. The eventual enforcement of legislation would bring the legal rights and equality that blacks had long sought. "The war is over," declared an editorial in the *Century*, "the sooner the south accepts this fact and loses itself in the nation the better for it and for the nation." The Voting Rights Act certainly did make a difference once it was passed. By 1967, more than 170,000 new black voters had registered in Mississippi.[39]

But guaranteeing individual rights for blacks by law did not solve all the problems associated with racism.

As one scholar put it, sometime in the mid-1960s, the struggle shifted from "rights" to "resources." Or, put another way, the legal struggle seeking individual rights shifted toward the demand to recognize group (blacks as a community) rights.[40] This latter demand, as it developed, had several different facets. Some in the movement emphasized the group's economic needs, seeking new centralized policies like affirmative action. As the movement moved north, black leaders sought more radical goals, including a massive rejection of the values associated with white middle-class culture. There were signs that serious trouble lay on the horizon. Because white leaders in the church had mostly viewed the civil rights battle as one seeking individual rights alone, they found themselves muddled and threatened by the new turns taken by the movement.

The Muddled and Threatened Period: (Summer 1965-1970)

Increasingly, throughout the mid-1960s, black leaders were recognizing that civil rights did not translate into economic equality. In

1965, "43% of all black families were poor, earning under $3,000 per year" and "black unemployment was twice that of white unemployment, with black teenage unemployment 100 percent higher than black adult unemployment." More than sixty percent of black teenagers dropped out of high school before finishing. While Lyndon Johnson declared war on poverty, his war mostly emphasized that increased opportunity would result in the eventual eradication of black poverty. Black leadership, on the other hand, saw poverty more as the result of "unequal distribution of power and wealth." In other words, the war on poverty had to address the system that created poverty rather than just the symptoms emerging from that system.[41]

Johnson's war on poverty, despite the fact that Congress never appropriated more than twenty percent of the originally allotted appropriations, experienced some success. By 1968, only twenty-three percent of black families earned less than $3,000 per year. But part of the split in the movement after 1965 occurred between those who were in a social position to take advantage of those gains and those who were not. Black youths living in urban ghettos felt this inequality most acutely. After Watts, Martin Luther King began to see this problem more clearly. The violence of the riot drove home the point for him. Recently passed legislation had little effect on racism and poverty in the North. According to James Cone:

> What was it that Martin King understood? First, he realized that formal equality (i.e, the achievement of constitutional rights) did not change the *material* conditions of black people, especially those packed in the ghettos of the North. In fact their poverty continued to get worse, partly because of the progressive displacement of unskilled labor, further eroding their sense of somebodyness. After Watts, Martin concluded that without *economic* justice, the right to a job or income, talk about "life, liberty, and the pursuit of happiness" was nothing but a figment of one's political imagination.[42]

Though King did not share the violent revolution scenario of the black separatists, he emphasized the need for some form of Christian socialism, "what in later years would be called 'liberation theology.'"[43] But when King died in April 1968, before he had the opportunity to develop more systematically his thinking in this direction, the white church lost its most trusted interpreter of black life. The tragic death of King no doubt contributed to the depth of confusion white Christians found themselves experiencing during this period.

The first undeniable signs that the Civil Rights Movement would soon turn North to focus on economic equality appeared in the fear Americans expressed about the potentially "long, hot summer" of 1964. Liberal Christian leaders especially feared the riots, not only because of the violence such riots might cause, but also because of a "white backlash" that might favor Goldwater in the national presidential election in the fall. Moderate black leaders shared that judgment and decided to ban all demonstrations over which they had any control. Others, like James Farmer and John Lewis, leaders of CORE and SNCC respectively, insisted that mass demonstrations should continue, or else leadership in the movement might pass to the extremists. The moderates prevailed and demonstrations ceased temporarily. Small riots broke out in Harlem, Bedford-Stuyvesant of Brooklyn, Rochester, Philadelphia, and five other communities.[44]

In response to the riots, some Christian leaders alternated between minimizing the significance of the riots and recommending better jobs, better education, and the right to move into white neighborhoods.[45] Neither approach offered much understanding of the real problem. More to the point, however, was the official interpretation offered by the F.B.I. and accepted by many in the churches, that the riots were not race related. Quoting the *Century's* endorsement of the report is illustrative here:

> The bureau concludes that the riots were not racial in character, were not related to civil rights protests and were not planned or engineered by the Communist party. It states rather that the riots were dominated by youths—Negro and white—who were "variously characterized by responsible people as 'school dropouts,' 'young punks,' 'common hoodlums' and 'drunken kids.'" Urged on by adult troublemakers, "looking for excitement or violence or worse," these young people succumbed to a mob spirit and to senseless "attack on all constituted authority without purpose or object." ... According to the F.B.I. report, the riots reflect "an increasing breakdown across the nation in respect for the law and the rights of other people to be secure in their person and their property."

The report, as an aside, recognized that blacks live in "demoralizing" poverty, but expressed confidence that the current war on poverty would "result in steady improvement."[46] Robert Spike, the director of the NCC's Commission on Religion and Race, offered one of the few published dissenting Christian opinions. "These were race riots," he wrote.

> The problem is precisely that thousands of Northern Negroes have ceased to believe in the reality of the liberal social creed as having any meaning for them. . . . What is so sorely missing in our Northern cities is any will to deal dramatically and decisively with the issues that are bothering people right now.[47]

A few other white Christian liberals were beginning to recognize that significant numbers of blacks, especially in the North, believed strongly not only in economic improvement, but in the outright rejection of white cultural values as well. As one of them put it in the fall of 1964:

> White liberals have usually assumed that improvement in the individual Negro's educational and economic opportunities would result in his sharing the liberal's enthusiasm for bourgeois values, and in the virtual elimination of a Negro community as such. . . . Many Negroes believe that they have been betrayed by the white man's culture, by the white man's churches, and, in all probability, by the white man's Civil Rights law.[48]

The "long, hot summers" of 1965 through 1967 resulted in riots in some fifty-seven communities and over 140 deaths. The responses of Christians throughout these events varied considerably. The liberal among them knew that Billy Graham's assessment that Watts was "symptomatic of the revolt of man against God" hardly deserved consideration. There were more appropriate responses. The Southern California-Nevada council of churches, formed as a result of Watts, vowed "to mobilize the full resources of the churches to meet the present crisis and work forcefully for a community where all citizens have the opportunity to attain their full stature as human beings." This new council representing ten major denominations recognized that part of the problem of Watts could be traced to "the unconcern of economically advantaged white citizens . . . and the failure of the churches to respond to the repeated cries of pain which have come from our fellow man."[49]

The more common response among Christians failed to make these kinds of connections. Many Christians endorsed the well-publicized Moynihan Report that family instability in the black community was responsible for these outbreaks of violence. The report, written by Daniel Moynihan, at that time an under-secretary in the Department of Health, Education, and Welfare, did state clearly that white racism was to be blamed for creating that instability, but economic factors, as well as ongoing acts of racial discrimination were largely ignored in the report.[50] Vietnam rapidly came to dominate the administration's attention.[51] The problems in the urban ghettos raised by rioting in Watts were left largely unattended.[52] And the majority of the church's leadership had little to say about it. Malcolm Boyd asked in exasperation:

> Why do white Christian leaders maintain silence as the holocaust comes closer and closer? Is it really true that they do not know the facts? If it is, is it because they, as moral guardians of the power structure, are enmeshed in a deliberate conspiracy of ignorance?[53]

The complexity of the black concern for economic equality that so confounded white society found three particular expressions that confronted the church in the period from 1966-1970, with manifestations that continued well beyond that period: the three expressions were Black Power, black theology, and the black manifesto.

When James Meredith was shot as he marched to inform blacks in Mississippi that they could vote freely under the Voting Rights Act of 1965, civil rights leaders organized a Freedom March, from Memphis to Jackson. While marching, on June 16, Stokely Carmichael first publicly proclaimed the words "Black Power." Putting those two words together brought a serious division between civil rights leaders and caused many in the white churches to begin to withdraw their support from the objectives of even the moderate black leaders. *Commonweal* offered one of the few insightful editorials on Black Power:

> . . . in the end, Negroes must give primacy either to the appeal to white consciences or to the strength of block politics, either to petitioning the power

> structure or to confronting it with another power structure . . . the primary aim of Negroes cannot be the prevention of hurt feelings in white liberals. It must be, rather obviously, the vigorous promotion of justice for the nation's most aggrieved minority. In view of the Administration's muted enthusiasm, and the current mood of white voters, we should expect, and support, some form of the allegedly dread term, "Black Power."[54]

Most Christians, as well illustrated in their independent journals, were very confused and threatened by advocates of Black Power. They often quoted the moderate black leaders, especially Roy Wilkins of the NAACP and Whitney Young of the Urban League, concerning their opposition to it. King refused to join the moderates in signing a statement condemning advocates of Black Power.[55]

Instead, King tried to keep contacts with both groups, the more moderate blacks, Wilkins and Young on the one side, and the more radical, Floyd B. McKissick of CORE and Stokely Carmichael of SNCC, on the other.[56] Black Power advocates left the term deliberately ambiguous, believing it served their purposes better that way. McKissick tended to define it in terms of black identity leading to black economic and political power; others defined it in terms that emphasized black supremacy or separatism. King preferred to emphasize its connections to black self-esteem because he continued to hold out hope of white support for the movement.

James Cone has argued that Black Power ultimately had a profound impact upon King. He began to appreciate the fact that white liberals had never really supported complete equality for blacks. Cone quotes King as saying, even though "they took a stand for decency" by supporting legislation and marching in Selma, they "never really [took] a stand for genuine equality for the black man."[57]

White Christians began to realize that Black Power essentially meant a rejection of integration. "When the young Negro marchers say that they do not need the white liberals, they are not being racist," wrote author Margaret Halsey, "they are cutting their losses." After rehearsing the statistics on remaining segregation, and on Negro unemployment, Halsey boldly stated "that integration has failed." The white will not be able to integrate the black on the white's terms. "It will be the self-reliant Negro, consciously using available power like other minorities before him," concluded Halsey, "who will successfully integrate." But there was more to Black Power than the desire to integrate on one's own terms. Not only was Black Power a rejection of integration according to the white person's agenda, but it was also a rejection of the "whiteness of our cultural values," the "number one enemy of Negro selfhood."[58] This is what CORE meant when it denounced integration at its twenty-fourth annual meeting. It is also what Albert B. Cleage, Jr., a black UCC minister from Detroit, meant when he declared that Jesus was black. Most white Christian leaders missed his point. They greatly despaired concerning the disparaging rhetoric about integration throughout the late 1960s. Those whites who had been involved so actively in the Civil Rights Movement, left it disillusioned and disappointed.[59]

In early July of 1966, several black leaders gathered at the request of Benjamin Payton in his office at the NCC headquarters in New York City. Among them were Gayraud Wilmore and Henderson R. Hughes, an A.M.E. minister in Harlem. Together they formed a caucus of black church leaders which they called the National Committee of Negro Churchmen (NCNC). At the end of July, forty-eight black leaders associated with the NCNC issued a statement in support of the Black Power movement, indicting the white structures of the church for their distortion of what the movement represented. The statement appeared as an advertisement in *The New York Times*. By the summer of 1967, Benjamin Payton had resigned his NCC position to take the presidency of Benedict College in South Carolina. This action symbolized well the end of significant influence in this area for the NCC. Payton's associations with church activism from that point on were funneled through his association with black church leaders.[60]

The NCC did sponsor, following Payton's resignation, a gathering of black and white church leaders, about 100 persons from seventeen denominations. The meeting took place in Washington, D.C. on September 30, with the intention to discuss the meaning of Black Power and the church's response to it. The conference ended up honoring the desire to meet separately, during some of the meeting time, in two caucuses, one black and the other white. The meeting culminated in two separate statements. White leaders offered a confession of white America's guilt and a recognition that society needed to be transformed. Black leaders issued a lengthy plea expressing their "disquietude" about the "nature and mission of the church in a time of revolution." The conference, in all its discussions and in both reports, completely replaced use of the word "Negro" with the word "black." From this point on, white church leaders slowly became educated about the fact that the word had become "a badge of dignity, [and had] a psychological significance that should not be treated lightly."[61] By mid-1968, most mainline Protestant writing substituted "black" for "Negro." Catholics followed shortly thereafter. That year, the NCNC also changed its name, becoming the National Committee of Black Churchmen (NCBC).

In November 1967, the committee issued a call for the development of "a theology relevant to the black revolution."[62] From the time of Cleage's statements about a black Jesus, through the late 1960s, black theology was in its nascent stages. The first systematic treatment was James Cone's *Black Theology and Black Power*, which appeared in 1969 and declared "Christ is black, baby, with all the features which are so detestable to white society." And, "Black power . . . is . . . Christ's central message to twentieth-century America."[63]

But for all this kind of rhetoric, black theology was really about liberation from oppression, which Cone saw to be the essential meaning of the gospel. It also meant to define a theology from the perspective of black experience, and free of the ultimate controlling influence of white experience. In this way, "blackness" came to symbolize the liberation of any of God's people who bear the "scars of oppression."[64] As Cone described it, black theology became "the religious counterpart" to the secular movement of black power.[65] The NCBC defined black theology in a statement issued June 13, 1969 at a meeting at the Interdenominational Theological Center in Atlanta:

> Black theology is a theology of black liberation. It seeks to plumb the black condition in the light of God's revelation in Jesus Christ, so that the black community can see that the gospel is commensurate with the achievement of black humanity. Black theology is a theology of "blackness." It is the affirmation of black humanity that emancipates black people from white racism, thus providing authentic freedom for both white and black people. It affirms the humanity of white people in that it says No to the encroachment of white oppression.[66]

The emergence of black power, of black theology, and then of black caucuses within most of the white mainline denominations, including the Catholic Church, led to a renewed emphasis on the vitality of the black church, a new concern to enrich theological education for blacks, and the development of a whole new area of black studies. As the black church worked out its understanding of these things, the white church was slow to respond and occasionally offensive in its expressions. Cone, for example, a United Methodist, had quickly gained a national reputation among blacks for his written work but was completely ignored by the leadership of his own denomination. During these years, the mainline churches struggled as well to understand how to respond to the concerns of their respective black caucuses. For their part, black theologians have been a diverse group from the beginning, and have experienced considerable difficulty communicating their theological approach to black pastors and to lay people in the black churches.[67]

As if Black Power and black theology were not disconcerting enough, the white Christian churches experienced a more direct blow in the Spring of 1969. On May 2, James Forman, the international affairs director for SNCC, made an unscheduled presentation to the NCC General Board of his "Manifesto to the White Christian Churches and the Jewish Synagogues in the United States of America and All Other Racist Institutions." The document came to be known as the Black Manifesto. And, initially, it rocked the world of the white churches.[68]

Forman's manifesto demanded $500 million in "reparations" from all church groups because of their complicity in the "capitalist and imperialist power structure." The money was to be spent for black publishing houses, TV networks, the establishment of a land bank for financing small cooperative black farms, a strike and defense fund, a black university, centers for training and research skills, and the establishment of an International Black Appeal, funded with about $20 million and to be headed by Forman. This latter organization intended to concentrate particularly on economic development in the black community. Forman's style of confrontation made it difficult for white leaders to support the manifesto.

Two days after the unscheduled presentation at the NCC, Forman interrupted the worship services at the Riverside Church in New York City to read the document. Supporters of Forman, mostly students, occupied Union Theological Seminary's administrative and instructional building and demanded that $100,000 be provided immediately, with a pledge to raise a million dollars for Forman's economic organization. The seminary responded with several promises to raise and to invest funds in black organizations, and in the Harlem community, but none of the money was promised to Forman's organization or placed directly under black community control. Students and other Forman supporters also occupied the offices of the NCC and other denominational offices located in the Interchurch Center in New York City. On June 9, the occupations accomplished a total work stoppage. As the building's demonstrations continued, the NCC, in desperation, took legal steps to secure a restraining order and court injunction prohibiting further demonstrations. After meeting with employees, the NCC dropped the legal actions. The actions, however, demonstrate just how confused and threatened church leadership was by Forman's actions.[69]

The specifications regarding the reparations formed the center of the manifesto. The beginning and ending of the document were filled with Marxist rhetoric, advocating that the means of production must be "taken from the rich people and placed into the hands of the state for the welfare of all the people."[70] In other words, the manifesto demanded a complete rejection of American democratic capitalism. The strategy of the white churches had been to ignore the more radical dimensions of the manifesto and to concentrate on what they might be able to raise to help black causes, giving no money directly to Forman's organization. But, as Howard Schomer, NCC director of specialized ministries, noted after the occupation of the NCC offices: "There can no longer be any doubt that the real thrust of James Forman's . . . challenge . . . lies in the introduction and the conclusion rather than in the programmatic demands of the manifesto proper." He spoke to the causes behind the reticence of the church once this realization hit home.

> In our effortless superiority to most of mankind we are accustomed to giving handouts to the respectful needy, near and far. We have never had occasion to move over, to share both possessions and power. We have had no experience whatsoever in confessing our own massive social guilt, offering proportionate restitution or standing contrite before the justice of a God who visits "the iniquity of the fathers upon

> the children and the children's children, to the third and the fourth generation." Our imagination simply fails to function when we are summoned to work for a social order in which we shall not be first.[71]

The church responded with funds, but with very limited funds. About $4 million had been budgeted and spent by the white churches for all causes related to race over the two years following the manifesto, not much more money than they would have spent without having heard the demands of the manifesto. The Catholic churches and Jewish synagogues did not respond to the manifesto in any form. Gayraud Wilmore put it bluntly: The white Christian responses to the manifesto, he wrote, "constitute a rather dismal example of how a constructive proposal for empowering a frustrated community can be talked to death by frightened and ambivalent white churchmen."[72]

It is not that the white churches were totally uninvolved in programs related to race relations during these years. Most mainline denominations had some kind of program addressing black and white relations. Most worked independently from one another and operated on limited budgets, competing for the same funds sought by the NCC. The NCC launched two programs, its "Crisis in the Nation" program in 1967, responding to the riots, and a ghetto program in 1968 that attempted to help low-income businesses in the ghettos. Neither program had much success.[73]

Muddled about, and somewhat threatened by, black power and black theology and what to make of them, and definitely threatened by the manifesto and the tendency toward growing black disgust with the white program of integration, the churches struggled in attempting to offer a proper response. After the manifesto, most denominations supported their black caucuses and temporarily found ways to support minority empowerment programs and to educate congregations about the perils of individual and institutional racism. They placed blacks in leadership positions. But none attempted answers to the main question raised by the manifesto, the question of economic justice.[74]

White Christian activism usually originated more from the activity of Christian leaders, ministers, and bureaucrats, than from the insistence of the people sitting in the pews of the church. Among others, this was one major difference between white and black churches working in civil rights.[75] Black church activism was always sustained and energized by an enthusiastic lay involvement. By 1968, polls showed that lay people wanted their leaders to be quiet about both blacks and Vietnam.[76] After 1965, white Christian leaders found themselves barraged by a variety of black activity they were unable to decipher. Some of it attacked them directly and put them on the defensive. This pressure from all sides, combined with the fact that white leaders were perplexed, meant there was very little chance that the white churches could invest much energy in this struggle for black equality.

Given this context, white Christian leaders were unable to imagine how to address economic equality for the black beyond funding various and limited philanthropic projects. Many, in good American fashion, actually believed economic equality would naturally result from the guarantee of individual rights. In other words, they settled comfortably into the muddle of a safe and middle position. They preferred charity, and support of the *status quo*, to the more difficult task of identifying and challenging the systemic heresy that, from a Christian perspective, infected many of the civil religious tenets undergirding the sanctity of the American economy.

The black experience enabled African American leaders in this country to separate "liberty" from "equality." They knew in their hearts that one could be free without being equal. Advocates of black power and systematizers of black theology tried to make that point. It was also the message of the "Black Manifesto." Together, these black radicals understood Madison much better than those in the church who occupied the muddled middle. Cleage, Carmichael, Cone, and Farmer, each in their own ways, attacked the myth that Americans had come through time to hold so dear, that liberty, in fact, meant equality. White liberty, when combined with both economic power and the mores of a community that assumed inequality, translated into a very unequal liberty for anyone who was both poor and black.

When the movement was about "liberty," the church, though slow to respond, finally transformed sympathy into activism and enthusiastically joined the fray. When the struggle for liberty was mostly won through a combination of the Civil Rights Act of 1964 and the Voting Rights Act of 1965, black leadership turned toward the struggle for "equality," and church support began to wane.

When the first symptoms of that struggle erupted in the urban ghettos of the North, the thinking of church leaders became muddled. Their clearest thinking cited the need for education in the ghettos, the need to provide jobs for black youths, and the need to integrate white neighborhoods. Blacks involved in the struggle increasingly translated these suggested solutions in light of their own experiences: "[L]et us teach you how to be white, exactly what you need to know to be like us," or "[W]ork for sorry wages in a dead-end job and things will be better," or "[I]f you can afford to live here and act like us, move on in." Few white leaders understood the inadequacy of these kinds of solutions, all of which were built upon the premise that liberty would automatically ensure equality eventually.[77]

White Christian leaders in the churches never really understood the distinctions blacks were making between liberty and equality. The actions of black youths in the ghettos of American cities were cries for equality, not for liberty. They were, perhaps above all, crude demands for equal access to the country's resources, something, after all their years of liberty in the North, they were still being denied. When these moderate to liberal leaders encountered the proposals of the black radicals suggesting a solution, they responded just like any other good American: They saw them as a threat to the American values of liberty and democracy. Should they have accepted these black proposals outright? No, probably not. Should they have at least understood them? Perhaps so. If they had, they may have had alternatives to suggest that would not have been "worse than the disease." Trouble is, they did not understand the disease. The bottom line is they acted as if the gospel itself had nothing relevant to say about the differences between liberty and equality. But surely it does—doesn't it?

Endnotes

1. Gayraud S. Wilmore, Jr., "The New Negro and the Church," *Christian Century* (6 February 1963): 169-171.

2. The NCC story relating to these points is told in James F. Findlay, Jr., *Church People in the Struggle: The National Council of Churches and the Black Freedom Movement, 1950-1970* (New York: Oxford University Press, 1993), 15-17.

3. Reinhold Niebuhr, "The Race Problem in America," *Christianity and Crisis* (26 December 1955); Niebuhr makes this point again in "School, Church, and the Ordeals of Integration," *Christianity and Crisis* (1 October 1956): 121-122. For actions

taken by denominations in these areas, see "The Churches and Race Relations," *Christianity and Crisis* (4 February 1957): 4-7.

4. Charles V. Hamilton makes a distinction between *de jure* segregation and *de facto* segregation in "Federal Law and the Courts in the Civil Rights Movement," in *The Civil Rights Movement in America*, ed. Charles W. Eagles (Jackson: University Press of Mississippi, 1986), 97-117.

5. The bishops' statement is quoted in "The Bishops on Race," *Commonweal* (28 November 1958): 219-220.

6. Incredible as it may seem, *Christianity Today* completely ignored the activities of Martin Luther King, Jr. King's name was not even mentioned in those pages until 1964 when editors noted in two sentences that he had been chosen *Time's* "Man of the Year." In November, one sentence announced his winning of the Nobel Peace Prize. And in 1966, the example of King was used by editors to demonstrate concern with "lawlessness as a sign of our times." In short, Martin Luther King was not highly regarded by the magazine.

7. The following listings are not comprehensive but representative of writing about these topics. On praise for non-violence, see, for example, Waldo Beach, "The Courage of Self-Restraint," *Christianity and Crisis* (14 October 1957): 129-130; "Race Violence Will Defeat Itself," *Christian Century* (17 September 1958): 1046; Lauren A. Smith, "Saints in the Basement," *Christian Century* (17 September 1958): 1050-1052. On unqualified support for King, see "Decision on Bus Segregation," *America* (15 December 1956): 315; Waldo Beach, "Grace Amid Judgment," *Christianity and Crisis* (4 February 1957): 1-2; Wayne H. Cowan, "Racism in Reverse," *Christianity and Crisis* (23 June 1958): 87; Harold E. Fey, "An Announcement," *Christian Century* (8 October 1958): 1135; "Negroes in America," *Commonweal* (14 April 1961): 67-68. For King's essays, see King, "Nonviolence and Racial Justice," *Christian Century* (6 February 1957): 165-167; King, "The Church and The Race Crisis," *Christian Century* (8 October 1958): 1140-1141; King, "Pilgrimage to Nonviolence," *Christian Century* (13 April 1960): 439-441; King, "Suffering and Faith," *Christian Century* (27 April 1960): 510; and most importantly, King, "Letter from Birmingham Jail," *Christian Century* (12 June 1963): 767-773, the first appearance of which was in these pages. For examples of support concerning NAACP, see "NAACP's Right to Exist," *America* (27 October 1956): 88; "Basic Freedom Menaced in Attack on NAACP," *Christian Century* (17 July 1957): 860; "The Spirit of the NAACP," *America* (27 July 1957): 435-436. On Montgomery, see "The Montgomery Victory," *Commonweal* 11 November 1956): 222; "Decision on Bus Segregation," *America* (15 December 1956): 315; "Alabama's Plea Denied by Court," *Christian Century* (9 January 1957): 60-61; and Waldo Beach, "Grace Amid Judgment," *Christianity and Crisis* (4 February 1957): 1-2. For Little Rock, see, for example, "Treason in Arkansas," *Christian Century* (18 September 1957): 1091-1092; "The President and the Governor," *Commonweal* (4 October 1957): 5-6; John LaFarge, "Decision at Little Rock," *America* (5 July 1958): 384; Waldo Beach, "Authority, Consent and Racial Justice," *Christianity and Crisis* (29 September 1958): 125-126; Ernest Q. Campbell and Thomas F. Pettigrew, "Men of God in Racial Crisis," *Christian Century* (4 June 1958): 663-665; and Colbert S. Cartwright, "Lesson from Little Rock," *Christian Century* (9 October 1957): 1193-1194. On sit-ins, see "Unrest Grows Among American Negroes," *Christian Century* (24 February 1960): 212-213; "Negro Protests," *Commonweal* (1 April 1960): 4-5; "Platforms and Sit-Ins," *America* (13 August 1960): 527. On freedom riders, see "Violence in Alabama," *Commonweal* (2 June 1961): 244; "Violence in Alabama," *America* (3 June 1961): 388; "ICC Acts to End Discrimination," *Christian Century* (4 October 1961): 1165.

8. For Simon's article, Paul Simon, "Montgomery Looks Forward," *Christian Century* (22 January 1958): 104-105; for a record of Andrew M. Greeley's comments, see Greeley, *America* (19 March 1960): 233-235. For the southern minister's diatribe, see

Roy C. DeLamotte, "Southern Liberal: Prophet or Apostate?" *Christian Century* (1 May 1957): 555-556. On Niebuhr, see Niebuhr, "The Race Problem in America," *Christianity and Crisis* (26 December 1955): 169. For Wilmore, see "The New Negro and the Church," *Christian Century* (6 February 1963): 168-171.

9. Most essays during this period in mainline Christian journals stressed the immorality of segregation. Cushing is quoted in "Episcopal Leadership," *America* (12 September 1964): 249; see also, "A Sense of the Essential," *Christian Century* (18 September 1957): 1092, where the editor stresses that "moral factors make the crucial difference in a world choosing up sides;" and Robert McAfee Brown, "Levittown and Little Rock," *Christianity and Crisis* (28 October 1957): 138. For nonviolence will win out, see "Race Violence Will Defeat Itself," *Christian Century* (17 September 1958): 1046. For the quote of the minister, "Money Talks on Race," *America* (17 June 1961): 435; for another example of economic optimism, "Race Tension is Costly," *Christian Century* (13 September 1961): 1068.

10. The limits of congregational life for the Protestant are discussed in Niebuhr, "School, Church, and the Ordeals of Integration," *Christianity and Crisis* (1 October 1956): 121-122; and Beach, "The Southern Churches and the Race Question," *Christianity and Crisis* (3 March 1958): 17-18.

11. Niebuhr, "Bad Days at Little Rock," *Christianity and Crisis* (4 February 1957): 131.

12. The poll of Southern clergy conducted in 1958 by *Pulpit Digest* is referenced in "Episcopalians on Racial Peace," *Commonweal* (1 November 1958): 123. Reinhold Niebuhr wrote in 1957, ". . . the white Protestant churches are not found wanting in regard to their leadership, but are found wanting in regard to their lay opinion;" see Niebuhr, "The Effect of the Supreme Court Decision," *Christianity and Crisis* (4 February 1957): 3. For the results of the Maryland preferential poll, see ""Episcopal Leadership," *America* (12 September 1968): 249. On the United Church of Christ, see "Who Won the Election? The Negro or White Bigotry?" *Christian Century* (9 November 1966): 1369.

13. Stressing the success of the movement, see "Reporting Desegregation," *Commonweal* (10 June 1955): 245-246; and "Integration Advances," *America* (17 March 1956): 655. On tokenism, see "Then There Were Three," *Christian Century* (1 February 1961): 133-134; "Rights Commission Findings," *Christian Century* (15 February 1961): 196-197; as time passed, tokenism was less worthy of applause: see "Tokenism Frustrates Negro Hopes," *Christian Century* (20 March 1963): 357. Optimism in education and the power of the law, see "Mississippi Musings," *America* (29 March 1958): 742; "Civil-Rights Debate," *America* (27 July 1957): 439; "Civil Rights: A Giant Step," *Commonweal* (19 August 1960): 414. Support for early civil rights legislation is clear throughout these years; on lamenting the lack of government enforcement power in new civil rights law, see "White Thursday for Civil Rights," *America* (14 September 1957): 611; on supporting the lack of enforcement in favor of giving the South time for education and conversion to wisdom in race relations to occur, see "A Stitch in Time," *Christian Century* (26 February 1958): 245-247. Later, the *Century*, still with liberal confidence in the law, urged stronger laws to be passed: "Urge Congress to Aid Civil Rights," *Christian Century* (10 February 1960): 157; and "Strong Federal Vote Law Needed," *Christian Century* (10 August 1960): 916-917. Recognition of the political give-and-take of the battle is found in "Civil Rights Program," *Commonweal* (27 April 1956): 88-89; "Civil Rights," *Commonweal* (19 July 1957): 387-388; "Permission From Above, Pressure From Below," *Christian Century* (11 September 1957): 1059-1060. Ethical realism based on "accepted values" see F. Ernest Johnson, "Segregation and Federal Aid," *Christianity and Crisis* (25 June 1956): 82-83; for another example of the lack of analysis on the foundation of these accepted values, see where one liberal Protestant argues for integration of white neighborhoods by using an "impartial commission to review applications and to see

to it that all candidates belong to a certain general economic and cultural level;" see Robert E. Fitch, "My Negro Neighbor Next Door," *Christian Century* (8 May 1957): 589-591. For realism expressing some optimism in the law, but recognizing the need to act as quickly as possible is expressed by Roger L. Shinn, "Civil Rights in the Election," *Christianity and Crisis* (19 September 1960): 126-127.

14. King noticed the problem as well: "We see the new nations of Africa and Asia moving at jet speed toward independence and, on the other hand, we see ourselves to be moving at horse-and-buggy speed just to get a cup of coffee at a lunch counter." Quoted in Stephen C. Rose, "Test for Nonviolence," *Christian Century* (29 May 1963): 714-716; a very similar quote appears in King's "Letter from Birmingham Jail;" see that essay in *Christian Century* (12 June 1963), particularly p. 768.

15. James O' Gara, "Muhammad Speaks," *Commonweal* (26 April 1963): 130.

16. See Stringfellow, "Race, Religion and Revenge," *Christian Century* (14 February 1962): 192-194. James Cone indicates that white America's introduction to Malcolm X and Black Muslims came with their appearance in a documentary presented on the "Mike Wallace Show" in late 1959. See Cone, *Martin & Malcolm & America: A Dream or a Nightmare* (Maryknoll: Orbis Books, 1991), 100. For some of the earliest references found in these journals, see "Nationalism, Not Separatism," *America* (20 August 1960): 550-551; "Negroes in America," *Commonweal* (14 April 1961): 67-68; "The Fight's Not Over," *Commonweal* (5 May 1961): 141; "All, Here and Now," *Christian Century* (28 June 1961): 787-788.

17. There were, of course, exceptions. Not all Protestant leaders had sympathy for the movement during these years. Carl F.H. Henry, a Presbyterian and one of the most influential evangelical leaders in America, expressed serious reservations about the wisdom of government policy. Other evangelical authors agreed with him. The major outlet for their opinions was the evangelical fortnightly, *Christianity Today*, a magazine with a circulation of more than 200,000 copies in the late 1950s. The arguments these evangelical editors and authors set out can conveniently be divided into social and theological categories. From a social perspective, they opposed growing governmental power and decried the tendency in this country to turn the Supreme Court into a "policy-making" body. They urged protection of individual rights above all else; in their dictionary, that meant the government should not step in to impose restrictions on what individuals could do with their own personal property, whether that property was home or business. With the events in the South, that position generally translated into a strong expression of support "for state's rights over an ever-increasing power of the federal government." See, "Color Line in State University: A Wobbly Defense of Freedom," *Christianity Today* (12 October 1962): 30. It is interesting, given an evangelical pietism stressing the individual's relationship before God with no intermediaries, that *Christianity Today* often argued segregation as a state's rights issue. Evangelical theological arguments emphasized a need for the Christian to recognize a distinction between the kingdom of God and the kingdom of this world. As Carl F. H. Henry described it, the "movement of fallen history is downward; entrance to the kingdom of God comes only through individual rebirth." Such a separation between history and the kingdom of God meant clearly that no secular programs should ever be identified "as essentially and authentically Christian." See, Henry, "Perspective for Social Action: Part I," *Christianity Today* (19 January 1959): 9-11. The evangelical understanding of integration represented in *Christianity Today* during these years serves to verify anthropologist Mary Douglas's insight that "people really do think of their own social environment as consisting of other people joined or separated by lines which must be respected." See Mary Douglas, *Purity and Danger* (Baltimore: Penguin, 1966), 165. Evangelicals did not consider themselves racists. But they were mostly blind to the immorality of segregation as a cultural practice. Part of the iconic symbol system operating at this time clearly defined where blacks stood in relation to the white culture. Though these evangelical voices defended equality for blacks, they usually

meant an equality that did not or could not impact where they themselves lived. The power of the iconic assumption that blacks had "their place," and it was in a location other than whites enjoyed, carried considerable weight with these editors, even though they never phrased it quite so blatantly. The assumption, of course, was not limited to the evangelical community.

18. Niebuhr, "The Mounting Racial Crisis," *Christianity and Crisis* (8 July 1963): 121-122; see also Catholic notice of the dying patience among African Americans, "Law is Not Enough," *America* (22 June 1963): 879.

19. This action is covered in "Peace with Justice," *Commonweal* (31 May 1963): 268.

20. Martin Luther King Jr., "Letter from Birmingham Jail," *Christian Century* (12 June 1963): 767-773, see particulary p. 772.

21. See the discussion of bail money made as an aside in "Congress' Fateful Decision," *Christian Century* (30 October 1963): 1323-1324. Findlay discusses this aspect of the NCC's work in greater detail on pp. 78-80.

22. Details on the NCC developments are found in Findlay, *Church People in the Struggle,* 34-38; all these activities are briefly addressed in "The Testing of the Church," *Christianity and Crisis* (8 July 1963): 122-123. On the Catholic Theological Society resolution, see "Catholics and Race," *America* (13 July 1963): 33. The bishop's pastoral is mentioned in Elmer A. Spreitzer, "On the Road to Washington," *America* (12 October 1963): 426. For the story on nine Catholic priests, Trueblood Mattingly, "Gwynn Oak," *America* (10 August 1963): 136-137; Cardinal Ritter's comment is found in "Priests' Pledge on Race," *America* (5 October 1963): 376.

23. These words were written before the march on Washington in late August, but were not published until October: Robert McAfee Brown, "The Race Race," *Commonweal* (11 October 1963): 73-75.

24. See John LaFarge's account of this meeting, "Church Leaders Stand Up To Be Counted," *America* (29 June 1963): 897. This story is also told in Findlay, 48.

25. James Findlay's considerable research indicates the efforts of the NCC produced measurable success on both fronts. See Findlay, *Church People in the Struggle*, 48-75. The *Century* took notice of the success of grass-roots efforts when it pointed to the large numbers of church letters legislators were receiving, "A Straw in the Racial Wind," *Christian Century* (18 September 1963): 1123.

26. For an example of handwringing, see "Demonstrations or Threats," *Christian Century* (10 July 1963): 877-878; this editorial was most likely written by Harold Fey, who supported the march with his writing and his presence, but nonetheless worried that it might turn violent. The figure of 40,000 is found in a discussion of the event in "Congress' Fateful Decision," *Christian Century* (30 October 1963): 1323-1324. Findlay uses the same figure; see Findlay, *Church People in the Struggle*, 50. The Catholic organizational count was made by Elmer A. Spreitzer, "On the Road to Washington," *America* (12 October 1963): 426-427. The evangelical critique is presented by William Henry Anderson, Jr., Pastor of a Presbyterian church in Pittsburgh, "Evangelicals and the Race Revelation," *Christianity Today* (25 October 1963): 6-8; as one might expect, *Christianity Today* editorial staff was opposed to the March on Washington, see "Mob Pressures For Social Change," *Christianity Today* (30 August 1963): 34; and "Protestant Conscience on Race Issues," *Christianity Today* (25 October 1963): 26-27. Support for the March was regularly expressed in the other journals. See, for example, "March on Washington," *America* (10 August 1963): 131; "Marching Orders," *Christian Century* (21 August 1963): 1021-1022; "A Last Resort," *America* (24 August 1963): 188; "The Meaning of the March," *Christian Century* (28 August 1963): 1043; Bennett, "The Churches and Civil Rights," *Christianity and Crisis* (16 September 1963): 153-154; Robert McAfee Brown, "The Race Race," *Commonweal* (11 October 1963): 73-75.

27. See, for example, William J. Davis, "Mrs. Murphy's Private Rights," *America* (19 October 1963): 454-456; "Showdown in the Senate," *America* (22 February 1964): 247; for this particular evangelical view, see "In Defense of Property Rights," *Christianity Today* (11 September 1964): 32; for example of evangelical support of the civil rights legislation, see "Civil Rights Legislation," *Christianity Today* (22 November 1963): 31-32.

28. For an accounting of various church activities in this regard: "Congress' Fateful Decision," *Christian Century* (30 October 1963): 1323-1324; and Roger L. Shinn, "Civil Rights: Morality and Practical Politics," *Christianity and Crisis* (11 November 1963): 197-198. For Strom Thurmond's comments, see "Civil Rights Strategy," *America* (11 April 1964): 500.

29. Findlay believes the radical religious right in the 1980s went to school on the example of these kinds of liberal efforts in the summer and fall of 1963. He is likely accurate in that conclusion. See Findlay, *Church People in the Struggle*, 63.

30. On Humphrey's comments, see "Only a Beginning," *America* (13 June 1964): 809; Niebuhr, "Man, the Unregenerate Tribalist," *Christianity and Crisis* (6 July 1964): 133-134. The *Century*, on the other hand, wrote optimistically that the passage of the bill would likely stop the threat of violence; see "A Man's Step Forward in Civil Rights," *Christian Century* (24 June 1964): 820. The vote of the Senate was also recorded in this editorial.

31. James Cone offers a summary of King's response to the civil Rights Act of 1964, and of the conversation between King and Johnson, in Cone, *Martin & Malcom of America: A Dream or a Nightmare,* (Maryknoll: Orbis Books, 1991), 216.

32. Findlay has written a very helpful, analytical, and detailed description of the involvement of the churches in these events in *Church People in the Struggle*, 76-110. These paragraphs rely on his work for basic information. Evangelical criticism is found in "Troubled Waters," *Christianity Today* (17 July 1964): 23. The second quote is from "Murder is Murder - Anywhere," *Christianity Today* (28 August 1964): 30-31. The Harris poll results are covered in "Whose Backyard?" *America* (22 August 1964): 178.

33. For the statistics cited here on voters in Mississippi, see "Disgrace of Mississippi," *America* (4 July 1964): 8-9; and the 6.7% figure comes from "Hopes of Progress," *Commonweal* (4 September 1964): 591-592; see also Robert W. Spike, "In the Midst of Revolution," *Christianity and Crisis* (8 June 1964): 114; and Stephen C. Rose, "Why They Go to Mississippi," *Christianity and Crisis* (3 August 1964): 158-159.

34. See Findlay's extended analysis of the Delta Ministry, *Church People in the Struggle*, 76-168.

35. The statistics are from "The Selma Campaign," *Commonweal* (26 February 1965): 684-685; and Dean Peerman and Martin E. Marty, "Selma: Sustaining the Momentum," *Christian Century* (24 March 1965): 358-360. King had stayed in Atlanta rather than make the march himself, because those around him feared for his safety. As soon as he heard of the violence, he went directly to Selma.

36. On the diversity between SCLC and SNCC, see Arlie Schardt, "Tension, Not Split, in the Negro Ranks," *Christian Century* (12 May 1965): 614-616.

37. For church coverage of Reeb's memorial service, see Niebuhr, "Civil Rights Climax in Alabama," *Christianity and Crisis* (5 April 1965): 61; and Mary McGrory, "So Much Christian Unity in Selma," *America* (3 April 1965): 448. On LBJ and the Voting Rights Act, see Findlay, *Church People in the Struggle*, 169.

38. Evangelicals continued their opposition to these demonstrations: "The Clergy March on Alabama," *Christianity Today* (26 March 1965): 40-41; and "The Awakening of National Conscience," *Christianity Today* (9 April 1965): 32. On Jonathan Myrick Daniels, see "Catalyst for Reconciliation," *Christian Century* (8 September

1965): 1084-1085. Cone's analysis of King's change is found in *Martin & Malcolm & America*, especially 220-243.

39. "The South's Option," *Christian Century* (21 April 1965): 483-484; for another expression of optimism, see J.N. Eller, "The Test: A Vote for Everyone Anywhere," *America* (10 April 1965): 476. On Mississippi voters, see "Two Primaries in Mississippi," *America* (9 September 1967): 234.

40. Charles V. Hamilton, "Federal Law and the Courts in the Civil Rights Movement," in *The Civil Rights Movement in America*, ed. Charles W. Eagles (Jackson: University Press of Mississippi, 1986), 116. William H. Chafe's essay in the same book examines this shift in greater detail: Chafe, "The End of One Struggle, The Beginning of Another," in *The Civil Rights Movement in America*, 127-148.

41. Chafe stresses the connection civil rights leaders made between racial equality and economic equality in "The End of One Struggle, The Beginning of Another," 132f.

42. Cone makes this point in *Martin & Malcolm & America*, 222.

43. See the response of J. Mills Thornton, III, to Chafe, in *The Civil Rights Movement in America*, 150.

44. On fear of the upcoming "long, hot summer," see "Summer and Civil Rights," *Commonweal* (19 June 1964): 384; "Of Many Things,"*America* (2 May 1964): 583; and "The Time for Pretending is Past," *Christianity and Crisis* (8 May 1964): 109-110; and "Racial Violence," *Commonweal* (7 August 1964): 528. For fear of white backlash, see "Race Violence in New York" *America* (8 August 1964): 98; "Negro Leaders Ban Demonstrations," *Christian Century* (12 August 1964): 1005; and "To Demonstrate or Not,"*America* (15 August 1964): 146.

45. On the riots and white Christian response to them, the Catholic response is a good example: see Thurston E. Davis, "Of Many Things," *America* (8 August 1964): 117; "Harlem: Some Reflections," *America* (8 August 1964): 125; and "The Dreaded Summer," *America* (12 September 1964): 244; see also the *Century* editorial downplaying the significance of the riots that had occurred: "What Happened to the Long Hot Summer?" *Christian Century* (14 October 1964): 1261. This response was true of Protestants and Catholics throughout the riots of 1964-1967; see, for example, "Anatomy of a Riot," *Christian Century* (9 February 1966): 164-165.

46. The indented quote is from "F.B.I. Reports on Summer Riots," *Christian Century* (14 October 1964): 1261-1262; the F.B.I. report was also quoted and endorsed in "The FBI Report," *America* (10 October 1964): 404-405; and "FBI Report," *Commonweal* (23 October 1964): 119.

47. Robert W. Spike, "Probing the Riots," *Christianity and Crisis* (21 September 1964): 170-171.

48. C. Lawson Crowe, "Rights and Differences: Some Notes for Liberals," *Christian Century* (4 November 1964): 1359-1360.

49. "Does Anyone Really Care?" *Christian Century* (22 September 1965): 1148.

50. See, for example, "The American Negro Family," *America* (30 October 1965): 492; "Negro Family Life," *Commonweal* (26 November 1965): 229-230; Mary McGrory, "Blackout on the Moynihan Report," *America* (11 December 1965).

51. This paragraph is dependent on the discussion of Findlay, *Church People in the Struggle*, 178-182. *Commonweal* denounced the NCC rejection of the Moynihan Report. See "Negro Family Life," *Commonweal* (26 November 1965): 229-230.

52. Various essays were written in the independent journals encouraging more housing, better jobs and better pay, the need for addressing education in the ghettos, etc., but church (and government) action was limited. See "Anatomy of a Riot," *Christian Century* (9 February 1966): 164-65; Thurston E. Davis. "Of Many Things," *America*

(25 June 1966): 869; Maurice R. Berube, "White Liberals, Black Schools: The Proliferation of Ghetto Schools in the North," *Commonweal* (21 October 1966): 71-73.

53. Malcolm Boyd, "Violence or Nonviolence in the Deep South?" *Christian Century* (15 September 1965): 1126-1128.

54. "Negro Strategy," *Commonweal* (30 September 1966): 626-627. Editors at *Commonweal* expressed their belief that nonviolence was the better route, but did not feel they had the right to advise blacks on the matter: "Which Way Now?" *Commonweal* (8 July 1966): 430-431. Roger L. Shinn defended black power in an editorial in *Christianity and Crisis*, see Shinn, "Is Racial Hostility Ever a Gain?" *Christianity and Crisis* (16 October 1967): 225-226. Essay length defenses of Black Power came from Frank Millspaugh, "Black Power," *Commonweal* (5 August 1966): 500-503; and Margaret Halsey, "Integration Has Failed," *Christian Century* (28 December 1966): 1596-1597; Charles E. Fager, "White Reflections on Black Power," *Christian Century* (10 August 1966): 980-983; and John D. Maguire, "Thoughts on Black and White," *Christianity and Crisis* (8 January 1968): 311-312.

55. See "Negro Leaders on Black Power," *America* (29 October 1966): 501, where editors described this statement and King's refusal to sign it.

56. For example, see "The Pseudo-Power of Black Power," *America* (23 July 1966): 89; *America* talks of the withdrawal of white support in "Dr. King's Case for Nonviolence," *America* (12 November 1966): 578. *Christianity Today* described Black Power as "profoundly disquieting," see "Playing with Fire," *Christianity Today* (29 September 1966) 33-34. The *Century* spoke of the divisions in the Civil Rights Movement between SCLC, NAACP, and the Urban League on the one hand, SNCC and CORE, and black nationalist movements on the other. The *Century* editors sided with the former: "Black Power for Whom?" *Christian Century* (20 July 1966): 903-904; see also "Negro Leaders on Black Power,' *America* (29 October 1966): 501. When Dick Gregory, a Black Power advocate, was arrested for battery and resisting arrest and found guilty by an all-white jury, he declared that an all-white jury was unconstitutional. A *Century* editorial saw no justification for such an argument: "Inverted Racism," *Christian Century* (4 May 1966): 575-576.

57. Cone, *Martin, Malcolm, & America*, 227-235.

58. Margaret Halsey, "Integration Has Failed," *Christian Century* (28 December 1966): 1596-1597. The last quotes concerning white cultural values are from Charles Fager, "White Reflections on Black Power," *Christian Century* (10 August 1966): 980-983.

59. See, for example, the *Century* editorials dealing with these two events: "CORE Leaps without Looking," *Christian Century* (19 July 1967): 931-932; and, on Cleage, "Integration: Desirable and Possible," *Christian Century* (12 April 1967): 459-460; and, "The Incredibility of Integration," *Christian Century* (6 September 1968): 1391-1392. Cleage's book was published the next year, *The Black Messiah* (New York: Sheed and Ward, 1968). Occasionally, this white attitude degenerated into outright paternalism: "They [whites who want an excuse for indifference] ignore the fact that men in the grip of despair, proud men whose last hope has been crushed, do not always say precisely what they mean . . . This new mood among many Negroes poses problems for whites who are conscientiously devoted to the welfare of Negroes. How to be helpful without being condescendingly charitable, . . . how to let Negroes make their own mistakes without rushing in with abortive attempts to rescue them. These are some of the problems produced by the new mood among Negroes." "The Greater the Progress the More Difficult the Problem," *Christian Century* (29 November 1967): 1517-1518. For an example of those who left it disillusioned and disappointed, see Sarah Patton Boyle and John Howard Griffin, "The Racial Crisis: An Exchange of Letters," *Christian Century* (22 May 1968): 679-683.

60. See Findlay, *Church People in the Struggle*, 183-184.

61. The details of the conference are found in "A Fresh Look At Black America," *Christian Century* (25 October 1967): 1340-1341.

62. See the history of the NCNC in Grant S. Shockley, "Ultimatum and Hope," *Christian Century* (12 February 1969): 217-219.

63. James Cone, *Black Theology and Black Power* (New York: Seabury Press, 1969), 1, 68.

64. The quote is from Cone, in James Cone and William Hordern, "Dialogue on Black Theology," *Christian Century* (15 September 1971): 1079-1080, 1085. See also Cone's book *A Black Theology of Liberation* (New York: J.P. Lippincott Co., 1970). Mary Daly criticized Cone's second book for its blindness with respect to the oppression suffered by women: Daly, "Revelation Is A Black Event," *Commonweal* (26 February 1971): 529-530. Some ten years later, Cone reflected on how his mind changed about the oppression of women; see James H. Cone, "The Gospel and the Liberation of the Poor," *Christian Century* (18 February 1981): 162-166.

65. James Cone, "Black Theology and Black Liberation," *Christian Century* (16 September 1970): 1084-1088.

66. The statement is published in "Black Theology: A Statement of The National Committee of Black Churchmen," *Christian Century* (15 October 1969): 1310.

67. On renewed concern for the black church and for black theological education, see C. Shelby Rooks, "Theological Education and the Black Church," *Christian Century* (12 February 1969): 212-216; and J. Deotis Roberts, "Black Theological Education: Programming for Liberation," *Christian Century* (6 February 1972): 117-118. On the development of black studies programs: "Black Studies: Yes or No?" *America* (17 May 1969): 578-579; "Standards for Black Studies," *Christian Century* (10 September 1969): 1153; and "Black Studies: Fuse or Pacifier?" *America* (23 May 1970): 548-549. On Cone, Cornish Rogers, "James Cone and the Methodists," *Christian Century* (17 November 1971): 1340-1341. On confusion as to how to respond to the caucuses, see, for example among Catholics, Richard Rashke, "Trust for Black Caucuses?" *Commonweal* (20 March 1970): 35-37; "Federal Effort to End Racism," *America* (16 November 1968): 461. And, among the United Church of Christ, "Race and Riots Engage United Church," *Christianity Today* (21 July 1967): 38-39. An example of a negative evangelical response is in Barbara H. Kuehn, "A Separate Black Church Ahead?" *Christianity Today* (22 November 1968): 40-41. Not all blacks supported these developments either. Joseph Jackson, long-time president of the black National Baptists called upon his convention to repudiate black theology: "Negro Baptist Leader Calls Black Theology Racist," *Christian Century* (29 September 1971): 1128. The work of J. Deotis Roberts demonstrates the diversity of black theology early on: see his book *Liberation and Reconciliation: A Black Theology* (Philadelphia: The Westminster Press, 1971); see also William Jones, "Toward an Interim Assessment of Black Theology," *Christian Century* (3 May 1972): 513-517. On the difficulty of communicating the concerns of black theology to pastors and lay people, see, for example, Gayraud S. Wilmore, "Black Theology: Raising the Questions," *Christian Century* (20 June 77): 645-646; James Henry Harris, "Practicing Liberation in the Black Church," *Christian Century* (13 June 1990): 599-602; and Gayraud Wilmore, "Connecting Two Worlds: A Response to James Henry Harris," *Christian Century* (13 June 1990): 602-603.

68. Alan Geyer, "May Day in Manhattan," *Christian Century* (14 May 1969): 671-672; and "Will the Black Manifesto Help Blacks?" *Christian Century* (21 May 1969): 701. The manifesto and the response of the NCC is covered extensively in Findlay, *Church People in the Struggle*, 199-236.

69. See Howard Schomer, "The Manifesto and the Magnificat," *Christian Century* (25 June 1969): 866-867, where the story of the takeover of the building is discussed; see also Findlay, *Church People in the Struggle*, 204-206.

70. The manifesto is reprinted in Gayraud Wilmore and James Cone, eds., *Black Theology: A Documentary History, 1966-1979* (Maryknoll: Orbis Books, 1986), 80-89.

71. Howard Schomer, "The Manifesto and the Magnificat," *Christian Century* (25 June 1969): 866-867.

72. On Catholic and Jewish response, see "Black Over White," *Commonweal* (30 May 1969): 308-309; and Cornish Rogers, "White Ethnics and Black Empowerment," *Christian Century* (18 November 1970): 1372-73. The *Century* editorial referred to is "Get Ready for Economics!" *Christian Century* (14 April 1971): 451; and Wilmore, "The Black Manifesto Revisited," *Christian Century* (14 April 1971): 452-453.

73. On competition between the denominational programs and the NCC programs, see Alan Geyer, "May Day in Manhattan," *Christian Century* (14 May 1969): 671-672; for the "Crisis" program, see Findlay, *Church People in the Struggle*, 188; on the ghetto program, see "NCC Launches Ghetto Program," *Christian Century* (17 April 1968): 476.

74. On churchly analysis of benign neglect in the Nixon administration, see John David Maguire, "Benign Neglect or Malignant Concern?" *Christianity and Crisis* (13 April 1970): 65-66; and "A Question of Neglect," *Commonweal* (17 December 1971): 268. On a good analysis of denominational activities following the manifesto, see Gary L. Chamberlain, "Has Benign Neglect Invaded the Churches?" *Christian Century* (24 April 1974): 448-51.

75. The point is made in Findlay, *Church People in the Struggle*, 223.

76. "Making an Impact," *Christian Century* (1 May 1968): 576.

77. Harvey Cox is an example of one who did seem to understand the need for a different approach: see "The Riots: No Winners - Only Losers," *Christianity and Crisis* (7 August 1967): 181-182, where he recommended quadrupling the poverty budget and putting "it directly into the hands of black neighborhood groups rather than sifting it through the sticky tentacles of city hall poverty offices." He offered other suggestions here that seemed to imply the only solutions that would work needed to include black control over resources provided for them until they were able to provide their own resources. Of the independent journals used as primary sources here, *Christianity and Crisis* came closest to expressing an understanding of these problems. Roger L. Shinn, for example, following the riots of 1967: "Some day, we can hope, equality will be real. Then men will learn to reason together. The black man will state his mind, neither suppressing his thoughts out of traditional fear nor parading his militance because that is the current style. The white man will listen and respond, freed from prejudiced disagreement or guilt-induced strain to agree. And we shall all recognize each other as human beings, in part victims of our history and in part responsible for our sins." See Shinn, "Is Racial Hostility Ever a Gain?" *Christianity and Crisis* (16 October 1967): 225-226. But few of these authors offered suggestions touching on systemic change, or recognized a distinction between liberty and equality.

Imagination and Improvisation: Holy Play

Janet R. Walton
UNION THEOLOGICAL SEMINARY
NEW YORK, NEW YORK

The man bent over his guitar,
A shearsman of sorts. The day was green.

They said, "You have a blue guitar,
You do not play things as they are."

The man replied, "Things as they are
Are changed upon the blue guitar."

And they said then, "But play, you must,
A tune beyond us, yet ourselves,

A tune upon the blue guitar
Of things exactly as they are."[1]

A blue guitar. Out of the ordinary, strange, maybe disturbing. Its sounds are beyond us and yet ourselves. Things are changed upon a blue guitar. Throughout this poem, Wallace Stevens invites the reader to *play* with this metaphor, that is, to hear it, to see it, to grapple with it in a context of other images, rhythms, and sounds. By stoking our memories and evoking our imaginations, Stevens accompanies readers into a creative moment. He invites us to play, to let our creative capacities engage this blue guitar. Why blue? What kinds of sounds? Why is it urgent to play? How are the sounds beyond us, yet ourselves? Not every reader will care, but for some, those who suspend disbelief for even a moment, they will discover something; they will sense what a blue guitar says about themselves and about the world we live in.

Twenty years ago, liturgical scholar Joseph Gelineau called contemporary churches to a similar kind of *play* in worship. He challenged churches to play with its symbols as if throwing balls to one another.[2] Gelineau was concerned that churches were missing the point of coming together. They were not modeling a way of life in their liturgies. The problem, as Gelineau pointed out, was the way churches used their symbols. He decried the persistent attempts to control their interpretations as if there were predetermined meanings that a community must get. Such control undermined the symbols' power, in fact, contradicted their purpose. It would be as if Wallace Stevens *told* us what a blue guitar did rather than letting readers figure it out for themselves. Gelineau urged churches to find ways to engage their symbols, to play with them, so that persons could discover the symbols' meanings for themselves. He offered an example from his congregation's experience of water in the Easter Vigil.

> The congregation moved in procession to a room next to the nave. The room was in total darkness except for a spotlight in the ceiling over a large bowl of water.... The passage through the dark room with the bowl of water was entirely silent. When people entered the room, they looked at the water; some made the sign of the cross, some drank, some sprinkled themselves or splashed water over their heads; some did nothing.[3]

Gelineau comments: "Everyone had to find a meaning in this event, to situate themselves in relation to it, to take a stand".[4] When members of a congregation are *expected* to respond, to be interactive participants, they are involved in improvisation, that is, holy play. In this example, each person made a choice from a varied repertoire of possibilities. By making their own decisions, whether it was to do nothing or to splash water over their heads, they brought their own particular life experiences into some dialogue with what was happening in this ritual through the use of water. It was a time for discovery, for body-mediated knowledge, for play.

Of course, those who came into the room already knew something about the significance of water in general and about its role in this particular liturgical setting as a reminder of each person's baptism. But every experience is new, informed by whatever is currently happening. This specific experience invited each person to remember everything learned about water and about baptism and to let those memories flood into this experience to enrich it. A ritual experience does not stop with what we remember, it goes beyond the past and adds knowledge from the present moment. Maybe a sign of the cross with water reminds us of the beauty of our bodies and our ability to bless each other with these bodies. Maybe splashing ourselves with water, something never thought about until the moment of doing it, encourages breaking open other patterns in our lives. With no prescribed response, the choice comes from within each person. The leaders of the community act as coaches. They set the context through the environment: its sounds, its silence, the light, the way people are together. What happened depends. It depends on what each member of the community desires or can do in the moment.

A Call to Religious Institutions

The onset of the millennium, when many people are attending even more closely to their own spiritual resources, is challenging traditional religious institutions to look at what they communicate through their sacred texts, their sacred elements, their liturgical spaces. How is their heritage, the convictions they have developed over time, connecting to the needs of people now and in the next century? We live in a dangerous world where children murder children, where hatred and prejudice incite continual wars, where poverty dooms millions, where air and water and soil are polluted casually, where natural disasters wipe away whole villages in minutes, where depression silently kills our friends. And it is a world where many people feel like novelist Jane Smiley's character, Lidie Newton. When faced with the crisis of taking a stand (in her case, about abolition) she said, "Frank and I didn't pray. It didn't occur to us. We had swum in religion all our lives and had not gotten wet."[5]

Confronted with a decision that would, in Frank's case, cost his life, and, for Lidie, change her forever, they did not turn to God, or to a church for help. Though they were involved in religion all their lives, that connection had no significant value when they were confronted with a decision about whether or not to stand up for what they knew was right. Yet, the point of religious membership is to support such moments; the intention of doing worship is to practice a way of life that models justice, so that when the time comes we are empowered by it to take a stand. We get wet so we can act in the face of danger, so we can carry on even when dreams are dashed. We get wet so that we can move together, in the words of Martin Luther King, Jr., on dangerous pilgrimage toward the uncharted promised land that is always being created in the midst of the wilderness, calling others to join, to create, to overcome.[6]

The journey, as King points out, is always being created. There are always new challenges, new decisions, unpredicted failures and successes. Life is not static. Such rhythms of life call for worship that models a way to make continual choices, that gives each person a sense of agency, that affords not only permission, but the power to act in the moment. This power emanates from the tradition but not necessarily in ways that have been tried and tested. Gelineau invites us to let go of caution in our worshiping communities, not to be concerned with protecting our traditions as if they might break if we play with them. Instead, he urges us to throw what is most precious to one another. Tossing can be frightening. We do not know how to throw something precious: We might drop it. We do not know if and who will catch it. Throwing, catching or dropping—all assume active involvement of individuals and communities; all assume collective and collaborative movement along uncharted paths. Our liturgical forms have the capacity to help us to "get wet" if we want to play, toss, catch, and drop.

You have a blue guitar, you do not play things as they are.

Week after week, communities come together as people who share a pilgrimage. It is a pilgrimage fraught with danger but also with rich blessings. We want to discover the implications of belief in God for this pilgrimage; so we read and listen to sacred texts, the same texts, over and over; we meet around holy actions: blessing God, blessing one another, eating and drinking with all kinds of people, over and over. We do not do these things mindlessly but rather with an avid desire to layer our knowing and to act in light of what we do each time. We work together, we play together, to glimpse more and more dimensions of our relationships with God, with one another and with our created world. We practice living differently. We want to feel in our bones what life is like when every person is honored and is called upon, when hunger is satisfied, hope reinforced, love known for what it might be. For a time we try out being in such a world which does not yet exist. But we play as if it does, so that when we leave we can do our part to shape relationships anew. We return to share where we have been and to learn what we might try another time. Worship cannot be business as usual; congregations cannot depend solely on what they have always done. We live in a time where many people die from neglect, hate, and exclusion. It is a time that calls for something different, playing things not as they are but as they might be.

Holy play. Getting wet. We play because, in Diane Ackerman's words, play "carries one across fear and uncertainty toward the slippery edges of possibility, where one must use oneself fully and stretch human limits to achieve the remarkable."[7] Play is a vehicle for discovery and growth. In the midst of repetition and inevitably some tedium " we set bigger challenges, develop new skills, take greater chances, canvass worlds."[8]

"Holy play" which I use interchangeably with improvisation, is essential for effective ritualizing. Play is not a disregard for tradition, as liturgical scholar David Powers reminds us. It is rather "a texting of traditions, rites and texts for their adequacy in a fresh intertextuality."[9] The building blocks of rituals, its symbols, presume holy play. The word itself, derived from the Greek *symballo*, means something thrown together. Symbols accrue their meanings from what clashes and crashes, what is hurled and what is caught over centuries of use. So when communities use symbols, they, too, join in layering more meanings from what has been tossed and dropped. And continually they discover new meanings for changing times. It is active layering. There is always more to know and to add.

In worshiping congregations where people are the primary symbols they do not commonly play as a way of being in community with each other. Nor do they play with the things, the elements, the textures and texts around which they gather. Tossing what is precious takes courage and practice. Gelineau urges us to try it. In this essay I am offering a strategy for such play based on a study of improvisation among artists.

But play you must, A tune beyond us, yet ourselves

Improvisation is not an unprepared, unskilled, relentless imposition of one's point of view on others. That would be a nightmare for all. Rather, it is a process that intends to make space for new layers of experiences to be added to old ones, for boundaries to be stretched ever so slightly, for freshness, greenness, blueness, and clearness. Applied to worship, it means that leaders and members of worshiping congregations provide and take space and time to discover their own interpretations of symbols, to negotiate different sets of meanings among the many that are available and to take a stand in relation to them. Improvisation calls for doing what we practice in the midst of worship beyond the ritual time and space. It is a way of life that invites what is "most disturbing, more immediate, and also more powerful and rewarding" to get in.[10] It requires listening, waiting, taking in, trying something, practicing. As the jazz musician, Red Rodney says, "You keep playing, keep studying, keep listening, keep learning, and you keep developing."[11]

The term improvisation, as I am using it in this article, describes an attitude toward worship as well as the skills needed to embody it. Improvisation is a way of being that intends to pray and live in the moment from what each person remembers and from what is willing to continually envision. No one knows where the pilgrimage will end or even where it will wander, only that each person contributes to its twists and turns.

By drawing from the work of artists, most of whom spend many hours a day developing their skills of improvisation, I am not presuming that members of congregations or leaders can, or even need to, turn over large amounts of their time and energy to follow a similar regime of learning and developing in order to improvise. Rather I am exploring an approach to worship that uses what we know about improvisation in artistic venues to encourage active, collaborative, "holy play." I am proposing that worshiping congregations develop an artistic mindset and a schema for improvising as a way to enjoy the freedom and the power worship can provide. It is "holy play," a way of breaking the habits we have developed of missing the riches of our symbols. Improvisation or holy play intends to use engaged bodily ways of knowing to transform ourselves and our world, to be a vehicle for claiming the power of our partnership with one another and God.

In another Wallace Stevens poem, "St. Armorer's Church from the Outside," he offers the image of a church that once upon a time was a huge success but is now rotting. [12] In fact, it is so ravaged that there is a sumac tree growing upward from a ruined altar. A sumac tree. Something living in the midst of what seemed to be dead. An anti-structure. Stevens calls the image a "chapel of breath." The old St. Armorer's continues but not as anyone expected. Through its ruins something new appears.

> No radiance of dead blaze, but something seen
> In a mystic eye, no sign of life but life
> Itself, the presence of the intelligible
> In that which it creates as its symbol.[13]

A chapel of breath, "That which is always beginning because it is part. Of that which is always beginning, over and over."[14] A chapel of breath, where life is connected to death but not controlled by it, where resilience and freshness continue, regardless.

A chapel of breath expresses the essence of improvisation. In its purest and most formative state improvisation is a process rather than a product; it is a series of steps using a sound, an idea, an action, an element that develops and changes in both predicted and unexpected ways through the give and take of the performers. With rigorous attention to the moment, coupled with the free play of imagination, these sounds, ideas, actions expand to disclose what is heretofore unseen or unheard or untouched. What is born is often marked by familiarity but also surprise. In the words of Viola Spolin, "Spontaneity is the moment of personal freedom when we are faced with a reality and see it, explore it and act accordingly.... It is the time of discovery, of experiencing, of creative expression."[15]

The skills of the best jazz improvisors offer an example. To be effective they listen to each other very closely, they move into the dialogue from what they hear and add their own particular take at the moment. As they absorb the sound, the emotion, tension, beauty, they notice the familiar patterns and play with the texture. They may imitate the sounds, or they may draw from them and go on. In the process, the sound grows, it is a living response in the moment. The process repeats itself. More listening, more learning, more dialogue, more practicing, more risks, more conversation from within and without. Every performance offers another opportunity. No one can know for sure what will happen. Maybe nothing noteworthy. Maybe something good, that is satisfying, but not more. Once in awhile something extraordinary happens. "Entering into another world of awareness and sensitivity, they feel a deep reverence for "all living things". In spiritual communion they merge together in the shine of a universal life-force, timeless, peaceful, yet energizing and euphoric.[16]

Improvising artists and improvising worshiping congregations share a similar process, though the components are different. Something is given. As artists begin with an idea or a theme, congregations begin with texts intermingled with rituals of the body. From a repertoire of practiced patterns the experiences build among all the performers (here I am including the leaders and the congregation). What happens depends on what the performers expect, what they want to do, what skills they have to do it, and perhaps most of all their willingness to take in what happens in the moment and to try out a response. About improvisation in the theater, Paul Sills comments:

> True improvisation is a dialogue between people. Not just on the level of what the scene is about but also a dialogue from the being-something that has never been said before that now comes up. . . It's not what I know and what you know; its something that happens between us that's a discovery. As I say, you can't make this discovery alone. There is always the other.[17]

Improvisation in worship, as in art, comes from being in the moment. It involves attention, surrender, testing, give and take. Memories mix with imagination, old skills give way to new ones, what is and what was become the ground for what can be. This process—improvisation—leads to insight, agency, commitment.

A tune upon the blue guitar/Of things exactly as they are.

The following schema, based on the steps of creative processes is a framework for developing worshiping congregations where improvisation and imagination are at the heart of their lives, and thus, their liturgies. It involves four steps: take every offer, presume discomfort, go beyond the predictable, try it.

Take every offer

Improvisation at its core is a series of offers. An offer puts energy into space, it initiates play, it stirs ambivalence, lights "the possible's slow fuse."[18] Without any presumption of a particular response but expecting that something will certainly happen, an offer starts an interaction. It is the primary way of being together.

In a Christian setting, improvisation as a way of doing our worship seems quite natural. The goal of Christian worship is a momentary stop on our own pilgrimages to test our own choices over against the choices Jesus made in his lifetime. While Jesus learned from the generations of persons who preceded him, he made his own claim on a way of living and dying. So, the point of our gathering together is to engage a similar process. Through it we remember how holiness has been known, how it has been lived in unnumbered stories. Words, sounds, sights, smells, tastes remind us. Symbols urge us to believe in our own connection to ordinary and extraordinary power, to try on this connection to a Holy Spirit for ourselves. It is an ever-expanding vision, a movement that presumes a series of offers.

In a liturgical setting, to take every offer, presumes two phases. The offer is given. And the offer is received. The community does both.

a. The offer is given. The offer is clear and genuine. In the example described by Gelineau, the water was placed in an adjacent room. Some persons in the community had looked ahead on behalf of the rest of the community and prepared the space, the procession, the accent of light on the water, and the bowl of water itself. The offer was clear. It was also genuine, that is, there was no presumption of a "right" response. It was simply an offer. Even to not participate, at least visibly, was also possible. What happened depended on the desire and willingness of the congregation to play with the offer.

b. The offer is received. Each person negotiates a particular response from what they remember, from what they have practiced week after week, and from what they are moved to try. One person adds a subtle variation to the offer; another, perhaps empowered by the first, does something quite different. There may be lots of repetition, as in this example where many people made the sign of the cross, an action with which they were very comfortable. Perhaps no one will do what is familiar, there will be only a hint of where we have been. When enough has been done, the community senses it is time to move to another offer. The next offer will take a different form, but the process is the same.

Presume discomfort

Since improvisation is about making room for choices, the process inevitably moves through moments of discomfort. There is always time between an offer and the reception of it where not knowing what comes next. While this feeling of disquiet yearns for quick resolution, discomfort provides the incentive to be creative and critical and to break away from what is habitual and familiar. Maxine Greene regards this time of discomfort as a necessary step to stir our imaginations. She describes it as "an interrogative mode, the painful particularity; the sensation of falling into space; all these introduce a vantage point that subverts the systematic, the complete."[19] Discomfort is integral to the process of improvisation.

To accept the inevitability of discomfort as part of worship is quite a challenge for many worshiping congregations who come to churches or to temples for comfort. Surrounded by such a rapid pace of change in our world, people often want an oasis of ease. Comfort is one part of what liturgical experiences do provide. However, that comfort is wrapped in symbols that presume moments of discomfort. Relationships with God, marked by God's promise to be with God's people as modeled in the life of Jesus, certainly do not assure an easy pilgrimage. What is given to each of us for our comfort is the certainty of God's presence, but even that comes with a hook. God is often known most intimately through absence. In excruciating discomfort, realizing the extent and profound loss of life during the Holocaust Elie Wiesel prayed, "I believe in the Messiah even though the Messiah has not come."

To presume discomfort as an integral part of worship is necessary. In the spaces around knowing and unknowing there is time for holding back and daring, desiring and doing, free-fall and landing and everything in between. It is the fertile time that precedes choice. Using the water example again briefly, I suspect that many people in the procession were not sure where they were going when they were asked to leave the nave nor did they know what they would find elsewhere. For some, not knowing was exciting, even though also marked by discomfort. For others, the idea of moving was very disruptive. Why could not they sit in their pews as they had for years, and there, listen and watch the blessing of the water? To move to another space in procession imposed discomfort on all participants. When they reached the water, there was even more discomfort. What should they do? If there were any children present, to play with the water would have been quite natural, but for adults, especially for those who have lived with scripted actions in our liturgies, here was a real and genuine offer in a space where each person had to make a choice. The invitation required attending to oneself, opening oneself, accepting some discomfort, and moving with it. Many people in the same situation helped. Inevitably someone was bold enough to begin. That daring inspired and empowered others. Holy play ensued.

New awarenesses often begin with feelings of being off balance, uncertain, anxious, excited. It is the emotional space which makes room for choice and ultimately, freedom and power.

Go beyond the predictable

Aba Kahn, a wealthy prince and imam established a fund a numbers of years ago for a competition among architectural projects. Dissatisfied with the quality of architecture in the Islamic world he offered an incentive to change the situation. Among the awardees in 1998 was a mosque. (The awards were not given to architects but rather to projects.) The design of the mosque evoked considerable controversy. Nothing about it seemed to suggest that it was a mosque. There were no minarets, no dome, no solid wall to face while praying. Many Muslims were angry. But a jury of respected artists and architects had considered this mosque to be an extraordinary model of Islamic architecture. The building made an offer to the local community and to the world community. It invited Muslims to consider again the meanings of Islam and the role of a building in communicating those meanings. The mosque evoked dialogue about the symbols of Islam. Though any new mosque would have been the source of some conversation, with a familiar structure the questions may have focused on taste, style, and the varied choices of artists and architects. But this mosque made a different offer. Instead of passing on the symbols and their meanings cautiously, assured that they would endure as they been interpreted, the architects and all those involved in the design of the building, tossed the symbols. The ripples continue.

Worship described as boring, a tiring repetition of the same old ideas, the same old actions with the same old people doing all of it is not true to its name. How can an encounter with God through people's stories be boring? Only when congregations have settled down to what they have always known with no desire to discover how the symbols of worship unfold in their lives can it be described as boring. Improvisation assumes that there always is a series of offers, moments that invite participants to go beyond the predictable. The rationale is simple. There is always more of God than we have grasped, and more within us than we have thus far recognized. To uncover fresh meanings requires pressing beyond and under what we have always thought and believed.

Imagine a congregation where sacred texts are read as an offer to which the congregation is expected to respond: to ask questions, to listen for what has been left out, to wonder why certain details seem so important. The leaders coach the community. From their study, they urge the congregation to go beyond what they have thought earlier when hearing these stories, to wrestle with them to see what more they can learn and know about the choices they make daily. The coaches add layers of understanding from the tradition, explain what is obscure. But the real work, inner dialogue and public sharing is done by everyone.

Try something

When Maya Lin was only a student sculptor, she proposed a plan for the Vietnam memorial in Washington, D.C. Many scoffed at her idea. Though distinguished artists also submitted their designs, the committee chose Lin's concept. Today, this Vietnam Memorial is the most frequented memorial in Washington. People continue to flock to it to touch the names of the men and women who died in the war. Often they trace their names. To look at the names is not enough. Maya Lin made an offer. It was real and genuine. She invited people to feel the names. It is more difficult to place your fingers on the names of these dead, such young women and men. But, through that action, there is no way to miss the connection. Parents and relatives of these women and men weep openly. Others, too. The offer is powerful. The letters are symbols, there for our remembering, for imagining, and for grasping something about the choices we make in our lives.

What does it mean for worshiping communities to try something? How would the blessing of bread become an offer? What kind of arrangements of space encourage interaction? What forms of music inspire courage? How might praying require taking a stance? Two related examples provide illustrations.

a. The conversations that usually result from discussions about language for God and humankind often avoid the words of the Lord's Prayer. The arguments are that these were Jesus' words, that Jesus commanded us to use them and that everyone knows them by heart so no change is possible. So how can a community make an offer, try something through the Lord's Prayer? But how can it not make an offer, knowing that what is most precious is the first ball to toss, as Gelineau states it?

In the midst of a planning meeting with women who were responsible for the liturgy at a high school reunion, someone raised a question about the Lord's Prayer. How shall we pray? With what words shall we begin? Since we were a group of women planning for a group of women why not try something, why not substitute the word "mother" as we begin? Most of the people reacted to the offer by rejecting it without much time for discomfort or any thought of going beyond the predictable response. But one woman, one who had not spoken in this meeting, responded differently. She was shaken by this offer. She was a mother and had never thought about God as mother. The idea took her breath away. Here was an image for God that expressed her identity as a mother. She wanted to try it. The group could not imagine trying it and they did not. It was too great a risk. Imagine what might have happened if in the few moments before the prayer began, instead of the familiar introduction to the prayer, this woman had introduced it through her experience. A chapel of breath.

b. The second example explores a possibility for give-and-take in our community prayers. Instead of prayers prepared or printed for our use, or led by one person, the prayer is improvised: A member of the community calls the community to pray with a short introduction involving an invitation to pray in the form of a call and response, that is, someone calls out an image of God that she relates to particularly in this moment and someone else responds with a petition or a word of thanks related to this image. And so the rhythm begins, another image, another prayer. Sometimes there is silence between an image and a response. That, too, is understood as part of the prayer. To take every offer presumes that one is willing to try something, to presume discomfort, but to step up and go beyond the predictable, to throw oneself into the fray without knowing where it will end.

In another section of the Wallace Stevens poem, "The Man with the Blue Guitar", he urges:

> Throw away the lights, the definitions,
> And say of what you see in the dark
> That it is this or that it is that,
> But do not use the rotted names....
> You as you are? You are yourself.
> The blue guitar surprises you.[20]

This rationale and schema for improvisation and imagination in worship, or as I term it "holy play" dares to suggest that we play with the story of God. It assumes that this story is constantly layered from what happens among us day to day. When we gather to remind ourselves of our identity as people of God and to take our stand in relation to it, we throw the lights and the definitions; we throw them not away into oblivion but away to each other, so that they will live among us. From all the nooks and crannies of our life experiences we play with our symbols steeped in traditions and memories, so that we can claim what we see in the darkness. We do not use the rotted names, those that have no life left in them, but rather we draw from their ashes something new from the old. We are communities in search of ways to live, "You as you are? You are yourself." We are communities in search of God, "The blue guitar surprises you."

Endnotes

1. Wallace Stevens, *The Man with the Blue Guitar: Including Ideas of Order* (New York: Knopf, 1952), 3.

2. Joseph Gelineau, "The Symbols of Christian Initiation" in *Becoming A Catholic Christian Today*, ed. William Reedy (New York: Sadlier, 1979), 190-194.

3. Ibid.,193.

4. Ibid.

5. Jane Smiley, *The All True Travels and Adventures of Lidie Newton: A Novel* (New York: Knopf, 1998), 148.

6. Vincent Harding, *Martin Luther King: The Inconvenient Hero* (Maryknoll, NY: Orbis, 1996), 111.

7. Diane Ackerman, *Deep Play* (New York: Random House, 1999), 38.

8. Ibid., 39.

9. David Power, unpublished manuscript.

10. A. Frost and R. Yarrow as cited in Hazel Smith and Roger Dean, *Improvisation, Hypermedia and the Arts Since 1945* (The Netherlands: Harwood Academic Publishers, 1997), 40.

11. Paul F. Berliner, *Thinking in Jazz: The Infinite Art of Improvisation* (Chicago: University of Chicago, 1994), 485.

12. I am grateful to Peter Hawkins for introducing me to this poem. He used it in his response to my presentation on "Improvisation and Imagination" at the 1998 Luce Fellows Conference in Atlanta, Georgia.

13. Wallace Stevens, "St. Armorer's Church from the Outside" in *Collected Poems* (New York: Knopf, 1955).

14. Ibid.

15. Viola Spolin, *Improvisation for the Theater: A Handbook of Teaching and Directing Techniques* (Evanston: Northwestern University Press, 1963), 4.

16. Paul F. Berliner, 498.

17. Paul Sills as cited in Smith and Dean, 213.

18. Emily Dickinson, "The possible's slow fuse is lit by the imagination."

19. Maxine Greene, *Releasing the Imagination: Essays on Education, the Arts, and Social Change* (San Francisco: Jossey-Bass Publishers, 1995), 19.

20. Wallace Stevens, *The Man with the Blue Guitar*, 3.

Contributors to this Volume

Matthew Zyniewicz
The Association of Theological Schools

Gary A. Anderson
Professor of Hebrew Bible and Old Testament
Harvard University Divinity School

Patricia H. Davis
Assistant Professor of Pastoral Care
Perkins School of Theology, Southern Methodist University

Dawn A. DeVries
Associate Professor of Theology
Union Theological Seminary and Presbyterian School of Christian Education

Jean Porter
Professor of Christian Ethics
University of Notre Dame, Department of Theology

Choon-Leong Seow
Professor of Old Testament Language and Literature
Princeton Theological Seminary

Jane I. Smith
Professor of Islamic Studies
Hartford Seminary

Mark G. Toulouse
Professor and Associate Dean
Brite Divinity School, Texas Christian University

Janet R. Walton
Professor of Worship
Union Theological Seminary